# Two Tents

# Two Tents

## Twenty-one Years of Discovery on the Appalachian Trail

**Jim Haskell**

*Two Tents: Twenty-one Years of Discovery on the Appalachian Trail*

ISBN 978-1-63381-058-7

Edited by Bob Haskell
Cover illustration by Chelsea White
Photos by Donna Randall, Bob Haskell, other hikers, and the author



A portion of the net proceeds from the initial sale of print and electronic versions of this book will be donated to the Appalachian Trail Conservancy and the regional clubs that maintain the AT.

*Designed and produced by*
Maine Authors Publishing
558 Main Street
Rockland, Maine
www.maineauthorspublishing.com

Printed in the United States of America.

**"Life for two weeks on the mountaintop would show up many things about life during the other fifty weeks down below...There would be a chance to catch a breath, to study the dynamic forces of nature and the possibilities of shifting to them the burdens now carried on the backs of men. The reposeful study of these forces should provide a broad gauged enlightened approach to the problems of industry. Industry would come to be seen in its true perspective—as a means in life and not as an end in itself."**

—Benton MacKaye,
"An Appalachian Trail: A Project in Regional Planning,"
*Journal of the American Institute of Architects* (October 1921)

**"To those who would see the Maine wilderness, tramp day by day through a succession of ever delightful forest, past lake and stream, and over mountains, we would say: Follow the Appalachian Trail across Maine. It cannot be followed on horse or awheel. Remote for detachment, narrow for chosen company, winding for leisure, lonely for contemplation, it beckons not merely north and south but upward to the body, mind and soul of man."**

—Myron Avery, *In the Maine Woods*, 1934

## Author's Note

*Two Tents: Twenty-one Years of Discovery on the Appalachian Trail* is primarily a work of nonfiction. The stories that I relate about my adventures on the Appalachian Trail from 1990 to 2010 are true. Similarly, the stories told to me by other characters in this book were at some time told to me by other hikers, although I have sometimes changed the places where these incidents occurred to better fit the story.

In most cases, I have used the real names of the people I encountered. Frequently, I only knew those people by their trail names. In rare instances, I have deliberately changed a character's name to provide anonymity when I felt that was prudent.

I started writing *Two Tents* in early 2009 and had mostly completed it by the end of 2011. For a number of personal reasons, it then sat on my shelf until 2015. In the meantime, Cheryl Strayed's excellent memoir, *Wild*, which chronicles her hike on the Pacific Crest Trail, was published and subsequently made into a movie. While reading *Wild*, I noted several similarities between my story and hers. The reader should be assured that these are purely coincidental.

I have incorporated some fictional elements into *Two Tents*. The characters of Rex, Karen, and BB are largely fictional. Furthermore, while the opening scene at Skyland Resort did occur in much the same way as depicted, the subsequent hike that Rex and I took through Shenandoah National Park in November 2009 never occurred. Employing these fictional elements helped me frame the book's narrative. They are not intended to embellish my stories about the trail. On the AT, the truth is much more fascinating than any fiction.

—Jim Haskell, 2015, Ipswich, Massachusetts

# Foreword

Talk about leaving no stone unturned. Jim Haskell was very much our father's son on August 14, 2010, a pristine Saturday in northern New England. We drove from his home in Ipswich, Massachusetts, into Maine's western mountains so that Jim, trail name "Two Tents," could hike about two hundred feet of the Appalachian Trail that he had "orphaned" fourteen years earlier and revisit that part of the AT where he had nearly killed himself.

"Finish what you start" and "never give up" were two lessons that Percy Haskell of Levant, Maine, hammered into his two sons before he died in 1981. Jim, who is eleven years my junior, has taken the old man's life-defining words to heart. Jim has our father's six-foot frame and solid build, and he is every bit as determined to see a project through.

That's why we spent fourteen hours and drove four hundred seventy miles that Saturday so that Jim could walk two-thirds of a football field across the Pierce Pond Dam.

"Part of it is obsessive, I know, because I want to walk every foot of that trail," Jim observed during lunch in Bingham, Maine, about twenty miles shy of our destination. "Part of it is curiosity. That section defeated me. I want to see what it really looks like."

It was the twenty-first consecutive year that Jim was section-hiking the AT, the famous 2,179-mile footpath between Springer Mountain in Georgia and Mount Katahdin in Maine that was seventy-five years old in August 2012. He began his adventure with his first wife in Maine in May 1990. He hiked about one hundred miles every year. He finished the trail with forty family members and friends at the Appalachian Trail Conservancy's headquarters in Harpers Ferry, West Virginia, a few months after hiking across the dam in western Maine. He walked his final mile on 10-10-10.

Jim got a few minutes of fame for his accomplishment. Numerous newspapers and television and radio outlets across the country picked up an Associated Press story about Jim's five-million-step feat with his feet. Five newspapers, including the Boston Globe, published their own versions of the story.

As far as Jim Haskell was concerned, however, the story would not have been complete unless he had walked those two hundred feet along the southern end of remote Pierce Pond so he could truthfully claim he had walked every foot of the trail. It just may have been the shortest section hike ever taken on the trail.

The fact that Jim didn't die from stupidity there on August 9, 1996, is something of a miracle because he wasn't paying attention to the messages that Mother Nature was sending him.

The Kennebec River was running fast and high as he was ferried across in a canoe on that Friday afternoon, and the stretch of the trail leading to the pond ran beside a rampaging stream. The fact that these conditions were unusual for Maine in August didn't register with Jim as he dutifully followed the AT's white blazes toward his destination for that night—a lean-to on the other side of the dam.

He could not see the dam when he got to it at about 5:00 p.m. Water was cascading over the top of it toward a waterfall and gorge just below. Still, Jim didn't even consider the idea that this was not right. He was just following the blazes. Uprooted trees extending over and above the dam seemed the only way across. So Jim started working his way along one of them, all the while carrying a fifty-pound backpack with the food, water, and other essentials for living on the trail.

He inched his way farther and farther out over the cascading water until he approached the top of the tree. It started dipping toward the water. That's when it occurred to Jim, during his seventh year of hiking the AT, that something was terribly wrong here; that the top of this tree could not support this 250-pound load; that if he didn't turn back, a lot of people would be looking for his body. So he worked his way back along the tree to the shore.

"I cursed myself with every step I took for being so stupid," he said after the fact.

Half an hour later Jim was at the lean-to on the other side of the dam after finding a footbridge over the roiling water a ways downstream. Two other hikers at the lean-to filled him in. A monster thunderstorm had dumped five inches of rain on that region a couple of days earlier. It had filled Pierce Pond to overflowing like a fully opened faucet fills a bathtub.

Still thankful that he was alive, Jim continued hiking the next day, vowing to one day return to that orphaned stretch of the trail. He got back to the dam fourteen years later.

This dam is hardly of hydroelectric dimensions. It is built of plywood and rocks, and stands about two feet high. It prevents the southern part of one of western Maine's more obscure lakes from escaping downstream toward the Kennebec River.

Jim Haskell is not the first person to spend many years hiking the Appalachian Trail by sections. Fact is, the Appalachian Trail Conservancy claims that over fifteen thousand souls have hiked the entire trail. Most accomplish that feat in a single year. However, about 20 percent do it over several years as Jim did. Nor is Jim the first to walk across Pierce Pond Dam where the footing over rocks and driftwood is tricky under the best of conditions. But it is hard to imagine that anyone else has ever spent so much time and traveled so far just to hike those two hundred feet.

—Bob Haskell

# 1

# Snowbound on Speck

"You hikin' the trail?"

The voice sliced through the deep fog that had settled over my mind, much like the real fog that I had been cutting through for most of this day. I looked up from my reading and saw that the question had come from a man sitting at the next table. He and a woman, his girlfriend perhaps, were midway through their meal, while I had been seated for only a couple of minutes.

"Yes, I am," I answered, abruptly enough to discourage further conversation. I wasn't in a hospitable mood, and I have learned from years of experience that it's possible to discourage potentially irritating questions by answering the first one as curtly as possible.

I had just hiked eleven miles carrying a twenty-pound pack. It was midafternoon on this November Saturday in 2009—my final day of a five-day hike on the Appalachian Trail. I was sweaty and sore. I stunk. I was feeling very much out of place in this posh restaurant and lounge in Virginia's Shenandoah National Park. The Tap Room at the Skyland Resort was much nicer than most of the other eateries I'd discovered along the trail.

I really wasn't interested in making small talk with some guy who saw me as an oddball hiker. All I wanted to do was enjoy my meal and then begin heading north. There are days when it's OK to be the freak show at the carnival. Then there are days when you just want to be left alone. This was one of those days.

"So am I," he replied. "I knew you must be because of the trail maps. I love those things."

Fanned out in front of me on the wooden pub table was the trail map for the Central District of Shenandoah National Park. Set off to the side was its accompanying trail guide. My defenses dropped a little. Maybe I was talking to a kindred spirit. Maybe this wasn't an idle question from someone who knew nothing about hiking or the Appalachian Trail. Maybe this guy wouldn't be so bad after all.

"So do I," I said, warming slightly to the conversation. "These maps are great. They have so much information. I can usually tell exactly where I am on the trail, how much I have to climb, and when I'm going to get to my trailhead. These things have saved my life quite a few times."

The Appalachian Trail runs for nearly twenty-two hundred miles between the top of Springer Mountain just north of Atlanta, Georgia, and the summit of Mount Katahdin in central Maine. The trail passes through fourteen states, including ten of the original thirteen colonies. There are eleven regional AT guidebooks published by the nonprofit Appalachian Trail Conservancy, which oversees the trail on behalf of the National Park Service, or by the regional clubs that actually maintain it.

The guidebooks are a study in detail. They provide an overview of the history and ecology of different areas, a description of significant milestones along the trail, locations and evaluations of the trail shelters, and information about how far the trail crossings—where the trail crosses roads—are from towns and other services. The guidebooks have been my bible.

"How much of the trail have you finished?" asked the man. By now I was folding up my map. I had also gotten a better look at him. Early thirties, I guessed. Far from obese. You couldn't call him stocky, but he didn't have six-pack abs, either. This was a guy who liked to eat and drink but who had kept himself in pretty good shape by exercising on a fairly regular basis. He was built much like me.

"Well, yesterday I passed the two thousand-mile mark."

I knew that answer would impress someone who was familiar with the trail. It's kind of like a high school senior claiming, "I got a sixteen hundred on my SATs." It told him I was just a few miles short of finishing the whole thing; that I was on my last lap.

"Wow, that's impressive. What sections do you have left to do?"

"Well, unfortunately, what I have left is split up in a bunch of different sections. I've got a little section just north of here and about twenty miles of trail in the Pearisburg area. But the biggest two sections are sixty miles from Black Rock here in the Shenandoahs down to Tye River off the Blue Ridge Parkway and then fifty-five miles from Front Royal to Harpers Ferry." What I had just described were segments of the AT that stretched several hundred miles from southwestern Virginia up to the panhandle of West Virginia. I could tell the guy was familiar with some of the places but that he had never heard of some of the others.

"You plan to finish them this year?" he asked, somewhat confused. It sounded like a strange way to be hiking the trail.

"No, I'm section-hiking. I hope to finish the whole thing next year."

"Oh my God, I'm section-hiking, too!" he shot back excitedly.

"Really! That's great. I've been doing this now for twenty years, knocking off around a hundred miles a year."

"You've got to be kidding me. My brother and I have been doing the same thing. Except we've only been doing it for five years. We go out for nine or ten days and do another section. We started up in New York, and we've been working our way south since then."

Just then the waitress came to take my order.

"I'll have the Pub Burger. Medium well."

Normally I like to try different dishes in restaurants, and there were a number of interesting choices on the menu. But there's nothing quite like a good old-fashioned cheeseburger to satisfy my appetite after a long hike.

"Do you want bacon with that?"

"Sure. What the heck." I had burned up plenty of body fat on this trip. I wasn't too concerned about putting on a couple of ounces now.

"Fries or coleslaw?"

"Fries." There's something to be said for tradition.

As culinary fare goes, the Pollock Dining Room at the Skyland Resort is haut cuisine on the Appalachian Trail. A long line of resort guests were waiting to be seated for breakfast that morning when I had gone into the lodge to use the restroom before beginning my day's hike. The large windows in the dining room afford a breathtaking view of the Shenandoah Valley from one of the highest points in the national park. The prices are high by hikers' standards, but they're pretty reasonable for most tourists. Compared to the rest of the trail, this is gentility at its best.

I had chained my bike to one of the handrails near the resort's lodging office and driven to the crossing at Milam Gap to begin my eleven-mile hike back to Skyland. This was my fifth and final hike during this trip to Virginia. Eight days earlier, I had driven down from Massachusetts and hiked two sections of the national park the previous weekend. I had planned to hike for two days and then take a day off. That meant I'd be hiking again on Tuesday and Wednesday, and then again on Friday and Saturday.

As planned, I took Monday off and spent part of that day exploring a Civil War battlefield near New Market, Virginia. I hiked on Tuesday, but then Hurricane Ida stalled over the outer banks of the Virginia coast, and I ended up spending Wednesday and Thursday holed up in my motel room. Even though it was still pouring rain on Friday, I hiked that day because I wanted to complete enough of the trail this year so I wouldn't have too much to do next year. That's when I completed my two-thousandth mile. I raised my arms in celebration and let out a whoop in the rain. Then I kept hiking.

Saturday would be my last day on the trail for this trip. The rain had abated overnight, but the area was socked in dense fog that morning as I set out. The entire day was foggy, with a threat of rain, until I nearly reached my destination. The fog, and the temperature with it, suddenly lifted as I approached the Skyland Resort's horse paddock. I hiked the final mile in warm, brilliant sunshine. However, everything on me was damp. I felt like an old mop that someone had just wrung out. My clothes were damp. My pack was damp. My boots were damp. And I was damp underneath. Quite unexpectedly, the rapid increase in temperature, coupled with the high humidity, sapped me of whatever energy I had left. I was completely drained by the time I reached the lodge.

I knew from experience that this dampness after a day of hiking creates a rather powerful body odor, so I felt very self-conscious as I entered the lodge. I was in what we hikers call "the land of the clean."

It's funny how the nose works. I don't smell other hikers or myself when I'm on the trail, even if I've been out for several days. But once I get into town and begin mingling with people who have showered in the last day or so, my body odor and the smell of other hikers around me becomes overwhelming.

*Should I sit down and subject these good people to my powerful B.O.?* I asked myself. On the other hand, the idea of a really good burger seemed awfully appealing. Besides, this was my last hike of the year. *OK, what the hell. I'm sure they've sat beside a stinky hiker before,* I reasoned. Even though the restaurants at Skyland are very nice, they are still on the AT.

The Pollock Dining Room had closed for the afternoon, but the Tap Room was open. It's an upscale yet comfortable lounge—almost as nice as the restaurant—where you can gaze at the Shenandoah Valley through large windows while nursing a beer or savoring a cheeseburger and fries. I walked in carrying my pack in my arms, and asked one of the staff members if I could keep it with me. She said I could. They had obviously seen hikers before. Maybe I wasn't going to be so out of place after all.

The television over the bar was showing the Texas–Baylor college football game. Texas was up forty-to-nothing in the second half, and I decided I didn't want to witness the mauling. The thought that there really should be a mercy rule dashed through my mind. I sat with my back to the TV.

I was now in the uncomfortable predicament of being alone in a restaurant with nothing to do. Normally I have a book, and can read while I'm waiting to be served. Other times, I'll buy a newspaper, but the gift shop here didn't sell papers. The ATC guide and map for this section of the trail was all I had to read. Even though I didn't have much of the AT left to hike in this area, it was still better than nothing. I unfolded the map and began reading the trail description in the book.

That's when this guy who I didn't know asked me if I was hiking the trail.

I looked at the couple who by now had gone back to eating and talking to one another. I had to make a decision. Did I want to continue our conversation or not? Usually I'm pretty shy around people I don't know. Under normal circumstances, I probably would have gone back to my maps. But finding someone who was hiking the Appalachian Trail almost exactly the way I was didn't happen very often. I decided to take a leap of faith and reengage them.

"Hi, I haven't introduced myself. I'm Jim."

Between mouthfuls, the man stuck out his hand in my direction. "I'm Rex," he answered as we made our first gesture of friendship.

"And I'm Karen," the woman chimed in. She held out her hand, and we shook limply.

Karen was attractive but not beautiful. Her dark hair came down to her shoulders with a slight curl at the end. She and Rex appeared to make a good couple, but if they were to enter a room filled with strangers, hardly anyone would notice they were there.

"Do you go out on any of these hikes with Rex?" I asked. I was pretty certain what her response would be, but I figured it would be a good icebreaker. A lot of women hike the trail, but Karen did not appear to be one of them.

"No, I'm not much into hiking. I let Rex do the hiking and then tell me stories about his adventures when he comes back. I'm perfectly happy to stay at home where it's warm and dry," she replied. Exactly as I had thought.

"Yeah, my wife has pretty much the same attitude," I answered. "Especially since we became parents. She's perfectly content to stay home with our son and let me do the trail on my own."

"Have you done all of the trail by yourself?" Rex asked.

"Most of it. But I've also hiked parts of it with different people. My first wife and I did parts of the trail together during the first year. And I've done other sections with my niece, and then some others with college friends or people I work with. And my wife Donna and I did some hiking before we adopted our son."

I had now volunteered more personal information than I normally do during a conversation with complete strangers. But I felt comfortable with Rex and Karen. Talking with them reminded me of conversations I've had with hikers around campfires.

"I'm confused about what you said before," Rex resumed his questioning. "Are you hiking north to south, or south to north?"

"Actually, I'm hiking from each end towards the middle," I replied. "I started hiking the northern sections in 1990, and in 1992 I began coming down South and hiking sections down here. I finished everything north of Harpers Ferry in 2006, and since then I've been hiking the sections I have left in the South. I'm planning to finish in Harpers Ferry next October."

How I had actually hiked the Appalachian Trail was even more convoluted than that, but I figured that Rex and Karen didn't really want to hear all of the details about how I had hiked the trail over twenty years. So I had given them the *Reader's Digest* version.

"How are you and your brother hiking the trail?" I asked, trying not to dominate the conversation.

"Well, we started in New York five years ago, because my brother was working there at the time. So we started at the Bear Mountain Inn."

"On the west side of the Hudson," I interjected.

"Yeah. So we started there, and we've been hiking south every year since. We ended up here last year."

"What was the scariest hike you've ever had?" Karen asked.

The question caught me a bit off guard for a couple of reasons. For one, it abruptly changed the nature of our conversation. And seasoned hikers generally don't ask one another about their scariest adventures, especially after just meeting. But Karen wasn't a hiker, so I understood where she was coming from.

The risks and uncertainties of the trail keep many non-hikers from ever venturing out. A trail is an alien environment to many people. It seems so remote and devoid of the creature comforts that people take for granted. It's easy to become consumed with what-ifs. What if it rains? What if I get attacked by a bear? What if I break a leg?

For a hiker, the what-ifs are a given. To some extent, they are the adventure. A big part of hiking is putting yourself into situations where you have to deal with the unexpected. You can plan all you want to and for every situation that you can imagine. But there will always be situations that you haven't anticipated. So you'll probably have to deal with them with your wits and with the resources that you're packing on your back. Coping with the unexpected is the adrenaline rush that makes hiking so addictive for me.

"Hmmm, let me see, the scariest hike I've ever had..."

I thought back over my years on the Appalachian Trail. Which hike had been the worst? No, that wasn't the question. On which hike did I really believe I was going to die? That was the question.

"Well, I've had some close calls on several hikes, but I'd have to say my second hike was the scariest. It was when my first wife and I were hiking in the White Mountains near the Maine–New Hampshire border."

"Are the Whites that much different from what you see down here?" Rex asked.

"Oh, yeah. This area certainly has its challenges. But nothing down here compares with the Whites. That's some serious hiking. You'll see.

"Anyway, my first wife and I thought we knew something about hiking. But we were not at all prepared for what we found ourselves in. Snow. Really deep. In May. We'd had lunch near the summit of Old Speck

Mountain and had decided to continue following the trail even though there was still snow on the mountain."

"Follow close behind me. If you're too far back, the snow will collapse back onto the trail. Then you'll be cutting your own path, too."

I wasn't entirely sure that this was the case, but when you're unexpectedly wading through chest-deep snow, miles from any road, not sure if you're even on the trail, and afraid that nightfall will leave you stranded in the woods, you begin to take every possible precaution.

My first wife Aimee and I were hiking on the Appalachian Trail during this late May afternoon in 1990. It was Memorial Day weekend. We were coming down the southern side of Old Speck Mountain in Maine beside the still-frozen Speck Pond, a little kettle pond high in the White Mountains, a few miles east of the New Hampshire border. The pond lies in a basin that has steep ridges on three sides. Typically, snowstorms in these mountains become more intense as they climb the ridges, and then dump prodigious quantities of the white stuff once the ground gives way. We were in the middle of a heavily-wooded dumping ground.

The snow that we'd been wading through for the past couple of hours had deepened from our knees to our waists. I'm nearly six feet tall. With every step, I sank to my midsection, sometimes to my chest. I cleared as much snow in front of me as I could with my hands and arms. Then I lifted one leg as high as I could and took as long a step as I could to push forward, at most, another foot. I repeated this process again and again and again, slowly cutting a path across the basin, hoping that we'd find some way to get out of the mess we were in. Aimee, who is about a foot shorter than I am, trudged right behind me.

Aimee and I were experiencing one of the vagaries of the trail. Some sections are heavily hiked. Most are not. We had climbed to the top of Old Speck that morning on a stretch of the AT used by a lot of day hikers—people who park their cars at a trailhead or crossing, hike for the day, and return to their cars to go home. We had first encountered the snow more than halfway to the top. But it was never more than knee-deep, and it had been packed down by other people. The trail was easy to follow. After eating lunch with a family of day hikers who had gone back down the northern side of the mountain, Aimee and I had started down the southern side where the trail was used chiefly by AT thru-hikers during the late summer and early fall. No one, so far as we could tell, had hiked through this snowfield so far this year.

The snow on this side was considerably deeper, usually up to our hips, and it was getting deeper the farther down the mountain we went. Furthermore, sheets of ice had formed under the snow, creating a slippery bottom that could easily take our feet out from under us. The only way to get down this steep slope was to blindly feel beneath the snow for a foothold that would support our bodies, take a cautious step, and hope we didn't slip and fall. It was painfully slow going, and our fatigue made the ordeal even more difficult. Finally, we made it off the slope and onto the relatively flat basin. But here the snow was as deep as my chest.

"What happens if the snow gets so deep that we can't go any farther?" Aimee asked, so close behind me I could almost feel her labored breaths on my back.

"I guess we're going to have to turn around and go back," I answered.

The prospect of doing that didn't appeal to either of us. We had already defied death while descending from the summit of Old Speck. We weren't sure we could climb back to the top. If either of us slipped and fell, injuring ourselves, it would probably be a death sentence. It was highly unlikely that another hiker would come along to help us or to go get help, and by the time the healthy one of us could get out and bring rescuers back, it would certainly be dark and cold—very cold.

So our only alternative was to keep moving forward, hoping that we wouldn't have to turn around, because with every step forward it became more difficult for us to make it back.

We had certainly not anticipated these conditions when we'd started this hike late that morning, and we were not suitably clothed or equipped for this encounter with so much snow. It was Memorial Day weekend—almost June, for crying out loud! But at four thousand feet, Maine winters hold on for a long time.

To make matters worse, we were having trouble following the trail. Usually, staying on the Appalachian Trail is simple. Just follow the "blazes"—the two-inch by six-inch markings painted on trees and rocks along the way. The trail is famous for having the same color blazes along its entire length. That color is white. On the day we were hiking in the snow, those white blazes looked a lot like white blotches of snow on the trees. We wished the AT people had painted the blazes a different color.

Fluorescent orange would have been nice.

Following the trail usually means walking along a well-worn path in the woods that hundreds of thousands, perhaps millions, of feet have walked on before. On this day, however, the snow completely covered the path. The only way for us to follow the trail was to find the blazes. But it was very easy to miss a blaze in the sea of snow that we were wallowing through.

My story was interrupted when the waitress brought my cheeseburger. It was bulging with lettuce, tomatoes, and onions. The rest of the plate was filled with french fries: thick and long; better than the ones you get at a fast-food place.

"Can I bring you anything else?" she asked.

"Sure. Another iced tea would be great."

Rex and Karen had finished their meal, and the waitress turned to clear their plates. We had been talking for almost half an hour and had pretty much ignored the other diners around us. There weren't many. It was midafternoon on a Saturday in November. The lunch crowd had long since disappeared, and the dining room wouldn't open for dinner for another hour.

The waitress returned with a fresh iced tea. I resumed my story.

"OK, keep an eye out for a blue blaze. We've got to find the junction, or we're really screwed," I told Aimee. While blazes on the AT are white, any trail connecting to the AT has blue blazes. If the AT can be compared to the Interstate, then the blue blazes indicate the exit ramps.

As if trudging through chest-deep snow wasn't bad enough, we had to find the junction with the Speck Pond Trail. That trail would lead us off the AT and to the trailhead where our Mazda was parked. If we missed the junction, we'd continue on the AT for at least another mile before there was another cutoff trail. Given the amount of time it had taken us to hike the previous mile, and considering it was already after three in the afternoon, another mile would have us hiking in pitch black.

Aimee and I had hiked a lot together during previous years, and I had always been the one responsible for most of the logistics—where we would hike, how tough the trail would be, and how long it would take. This kind of planning came naturally to me, because I'd been the planner and navigator for my family's trips when I was a kid. The advantage of being the trip planner is that you usually get to go where you want. The disadvantage is that if something goes wrong, you get the blame.

Since the beginning of our relationship, Aimee and I had bickered about everything you could imagine. Neither of us was afraid to make our feelings known, regardless of the ramifications. We were brutally honest with each other, but we also felt a tremendous amount of genuine affection for each other. Our relationship didn't run hot and cold. It simply ran hot. But hot could be exhilarating or excruciating—depending on the moment.

When we were hiking, if anything went wrong—including misjudgments about the length or difficulty of the trail—the blame usually fell on my shoulders. If we got a late start and then had to push hard to get off the trail before sunset, Aimee would let me know that it was my fault.

As we found ourselves wading through deep snow at the bottom of the ridge near Speck Pond, it finally dawned on me that we were in a very dangerous predicament. This wasn't just a difficult situation. We could die out here. A sense of panic began to overwhelm me. How would we get through this snow? Would it get so deep that we just couldn't go on? What if we missed the junction with the Speck Pond Trail? What if we couldn't hike up and over the ridge on the other side of the snowfield? What if we had to turn back? What if we couldn't make it back up the ridge we had just come down? What if one of us got hurt? What if? What if? What if?

I started sweating profusely while trudging through snow that I could barely see over at times. I fully expected Aimee to start letting me have it, because I had certainly misjudged the hike and gotten us into this precarious situation. I had really messed this one up.

Amazingly, Aimee became very quiet and very, very focused. It wasn't the same kind of quiet I felt from her when she was seething and holding it in until it boiled over. I had certainly experienced that many times—as she had with me. No, this was an "I'm in a very dangerous situation, and I need to focus so I won't die" kind of quiet. It was a side of Aimee I had never seen before.

"Oh, my God, I think I see something," I told Aimee, almost in disbelief.

"What is it? What do you see?" Since Aimee was standing behind me, and because she was so much shorter, she couldn't see what I saw in the snow up ahead.

"Tracks. Human tracks." Up ahead was the unmistakable sign that someone had been here fairly recently: a path cut into the snow by people who, it seemed, had been hiking much like Aimee and I were doing now.

"And even better than that, I see a blue blaze."

I turned around, and Aimee and I hugged each other, jumping up and down as best we could in the deep snow. We cried. We kissed. We weren't exactly saved, because we still had to hike well over three miles to our car. But at least we knew that someone had been here before us. Now we didn't have to plow through the snow. We could walk in someone else's footprints. Now we knew where the trail was. And, most important, if someone else had gone over this section, we sure as hell could do it, too.

We followed those marvelous tracks and those gorgeous blue blazes along the Speck Pond Trail up the ridge. It was steep, but it wasn't nearly as icy as the trail we had descended from the summit. The tracks exposed the rocks that we had to climb over to make our way up the slope. I had never been so happy to see another person's tracks.

Of course, we could have followed those tracks and stumbled onto the body of the hiker who had made them. Or we could have followed those tracks to a point where the hiker had realized that he or she couldn't go any farther and had turned around. Neither of those scenarios would have led to a happy ending.

Fortunately, neither of those things happened. We made our way slowly up the ridge. As soon as we reached the top, the trail became much easier. It was practically rock-free, and it sloped gradually down through the woods. No major features. Nothing special. What had been a terrifying hike was suddenly mundane.

The snow was ankle-to-calf deep, and even that started to diminish within a few minutes. Pretty soon the snow became spotty, until somewhere around the three-thousand-foot mark it disappeared entirely. By now it was after six o'clock. We still had almost three miles to go, but under these conditions, we could easily do two miles an hour. The day was still warm, and the weather was beautiful. Our clothes began to dry in the spring air.

After fearing for our lives for much of the afternoon, the last hour and a half of the hike was a pleasant stroll. There was plenty of light when we got to the Mazda. We drove to Grafton Notch and retrieved our other car—a Toyota—that we had left there that morning. We got a motel room near Bethel by nine o'clock. We ate dinner and settled into our room shortly after ten.

Then Aimee let me have it with both barrels.

# 2

# Climbing Katahdin

I looked down at my plate and realized that I had barely touched my cheeseburger and fries. Everything was quickly getting cold, and I absolutely hate cold french fries. Still, as much as I had been looking forward to this meal, I was enjoying talking to Rex and Karen even more.

"I'm sure you and your brother have had some interesting situations in five years," I offered. I had been dominating the conversation, but perhaps I could actually eat if I got them to talking.

"Well, nothing like what happened to you. We've never done anything that would come close to getting us killed. I guess the strangest thing that happened was when we had to break camp and move at two in the morning."

"What? Where did that happen?"

"Right here in the Shenandoahs," Rex continued. "It was our next-to-last day out, and we had been hiking all day. It was turning dusk, the rain was coming down in buckets, and we were well short of any of the shelters. We got to Elkwallow Wayside. You know, one of those places in the park where there's a restaurant and a gift shop?"

"I know. I've had lunch there myself," I responded.

"Anyway, it was late afternoon, early evening, and the place was deserted. So we decided we'd pitch our tent and stay there that night. We got everything set up, and made our dinner under the awning where the locked restrooms were so we'd be out of the rain. Then we got into our sleeping bags and went to sleep.

"We're sound asleep and there's this noise outside our tent. Wakes us right up. It's pitch black, still raining hard, and at first we're thinking it could be a bear or some other animal. But then we see the flashlight, and so we open the flap. It's a park ranger, and he's telling us that we can't camp there.

"We hadn't seen any sign telling us we couldn't be there, but that didn't matter to him. He told us there was a rule that no one could camp at the wayside and that we had to leave. He was really serious. He made us pack up our tent and gear in the pouring rain, and then we had to start hiking again. Of course, by now we're soaking wet, and all our gear is, too, and we're walking in the dark and the pouring rain with our headlamps. And we're calling that ranger every nasty name we can think of."

"What did you do?" I asked, wolfing down my meal.

"Well, it's pitch black and raining like hell, and we had something like six miles to hike before we could get to the next shelter. We said screw that. So we walked into the woods for about five minutes and found a place where we could pitch our tent again. It wasn't the greatest spot, but we weren't being really picky at that point. We basically camped right in the middle of the trail, but we figured there weren't going to be a lot of people out hiking in the pouring rain at that time of night.

"Of course, now all our stuff is soaking wet, so we didn't get a whole lot of sleep the rest of the night. But then it stops raining, we get a little bit of sleep, wake up, and the sun is starting to poke through the clouds. We pack up our wet stuff and actually have a great day of hiking. So we end up here at Skyland, have a decent meal, and go home."

"Yeah, it's funny," I replied. "I've been so tired that I could barely put one foot in front of the other. I've had huge blisters on both of my heels at the same time, and I was in screaming pain with every step I took. I've been soaked to the bone. I've been just as miserable as you guys were. And then the next morning I wake up, and I'm ready to get back on the trail."

The journey that brought me to the lounge at Skyland Resort in Shenandoah National Park on November 14, 2009, had actually started more than two decades earlier in the shadow of Killington Mountain in Vermont. But in a way, I had been contemplating the idea of hiking the entire Appalachian Trail for most of my life.

I began learning about the trail when I was nine because of a camping trip that I did not take with my family. I grew up in a rural Maine town near Bangor. My family lived on a small farm, but my father worked full time as a carpenter and electrician. Farming was more or less of a hobby. When I was nine, my father decided he no longer wanted to grow crops and maintain his small herd of dairy cows. He sold them. That made the daily chores of milking the cows and the summer ritual of haying for winter feed a thing of the past. My family now had some leisure time.

My parents bought a little pop-up camper for what seemed like an exorbitant sum of eight hundred dollars during the spring of 1969, and we began camping. The Cox camper was little more than a collapsible tent atop a small metal box on wheels. When raised, the tent folded out to make two double beds. It was cramped but comfortable. Two seats with a folding table in between seated four adults. There was limited space for storage, but no built-in stove, refrigerator, or bathroom. It didn't matter. Every weekend we would load up the Cox, hitch it to the family car, and go camping.

Camping opened up the world for me. We'd usually arrive at a campsite on a Friday night. After we had set up the camper, I would go down to the playground. There I would meet someone—usually a boy around my age—who would become my best friend for the next two days. We'd spend time playing tetherball or shooting a basketball or swimming in the lake or exploring the woods around the campground. Nights were usually spent around one of our campfires with adults telling stories. Sometimes my sisters would visit. Sometimes the group would end up singing the night away. I came to appreciate the stark darkness of the Maine sky at night. You could easily make out the Milky Way and see what seemed to be a million stars—bright ones and faint ones.

I am the youngest of four children—the "mistake." My brother, Bob, is eleven and a half years older than me, while my sisters, Elaine and Patti, are ten and seven years older. Despite our age differences, my older siblings were always attentive to me—taking me places and playing with me. In many ways, they did more parenting for me than my parents who had had quite enough of raising children by the time I came along. However, by the time I was nine, the older siblings—particularly Bob and Elaine—were working and living their lives away from the family. Their participation in the weekend camping trips was sporadic.

During the summer of 1969, my siblings went on one camping trip that I wasn't invited to. Toward the end of August my father decided that he and the three older children would climb Mount Katahdin. He had hiked up the mountain when he was in his twenties. Now he wanted to do it with his children. I was considered too young for the climb, so I spent that weekend with my favorite cousin.

Despite the age differences between my siblings and me, I had grown accustomed to doing everything with my family. I was just one of the kids. So now, why could they go on this adventure and I couldn't? I was not a happy camper.

My family stayed at Katahdin Stream Campground in Baxter State Park, and my dad and the three kids hiked five miles up the Hunt Trail to the summit, Baxter Peak. When they came home and developed the pictures taken with the family's Kodak Instamatic camera, the photos from above the tree line seemed to have been taken on another planet. To be able to see forever in a place without trees and with boulders the size of houses was completely foreign to me. I was truly fascinated, and I tried to imagine being there. One of the pictures they took on the summit showed a sign stating that the peak was the northern terminus of the Appalachian Trail—a footpath leading over two thousand miles from there to Springer Mountain in Georgia.

I studied that picture, and after finding out what the word "terminus" meant, I went to the family's Rand McNally atlas to figure out exactly where Georgia was.

For a youngster who had been out of Maine only twice in his life and who had never been south of Springfield, Massachusetts, Georgia was a very long way away. A trail that was twenty-two hundred miles long was hard to fathom. I located Springer Mountain on the Georgia map in the atlas, and followed the Appalachian Trail to the North Carolina state line. Then I flipped to the North Carolina map and picked up the trail again. I kept flipping through the maps, state by state, until the trail led back to Maine and ended in Baxter State Park at the point where it read: "Mt. Katahdin, highest point in Maine, 5,276 ft."

I began to imagine what it would be like to hike that trail. As I read more, I found out that a few people actually hiked the entire trail within a single year. They were called thru-hikers. What would that be like? What would it take to do that? Most thru-hikers start in early April in Georgia and finish in Maine by mid-October. How many days is that? How many miles do you have to hike every day to get to Mount Katahdin within a year?

My family continued to camp during the next few years, usually spending summer weekends at some campground within an hour's drive of our home. We did make some extended trips—traveling to the Canadian Maritimes a few times. Around my sophomore year in high school, my parents sold the Cox camper and upgraded to a Winnebago. That was a recreational vehicle with many creature comforts—a bathroom, stove, and fridge—that the Cox didn't have.

It's hard to say what happened. Perhaps I was experiencing adolescence. Perhaps the Winnebago had so many amenities that camping just wasn't the same. But by the time I was in high school, camping had become drudgery. Camping meant being with my parents in places where I couldn't escape. Now that my siblings had all become adults and had started raising their own families, I was alone.

I had also seen a good deal of Maine, and I wanted to expand my horizons. When it came to choosing a place to go to college, I opted for the bright lights of a big city. I went to Boston University.

I met Aimee during my junior year. We dated a little during the first semester of my senior year. We began spending more time together as late spring evolved into the summer of 1982. However, I was going to law school in San Francisco that fall, and it just didn't make sense for us to get too serious. But after a week or so in California, I began missing Aimee more and more. I'd call her or write a letter, and I'd get a call back. Pretty soon we were talking at least once a day, sometimes at length, not wanting to get off the phone. Our phone bills were astronomical. By the time winter break arrived, I was counting the minutes until I could get back East to see her.

I returned to California after the Christmas break and started my second semester. As miserable as I had been during the fall, I was doubly depressed after I got back. I hated my classmates. I hated my teachers. I hated the law. I hated California. And I desperately missed Aimee. After six weeks, I left law school and returned to Boston—and Aimee.

Aimee and I were young, and we didn't have a lot of money. However, both of us liked to travel and get out of the city—especially to escape the student ghetto apartments of Boston's Allston section during the hot summer months. We scraped together some cash and bought a tent, a cook stove, and a cooler, and we went camping as often as we could.

We got married in August 1984. For the next several years, we would look through our campground directory, pick an area that seemed interesting, and set up our tent for the weekend. We preferred state parks to commercial campgrounds because the latter tended to be more crowded and catered to the RV crowd. We much preferred places that didn't have electricity and where the tent sites were reasonably far apart. Sometimes friends would come with us. More often we'd go by ourselves.

When we got to an area, we'd look for some hiking trails. If a mountain was nearby, we'd climb it. If a trail led to an overlook or a lake or just someplace interesting, we'd follow it. Sometimes the hikes were short. Other times they would take several hours. Sometimes they were easy. Other times they were difficult. These hikes awakened my thoughts from childhood about what it would be like to thru-hike the Appalachian Trail. I sometimes retraced the path of the AT from Georgia to Maine on our atlas. But as each year passed and we became gainfully employed and then started our graduate-school work, the idea of taking off for a year and thru-hiking the AT became a dream we knew would never come true.

One of our favorite camping spots was Gifford Woods State Park near Killington Mountain in Vermont. Gifford Woods had a lot of the attributes we liked. The campground was spread out and very low-key. There was no electricity and, therefore, no blaring radios or TVs from other campers. We camped there several times.

We were camping there during the summer of 1989 when Aimee met a guy who was thru-hiking the Appalachian Trail. It was late in the summer, and most thru-hikers had long since passed through. At some point this hiker had realized he wouldn't get to Mount Katahdin by the middle of October when the mountain is closed for the winter. So he had gotten off the trail, driven north to Katahdin, and started hiking south back to the point where he had jumped off—a "flip-flop" in thru-hiker lingo.

Aimee told him that what he had done was really smart. He just shrugged. He said he was sick of hiking; that all he wanted to do was finish. He said that most of the thru-hikers were in the same boat—depressed and anxious to get the trail behind them so they could say they had done it, and go home. He told her that if he could do it again, he'd hike maybe a hundred or two hundred miles a year so that he could really enjoy the trail.

Aimee came back to our tent and told me about this conversation. It was as if a light bulb clicked on for both of us at the same time. Hey, we could hike the entire Appalachian Trail that way. Not all at once, but by doing different sections every year. Eventually we'd hike the whole thing.

We talked for the rest of the weekend about how we would turn that idea into reality. We knew that the most difficult sections of the trail are in New England. We decided to complete those sections before we had children. Then we'd hike the less difficult sections of the Northeast–New Jersey, New York, Connecticut, and Massachusetts—while our children were young. Then, as the youngsters got older, we'd shift our focus to the southern sections of the trail. Our sections hikes would be our family vacations.

We believed we could do this because we both considered ourselves experienced hikers. I had climbed Mount Katahdin several times since I was twelve, and Aimee and I had gone up Katahdin together twice—in 1984, the year we were married, and again in 1987.

After getting home from Vermont, we immediately bought the trail maps for Maine, New Hampshire–Vermont, and Massachusetts–Connecticut. We pored over those maps throughout the winter and decided to hike the sections of the trail in Maine and New Hampshire first. That's where the trail is the toughest. Those sections were also easy for us to get to. We could drive to New Hampshire and western Maine in three or four hours, and the northern section of the AT in Maine was an easy drive from my mother's house.

We completed the first of our Appalachian Trail hikes two weekends before Memorial Day in 1990—hiking from Daicey Pond Campground in Baxter State Park to Abol Bridge on the Golden Road in Maine. Our next hike was over Old Speck Mountain during Memorial Day weekend—when we nearly died in the deep snow.

"Actually, I'm a little bummed right now," Rex said. "I was supposed to meet up with my brother and do another ten-day hike with him, but he had something come up at work at the last minute and he can't make it. I decided I'd go out and see what it's like to go solo, but this'll be a first for me."

"That's too bad about your brother," I replied. Then I tried to offer Rex some words of encouragement. "You know, I've done a lot of this trail by myself, so it's possible to do it on your own."

I had hiked nearly three-quarters of the trail by myself. There is something to be said about being alone for prolonged periods of time. There have been times when I haven't seen another human being for an entire day. That is frightening in one way, because if something had gone wrong and I had been injured, it would have been a long time before somebody found me. On the other hand, that kind of solitude gives me time to really think through whatever issues I'm dealing with.

Still, I could tell that Rex wasn't looking forward to hiking on his own. Then I had a thought. If I've learned anything while hiking the Appalachian Trail, it has been to be flexible and take advantage of every opportunity.

"What would you say if I hiked with you for a couple of days?" I asked.

Rex's eyes widened as if he could not believe what I had just offered to do. I watched him closely. If I had sensed that he did not like the idea of me taking his brother's place, I would have come up with a reason why I couldn't go after all. Instead, his look of disbelief morphed into a slight smile and a sense of relief. He liked the idea almost instantly. "That would be great!" he exclaimed.

"I can only go out for a couple of days, and of course I need to check in with my wife. But I think it'd be fun."

Now that we'd decided to hike together, I realized we had a slew of logistical issues to resolve in short order.

"OK, so you were planning to start from here tomorrow morning?" I inquired.

"That's right. I was planning to hike from here to the Tye River."

"Oh, I'm very familiar with that crossing. That's where I finished up last year while coming from the south. There's a great B&B called the Dutch Haus close by in Montebello.

"But I'm not going to hike nearly that far," I continued, unfolding the trail map that had been the impetus for this conversation in the first place. "I can only go out for a couple of days, so let's see where that would take us."

"I have a reservation to stay at Pocosin Cabin on the second night," Rex informed me. "It would probably make sense for us to park your car there. That's where you could finish."

I found the cabin on the map. It was a little less than nineteen miles from Skyland—a very comfortable distance for a two-day hike. I had just hiked that part of the trail in the rain and the fog over the past two days. It would be nice to do it again in good weather so I could enjoy it.

"Sure, that would make sense," I agreed.

The beginning and end points were set. Now all we had to do was work out the middle. There were a couple of places where we could stay the first night, depending on how far we wanted to hike. It was only eight or nine miles to Big Meadows, the huge Park Service campground in the middle of Shenandoah National Park. Or we could hike sixteen miles to Bearfence Hut, a three-sided lean-to that is much more typical of the accommodations on the AT.

The waitress interrupted our deliberations long enough to take my plate, wipe the table, and leave the check while I lifted the map out of her way.

"Oh my God!" I exclaimed, getting back to business. "I just realized—I don't have any overnight gear with me. All I was planning on doing were day hikes this trip, so all my overnight stuff is back at home."

"That's OK," Rex answered. "I have my brother's gear with me. He was going to fly to get here, so he shipped me his stuff, and I drove it down. Like I said, he bugged out on me at the last minute. You can use his stuff."

"OK, then I guess it's meant to be," I said as I stood and pulled enough cash from my wallet to cover the bill plus a good tip. "I'd better get going. There's only a couple of hours of daylight left, and I still have to ride my bike about ten miles to get to my car."

"Before you go," Rex interjected, "I wonder if I've already heard of you. Do you have a trail name?"

"Sure do. But I don't think it's very well known. I've only had it for a couple of years. It's Two Tents," I said, sitting down again.

"Two Tents, like in t-e-n-t-s?" Rex asked.

"Yup, like in t-e-n-t-s."

"Kind of like that joke?"

"Oh, the one where the guy goes to his psychiatrist and says, 'Doc, night before last I had a dream that I was a teepee, and then last night I had a dream I was a wigwam. What does it mean?' And the doctor says, 'Well that's obvious. It means you're two tents.' No, I've never heard that one."

Rex and Karen laughed at the play on words.

Trail names are a strange phenomenon on the Appalachian Trail. Almost every thru-hiker I have met has one. Some thru-hikers start out with a trail name, but I'd say most of them acquire their names during their first few weeks on the trail.

There are a number of ways to get trail names. Hikers can choose a name, or a name can be pinned on them by other hikers because of something they have done or some personality trait they have. I've spent a night in a shelter with Lollygagger, who didn't like to get up and out on the trail until it was approaching noon. I've given a ride to Sneakers, so named because of his footwear. I've had a long conversation with Bones, an orthopedic surgeon.

Trail names rarely, if ever, get changed. They identify hikers as if the names have been printed on their birth certificates. Thru-hikers will travel together for months, knowing each other only by their trail names, never knowing their real names. They are like the nicknames—Bear, Shorty, Lefty, or Radar—that identify characters in war movies or in actual combat units.

But they are more than nicknames. They are an indication that the AT is a world unto itself—distinctly different from life off the trail. When I'm Two Tents, it doesn't matter what I do for a living or where I live or how much money I have. Two Tents is that person who straps on a pack and walks for days and days on end. To Two Tents, that's all that matters.

While most thru-hikers have trail names, most section hikers do not. Anyone who hikes any part of the AT is technically a section hiker. Millions of people do that every year, and the vast majority never consider taking a trail name. You don't assume a separate identity just because you've climbed Mount Washington.

Only a small percentage of section hikers, like Rex and me, plan to hike the entire trail. But even hikers like us don't necessarily take trail names. For example, Rex had not yet acquired one. Rex and I occupy something of a netherworld in the AT community. We may be as dedicated as any thru-hiker, but we haven't fully embedded ourselves into the AT hiking culture. We're on the trail for relatively short periods, and we don't necessarily develop lasting relationships with other hikers.

Two Tents the section hiker was a bit out of the ordinary on the AT.

I had tried on several trail names, much like I'd tried on new boots, during my twenty years on the trail. I called myself Blue Toad for a while after a small stuffed animal that my wife had given to me for good luck. But Blue Toad was left at home when he became so frayed that his stuffing started to fall out, and the name stayed there with him.

Another hiker named me Nipples during the first night of a four–day hike along the North Carolina-Tennessee border. That was my name for the rest of that hike. I conveniently forgot it after that.

Two Tents, on the other hand, was a trail name that fit me.

"There's got to be a story about how you got that name," Rex observed.

"Of course. There's always a story behind a trail name," I said as the waitress collected her money. I asked her to bring us some coffee. This was going to take a while. The car would have to wait.

# 3

# Two Tents

"Are you sure you can make it, Uncle Jim?"

"Yeah, Erin. Just give me a few minutes to sit here and catch my breath. I should be fine."

Erin's eyes were wide with worry, and the concern in her voice bordered on fear. She was worried that I wouldn't be able to reach our destination by dark on this first Saturday of October 2007 in western Virginia. She was concerned about what she might have to do if I couldn't get there.

I hoped this break would revive me, but I wasn't terribly optimistic. Lots of times when I'm tired and I have started up a long hill, a short rest will give me a second wind. Not today. My batteries would not recharge, no matter how many breaks I took. I was asking Erin to stop every five or ten minutes so I could rest. Even when we were hiking up a moderate grade, I had to stop frequently.

"Are you sure you're OK?" Erin asked again, even more urgently.

"Yeah, I'm just a little tired," I lied. "I haven't been running since last spring, and I didn't realize how out of shape I'd gotten. I'll be OK, though." I was trying to put a brave face on the situation, but I knew that she knew I wasn't being truthful. Both of us were getting concerned.

I knew the range of emotions that Erin was experiencing, because usually I was the one in her position. If the person I was hiking with was struggling, I could assume one of several roles to keep my partner moving. I could be a cheerleader: "Hey there, you can do it! We're almost to the top." I could be a psychologist: "Don't worry about it. Let's just sit here for a few minutes. We'll get our bearings. Then we can keep on going." In drastic situations, I could be a trail Nazi: "I don't care if you're tired. We have to keep moving." The role I most dreaded was terminator: "OK. You know what? We're not going to make this. We have to get off this trail." That required a drastic change in plans.

I have assumed all of those roles at various times, and I knew that Erin was trying to decide which one she should play in light of our situation. What made Erin's situation more difficult was that I had assumed one other role during our previous hikes that she hadn't: I had been the planner. I had decided where the hikes would start and end, where we would camp at night, what we had to bring, and how we would get back to our starting point. Whether I was hiking by myself or with others, I had been the planner for the past eighteen years. Planning these hikes was second nature to me. But as I sat on a rock on the side of Chestnut Ridge in Virginia, thoroughly exhausted and feeling very disoriented, Erin's and my roles were reversing. She was becoming the leader, and I was becoming the follower. Neither of us was very comfortable with that turn of events.

The one factor working in our favor was that we had hiked together many times before. We had formed a very close bond. It was an eleven-year-old Erin who had climbed Mount Katahdin with her mother (my oldest sister Elaine), Aimee, and me during Labor Day weekend in 1990. Erin was a junior in college when she had joined me and two of my colleagues from work for a three-day hike over several of Maine's highest peaks—Sugarloaf, Abraham, and Saddleback—in 2001. The next year she and I had completed an unforgettable five-day journey over Roan High Knob and several treeless peaks—what southerners call "balds"—between Erwin and Evergreen, Tennessee. That was our first hike as a duo. Since then, Erin had usually joined me for at least one hike every year. Having hiked so many times together, Erin and I had acquired a sixth sense about when the other was tired or struggling.

Of all of my nieces and nephews, I am by far the closest to Erin. But it hadn't started out that way. Erin is the fourth among my parents' seven grandchildren. However, she was the youngest among the oldest group. My brother had his first, David, when I was eleven. My oldest sister's first, Ginny, and my brother's second child, Brian, were born within weeks of each other when I was fourteen. I remember all three of those births in great detail. Erin was born in November when I was eighteen. After Erin, there weren't any other grandchildren for the next twelve years until my youngest sister, Patti, began having her two: Chelsea and Andrew. Donna and I added our own son to the mix quite a bit later when we adopted Jason.

Erin's entrance into the world coincided with my first semester at Boston University. I was fully embracing the freshmen and big-city cultures. I was making new friends. I was living in an exciting place. I was being challenged academically. I had just lost my virginity. The fact that I had a new niece barely blipped on my radar. The first time I saw Erin was when I went home to Maine for Thanksgiving break. She looked like most newborns—small.

My first real experience with Erin occurred after my junior year in college. My two sisters drove to Boston for the Fourth of July weekend, and stayed with me in my student ghetto apartment in the city's Allston section. Erin was almost three. If the "twos" are terrible for some children, they were particularly horrendous for Erin. At one point, my incredibly laid-back apartment mate, Stu, turned to me and asked, "Does she ever stop crying?" From previous experience, I had to acknowledge, "Not very often."

As my life progressed beyond college and into the early stages of my career, my sister Elaine embarked on her new career in the ministry. Elaine and her two daughters lived with my mom for several years while Elaine attended Bangor Theological Seminary. Then they spent two years in Torrington, Connecticut, while my sister served in her first position as an associate pastor. Finally, there was a move back to Maine when my sister became the pastor of the Congregational Church in Hancock.

The town of Hancock is situated on the coast, and is much closer to the tourists' idea of Maine than the town where I grew up. However, like Levant, Hancock is very small and pretty boring. Young people have to look for ways to entertain themselves. One of the first things Elaine did was to put up a basketball hoop in the parsonage driveway. That is where Erin discovered her calling.

Erin was small for her age. Yet, by the time she was nine it was evident she had some real basketball talent. She would spend hours dribbling and shooting at that basketball hoop in her driveway. It didn't matter if it was raining or snowing or dark. Whenever you'd go to my sister's house, you'd hear the "thump, thump, thump" of the basketball on the blacktop. Or the "swish" of the net as the ball went through the hoop. The basketball seemed nearly as big as Erin, but she learned to dribble it between her legs. If you made the mistake of playing one-on-one with her, you quickly learned that what Erin lacked in height she made up with speed and agility.

Maine high schools field the typical assortment of athletic teams, but basketball reigns supreme. Every high school in the state has a team. The Eastern Maine High School Basketball Tournament is played in Bangor during the February school break. The games are broadcast live on local television and radio. Some teams have to travel four hours to get there. Area motel rooms are reserved months in advance. It is that big a deal.

People in Maine can tell you the size of their high school by its alphabetical athletic designation: A, B, C, or D. The A schools are in the big cities like Portland and Bangor. The B schools are in the larger towns or, like Hermon High School, my alma mater, serve several small towns. The C schools are located in even smaller, mostly rural, communities. The D schools are located in tiny towns that are usually so far from anyplace else that they can't be consolidated into bigger districts. They are, in a word, remote—which defines much of Maine.

Erin played for Mount Desert Island High School, a Class B school. As Erin progressed through high school, her team improved every year. During her senior year, her team played for the state Class B championship. The MDI team was very good because of two key players: Brianne, a tall center who could shoot in traffic, defend, and rebound with a vengeance; and Erin, the point guard who was the de facto coach, taskmaster, and emperor on the floor. Erin could shoot from the perimeter, and she could drive to the basket. Once she started to break down the other team's defense, Erin could see the entire floor and feed the ball to teammates who were open. Not only was Erin very skilled, she made the rest of her team look good as well. She was the consummate team player. Erin's team won the state title in a laugher.

Erin continued to play basketball in college. Because her college team played several schools near Boston, I saw her in one or two games each year. By following her basketball exploits, I developed a closer relationship with Erin than I had with any of my other nieces and nephews.

Erin is a really great person to know. She is funny and talkative and has an amazing ability to relate to people of all ages. She is personable without being overbearing. When you talk to Erin, you don't feel that she is trying to be something that she isn't. Her gregarious nature isn't a cover for something she is trying to hide. You get the impression that she genuinely enjoys being around other people and that her innate curiosity fuels her desire to get to know them better.

As with several of our previous hikes, Erin and I started driving south on the Friday of Columbus Day weekend. Besides the chance for some fresh air and exercise, this weekend was giving Erin some time to seriously consider making a significant career change. She had been working with disabled people in a Greenwich, Connecticut, group home since college. She liked the job, but she knew it wasn't going to be her career. She was beginning the application process to become a Connecticut police officer, and she needed some time to reflect on whether law enforcement would be the right career for her.

Erin and I traveled all day and stayed in the vicinity of Roanoke, Virginia, on Friday evening. We got back on the road fairly early on the morning of October sixth. After hiding our bikes in the woods near the road crossing where we planned to end our hike, we got to our starting point near the small town of Ceres at about ten o'clock.

The eleven-mile hike that I had planned for this Saturday would take us up to the crest of Chestnut Ridge, to a place called Chestnut Knob. The shelter on the knob had originally been a fire warden's cabin. Other hikers had told me it is one of the premier places to stay on the AT. The shelter is in a fully enclosed stone building. Hikers are treated to a three-hundred-sixty-degree view of surrounding mountain ranges when they step outside. I had been looking forward to staying at this shelter for many years. Sunset would be around seven that evening, so we had nine hours of daylight to hike eleven miles. Given Erin's and my experience, this would not be difficult. We could get to the shelter in plenty of time to enjoy the sunset on the summit.

The only bad thing about this shelter is that there isn't any water nearby. Hikers have to carry their own water up there. I had packed extra water bottles and two plastic water bags so we could carry all that we would need.

I had read and reread the Southwest Virginia trail guide during the past month so that the locations of the water sources on our approach to the knob were embedded in my brain. The nearest water source was at a spring-fed pond less than two miles before the shelter. While water is by far the heaviest thing that hikers carry, Erin and I would have completed most of the two-thousand-foot climb up the ridge by the time we reached the pond. Lugging extra water for the last couple of miles would be a small price to pay for the great views we'd be getting on the knob.

The weather was clear, but it seemed unseasonably warm—even for the South. The little thermometer that I carry on the outside of my pack was already reading over seventy degrees. The air was thick with humidity. We'd be working up a sweat hiking up this mountain.

Erin and I had hiked a couple of miles when we came upon a shelter where we took our first short break. We met a couple of other hikers who had stopped for lunch.

"Hey, how's it going?" I asked.

"Good. You?" the young man answered. He was probably in his late twenties, and his companion was a woman of similar age. I could tell by his scraggly beard, their lean bodies, and the grimy clothes they wore that they were thru-hikers. Given the time of year, I figured they must be "Sobos"—southbound thru-hikers who had started on Katahdin in June and would finish at Springer sometime in November.

"Good. We're doing great. You Sobos?" I replied, trying to break the ice with some trail lingo.

"Yeah, we are," he answered. "You?"

"We're just out for a couple of days. We started out at Route 42 this morning." I'm sure they could tell we hadn't been out for long since we were still clean. "I'm section hiking. I've finished about seventeen hundred miles of the trail so far. But, then again, it's only taken me eighteen years." That had been my standard comment to thru-hikers for several years. It was as if I was saying, "No, I'm not one of you, but what I've done is pretty darned respectable. I'm not just some pretender."

"And I'm just along for the ride," Erin chimed in, repeating a line she had used many times as well. By now, Erin had hiked a significant part of the trail, yet she didn't want thru-hikers to think she was hiking the entire trail. Erin enjoyed being out with me for a couple of days at a time, but she was not as obsessed with walking all of the AT as I was.

"How's the water going north?" I asked.

Asking another hiker about the availability of water on the trail is as common as commenting about the weather just about anywhere else. In fact, weather is not often discussed on the trail. Even though severe weather—thunderstorms, freezing rain, extreme heat—can affect hikers, there's not too much they can do about it except be prepared. Weather will do whatever weather will do. Hikers who encounter bad weather can either tough it out or wait it out. Information about water, on the other hand, is much more important. Hikers who run out of water can die. You have to know where you can get more. You have to plan.

"The water is horrible," the man responded. That got my attention. Thru-hikers generally do not resort to hyperbole. At this stage of their hike they have been through so much that they pay little or no attention to minor inconveniences. For this guy to use a word like "horrible" meant that the water situation must be very bad.

I pulled out my trail maps and guidebook and asked him some very pointed questions.

"Is there any water at the spring-fed pond?"

"No, that pond is completely dry," he reported.

"Where's the last water on the trail?" I asked.

"Just up here a few miles when you cross Lick Creek. After that, there isn't any water until you get to Jenkins Shelter on the other side of Chestnut Knob."

"Thanks," I replied.

They began packing their stuff. The four of us made small talk until the thru-hikers got back on the trail. Then I went back to my maps and guidebook. What the young man had just told me totally changed our plans, and I had to make some adjustments—quickly. I also had to make it clear to Erin that we were up against something that we hadn't faced before—rationing our water supply.

I first had to determine how much water we'd need during the next couple of days. It was easiest to break that down into three stages: today's hike from Lick Creek to Chestnut Knob; our overnight stay at the shelter; and tomorrow's hike to Jenkins Shelter. It was six miles from Lick Creek to the knob. Tomorrow's hike to Jenkins Shelter would cover eleven miles. There would be no water on the trail for seventeen miles. Erin and I were each carrying two one-liter water bottles and a plastic water bag that could hold three liters. Each of us could carry five liters of water. If we limited ourselves to one liter during the hike up the ridge and two liters tonight, that would leave us with two liters for the hike down the ridge tomorrow.

A liter of water weighs a kilogram. A kilogram is about two and two-tenths pounds. Therefore, five liters weighs about eleven pounds. Yes, Erin and I would be able to carry enough water to get up to the shelter that night and then down to the next shelter on the other side, but we would have to carry eleven pounds of water up a two-thousand foot ridge. The weight of my pack is normally about forty-five pounds. Now I would be carrying nearly sixty. I hadn't carried that much weight in a long time. Erin's pack was somewhat lighter than mine, but the added water meant she would be carrying more weight than she had ever carried before.

When we got to Lick Creek, we knew what we had to do. We filled the water bags and bottles to capacity and then we drank as much as we could. Hydration was essential, so we intended to set out pretty well waterlogged. When we put our packs back on, the increase in weight was noticeable. This was going to be a very long climb.

The first couple of miles after Lick Creek were relatively flat until the trail reached the base of Chestnut Ridge. We had now completed seven miles and had only four to go. However, they were uphill all the way. The temperature had also risen into the low eighties, and the humidity was stifling.

We started to climb at around three in the afternoon. The first mile was particularly steep, rising nearly a thousand feet. With the combination of the heat, humidity, and a very heavy pack, I began to sweat profusely. This is a fairly common phenomenon for me on the trail, as it is for many hikers. If you don't like to sweat, you probably shouldn't be hiking. But the way I deal with sweating is to drink more water. As long as I keep myself well-hydrated, sweating just helps to keep my body cool.

Now, however, rationing water was of the utmost importance. If I drank too much today, we wouldn't have enough for tonight and tomorrow. If Erin or I ran out of water, very bad things could happen. As we continued climbing, I allowed myself to take only little sips of water. I knew I wasn't coming close to replenishing what I was perspiring, but I also knew that I could drink only a liter before we got to the shelter. Rationing water means adhering to the ration.

"Erin, I need to take a break." We had been climbing for only about a half hour, and normally we try to rest every hour or so. But I had to stop and rest much sooner.

"OK, Uncle Jim."

"I'm sorry. This is just taking its toll on me. I guess I'm not in as good shape as I should be."

The heat, humidity, and heavy pack weren't the only things working against me. I was in bad shape because I had stopped running the previous spring, and I hadn't done any other exercising. I had been running fairly consistently since my early twenties, but that spring I began experiencing incredible heel pain every morning. I finally saw a podiatrist. The x-rays showed a bone spur on each heel, and the doctor diagnosed me as having plantar fasciitis. The tendons along the bottoms of both feet were damaged. My leg muscles had turned to flab. So today, it was hot and humid; my pack weighed a ton; and I was out of shape. Oh yeah, and I couldn't drink much water. Other than that, everything was fine.

Our progress up the mountain was incredibly slow. While Erin and I usually hike well over two miles in an hour, we were barely going a mile an hour now. Sunset would be around seven, and we both wondered if we could get to the shelter by dark.

I hiked in a stupor, forcing myself to put one foot in front of the other and stopping when I couldn't possibly go any farther. I'd rest for a couple of minutes and repeat the misery all over again. There was no joy. There was no looking at the scenery. There was just the need to keep shuffling my feet toward the shelter. My exhaustion and thirst were starting to affect my judgment. I was hiking stupid.

Hiking without thinking means you can miss things that you should see or make decisions that could have disastrous results. But as much as I tried to snap myself out of the stupor, the exhaustion and dehydration had turned me into a plodding machine. I was just going through the motions. I wondered if this was how an ox felt.

Still, I was lucky in a couple of respects. I did not make any really stupid decisions, such as sitting down and refusing to go another god-damned inch. And, thankfully, I was not suffering through this alone. Erin was with me every step of the way. She was experienced enough to keep us on the trail, and she was incredibly patient while I kept stopping to catch my breath so that I could plod on a little farther. Our roles had reversed. She became my cheerleader even though she too was feeling the effects of the heat, the humidity, the dehydration, and a heavy pack. She constantly encouraged me to keep going. She may have saved my life.

Finally, we reached the summit and the shelter. The sun was resting on the horizon. The view of the mountain ranges was spectacular. I could have cared less. All I wanted to do was get into the shelter, take off my pack, and drink lots of water. Well, as the song goes: "Two out of three ain't bad." Yes, we had reached our destination for the night. But we still had to be very careful about how much we drank.

I sat in front of the shelter for a couple of minutes and tried to get my bearings. As exhausted and dispirited as I was, I knew we had to make dinner before it became completely dark. It is much easier to prepare food in the waning light of day than it is to fumble around in total darkness. Besides, I didn't want to risk spilling some of our precious water. That could mean even more trouble. So I began preparing our meal.

My pack has two main compartments: a small one on the bottom where I keep food and my stove; and a large one on the top where I store my lighter and bulkier gear such as my sleeping bag and extra clothes. Lashed to the outside of my pack are my inflatable sleeping pad and the three-person tent I carry when I'm hiking with another person. I took the stove and food out of the lower compartment, carefully measured the water we needed to mix with the prepackaged meals, and began cooking dinner.

Then I started taking out the stuff I'd need that night. Since we were the only ones in the shelter, we wouldn't have to put up the tent. I certainly regretted carrying that five-pound, three-person tent up the mountain.

I opened the top of my backpack and pulled out the clothes. Beneath them was my sleeping bag. After pulling that out, I could feel something else in the bag even though the compartment should have been empty. In the near darkness, I reached in and pulled it out. It was a nylon bag weighing about three pounds. I immediately knew what it was.

"Oh, holy shit!" I exclaimed.

"What is it?" Erin asked in the gloom of the darkened shelter.

"It's my other tent. I can't believe it. Not only did I carry up one tent we don't need, I carried up a second tent too. I just carried a second goddamned tent up that goddamned mountain. That mountain almost killed me, and here I am carrying two tents. I can't believe how stupid I am."

"How did you do that?" Erin asked, wondering how in the world anyone could pack a second tent by mistake.

"You know, when I was packing, I didn't actually take the sleeping bag out. I just put my clothes on top of it. So my one-person tent was underneath it. Then I tied the three-person tent to the outside. I need my smaller tent like I need a hole in the head."

"Well, what can you do now?" Erin asked.

"There's not much I can do. I guess I'm just going to have to pack the goddamned thing out."

"Do you want me to take it?" Erin offered.

"No, I'm not going to have you carry something because I was so stupid to bring it up in the first place. Besides, tomorrow we'll have a lot less water to carry, and we'll be hiking downhill. I'll be OK."

I was really pissed at myself for carrying this additional weight because, mentally, three extra pounds in this kind of a situation can seem like three tons. But the situation got me to thinking again. It was as if I had been slapped in the face and told that I had better start paying attention to what I was doing.

"So, that's how I got my trail name. Two Tents."

"Did you run out of water?" Karen asked.

"Yes, we ran out of water, and our bones are bleaching beside the trail where we died of thirst."

I tried to say that with a straight face, but after a couple of seconds I broke into a wide grin. "No, we did make it out, although by the time we got to the next shelter we were down to less than a pint of water between us. And the place where we got water wasn't very good—just three or four bathtub-sized pools of dirty water. But by that point we didn't care. We socked the iodine to it, drank as much as we could, and hoped for the best."

"That's quite a story," Karen laughed.

"Yes, it is. I guess it's just one of those times when the situation was already pretty bad, but I did something stupid to make it even worse. Anyway, the name Two Tents has stuck with me ever since."

With that, I threw down a couple of dollars to pay for the coffee, and we made our way from the Tap Room lounge to the long porch in front of the gift shop. The sun was quickly dipping toward the horizon, and I still had to ride my bike ten miles along Skyline Drive to get my car.

"Oh my God, I better get going or I'm going to be riding in the pitch black," I exclaimed.

"Hey, do you want us to give you a ride?" Rex asked. "You're taking off a couple of days for me, so the least I can do is take you to your car."

"You know, that would be great," I said, relieved that one good turn had led to another. It was a bit of trail magic I was not about to pass up.

The sun was setting when Rex pulled his car in beside mine at Milam Gap.

# 4

# Getting Going

I checked back into the same motel in Luray where I had stayed the previous week, and called home to tell Donna about the changes in my plans and what my new hiking itinerary would be. It was important that my wife knew where I was starting, where I was likely to stay overnight, and where I planned to finish. She wrote it all down in case she had to tell other people where to look for me. It was a routine we had been following for many years.

I got up early the next morning, packed my things, checked out, and wolfed down the continental breakfast as soon as it was set up. I drove into Shenandoah National Park a few minutes later. A fog had settled over the valley, but the day's forecast called for clear skies.

Rex and Karen were waiting on the porch when I pulled into the Skyland lot and parked just after six thirty. It was getting light even though the sun hadn't risen.

"Good morning," I called out as I approached the couple.

"Good morning," they replied in unison. Despite the early morning chill, Rex was wearing his hiking gear—shirt, shorts, and boots. He was upbeat and friendly. Karen yawned. She didn't seem quite so enthusiastic about being up and about this early on a Sunday morning.

"I take it that one of those is mine?" I asked, pointing to the two packs leaning against the railing.

"Yeah, that one's yours," Rex said, nodding toward the larger one. "My brother tends to over-pack. There should be everything you need except for your personal items."

"No problem. I brought my daypack with me. I can transfer my stuff into your brother's pack and leave my pack in my car. Then we have to hit the road. We've got a lot of driving to do."

"What exactly are we doing?" Karen asked groggily.

"Well, I have to get my car to Tye River, and Two Tents is going to drop his car at Pocosin Cabin," Rex replied. "So, first the three of us will drive our cars to Pocosin. Then you and I will drive to Tye River, and Two Tents will ride with one of us. Then the three of us will drive back here in your car, and Two Tents and I'll start our hike." It was clear that Rex had thought through the sequence of shuttling ourselves to our various trail-heads. He was doing what I have done many, many times. It was refreshing to let someone else take on that responsibility.

"Let's put the packs in Karen's car, mine in the trunk and yours in the backseat, so we'll have them when she drops us off back here," Rex said to me. I was impressed. This guy really did know how to think ahead.

Within ten minutes I had crammed the personal stuff I'd need for two days into Rex's brother's pack, both backpacks were placed in Karen's car, and the three of us were driving south along Skyline Drive in a sort of convoy. Our cars reflected the personalities and circumstances of the owners. Rex had a fire-red Camaro. It was very much a guy's car, and I surmised it would be gone if he and Karen stayed together. Karen drove a sensible beige sedan that said "family car" loud and clear. My silver Honda Civic hybrid told the world that my "guy-car" days were behind me and that I had settled into my life as a family man and professional person.

Rex made a sharp left turn onto an unmarked fire road a half hour later. I didn't know what he was doing, but I soon saw a few parking spaces beside the road. I assumed this must be the access to Pocosin Cabin. I parked my car and got out.

"I would have gone right by this road," I remarked as I locked my vehicle.

"Well, Karen and I drove down here yesterday. I just wanted to make sure the cabin's here. That's how I knew about this road."

Rex clearly knew what he was doing.

Now we were down to two cars. Rex's sports car was cluttered with hiking paraphernalia, while Karen's was empty except for the backpack in her backseat. It was only logical that I ride with her. But I had to wait for one of them to say so.

"Why don't you ride with me?" Karen offered, recognizing my awkward situation.

"You sure?" I replied.

"Yeah, there's a lot more space in my car than in Rex's."

"OK. It probably makes sense for us to lead since I know right where the crossing is at the Tye River."

"Good idea," Rex agreed. "Let's get going."

I settled into the passenger seat of Karen's car. Soon we were leading Rex out of the fire road and back onto Skyline Drive, heading south once again.

Skyline Drive and the Blue Ridge Parkway form a continuous two-lane paved road that runs over the crest of the Appalachians for nearly six hundred miles from Front Royal, Virginia, to Great Smoky Mountains National Park in North Carolina. Scenic overlooks are located on both sides of the road. They afford alternating views of the broad Shenandoah Valley to the west and of mountains to the east. We didn't have time to stop to savor the scenery, but we could still see a lot of the countryside, because the lazy curvature and gradual undulations of the roadway almost force people to drive at moderate speeds. The biggest risk on this road is hitting a deer should one leap out in front of you.

Karen and I would be spending almost two hours cruising along this road with Rex following behind.

"This is pretty early to be driving this far on a Sunday morning." I initiated the conversation, picking up on how groggy Karen had looked when we met at the hotel.

"Usually I haven't even opened my eyes this early on a weekend. Oh well, I guess that's just the price I have to pay," she sighed with mock exasperation. "I guess if Rex is going to be 'the one,' then I better get used to this."

That's when I noticed the ring on her left hand—a respectable but not overly pretentious diamond set on a thin golden band. She turned the ring around her finger with her thumb—as if to reassure herself that it was there.

"I take it you guys are engaged?"

"Yes, we are. For about six months now."

"Congratulations. How long have you known each other?"

"Well, I think we've known each other for about seven years."

"You think?" I queried, razzing her a little.

"Well, we both started working at the same company at about the same time. We were working in different departments, so I didn't really notice him at first. Then we worked on a couple of projects together and got to know each other a little better. But there wasn't anything romantic or anything like that. I had a boyfriend, and Rex was seeing someone, too. So it was just one of those things that we knew each other at work and liked each other.

"But then I broke up with my boyfriend, and Rex wasn't seeing anyone at the time, so a couple of years ago he asked me out," Karen continued. "We dated a little, and then things got more serious, and six months ago, he popped the question."

"From what little time I've known you two, you seem really well suited for each other," I interjected. "You know, sometimes you just get a good feeling about a couple?"

"Yeah, he's a pretty special guy," Karen concurred. "But I'll be honest. This stuff gives me a little pause at times," she added with a hint of concern.

"What stuff?" I asked. I thought I knew what she was talking about, but I wanted to make sure I didn't accidentally stick my foot in my mouth.

"You know, this hiking stuff," she said. "First, I'm not always sure whether Rex is hiking for himself, or if this is just part of the ongoing competition he has with his brother, Tom. Rex is a couple of years younger, and it seems like he not only has to do what Tom has done, but he has to go one better. Tom lettered in three sports in high school, so Rex had to letter in four. Tom became a Life Scout, so Rex had to make Eagle."

"Life Scout?" I asked.

"Yeah, it's the level just below Eagle Scout in the Boy Scouts."

"I didn't know."

"Neither did I 'til I met Rex," she confirmed. "It's not so much that I mind his going out hiking with his brother, but it's all of the things that other people have to do to help them make it happen. And then, of course, I constantly wonder if he's all right when he's out on the trail. From my perspective, it seems like I'm spending all of my time driving and waiting and worrying." Her concern had given way to something close to exasperation.

"Well, I'm not sure I have the magic solution," I said. "I know that my wife and son are doing the waiting and worrying thing a lot, too. And there have been a lot of people who have helped me out with the driving part, especially earlier when I was hiking in the Northeast. I imagine every hiker has to rely on at least one other person. But, then again, the most dangerous thing that I do when I'm hiking is get behind the wheel and drive to wherever I'm going. The trail itself is pretty safe."

"You're probably right on that one," Karen said. "Have you ever had a close call driving to one of your trailheads?"

"Well, I've had to avoid a few accidents, especially on I-81. But when you're used to driving in the Boston area, that's nothing new. Probably the strangest thing was the time my sister and I almost hit a moose."

"You almost hit a moose?"

"Yeah. But believe it or not, it was even stranger than that. I was going to be hiking a section in Maine, and my sister, Elaine, was giving me a shuttle. She was following me on a state highway up in the western part of the state. I was driving along, and out of the corner of my right eye I saw a cow moose run out of the woods. This moose was just kind of trotting along, and she was heading straight for the road. Of course, they're the size of a draft horse, but they're not the brightest bulbs on the planet. Anyway, I swerved my little Toyota pickup truck to avoid hitting the moose, because it was coming out onto the road. That finally got the moose's attention, so it made a right turn and started running along the side of the road, right beside us."

"Oh my God, that's amazing," Karen chortled. She sat up a little straighter and gripped the wheel a bit more firmly, as if she thought a moose would suddenly bolt out of the Virginia woods and onto the highway.

"Well, I passed the moose, but my sister pulled up beside it. She was driving a little Honda hatchback, so the moose was towering over her. The moose was running beside my sister's car and keeping pace with it. I was watching all of this in my rearview mirror. It looked like my sister was taking the moose out for a run. Anyway, I figured that I couldn't slow down, because if I did Elaine would probably run into me because she was keeping an eye on the moose. So I just kept driving along, and eventually Elaine slowed her car down. The moose kept running along and finally crossed the road in front of her car after Elaine stopped. The moose ran into the woods, and we kept on driving. The whole thing lasted less than thirty seconds, I'd guess. But I'll never forget it."

"That's really funny."

"It was one of those situations where you're kind of laughing while it's happening, although it could have turned out pretty bad if one of us had hit the moose. But everyone lived to tell the tale."

"Have you always been able to get someone to give you a ride?" Karen asked.

"No, certainly not," I answered. "Most of the time I've had to figure out how to get back to my starting point on my own. I think I've used just about every conceivable method to do that. Sometimes I've paid a shuttler who I've contacted from a list that the ATC keeps. I've even hitchhiked. But mostly, I've used my bike and ridden back to my starting point."

"Well, as long as Rex and I have been going together, I've driven down with him and his brother so they didn't have to take two cars."

"Where are you coming from?"

"We live in the Harrisburg area."

"Harrisburg, as in Pennsylvania, right? Not Harrisonburg in Virginia."

"Right. Pennsylvania," she confirmed.

"I always get those two mixed up. Wow, that's a long way to drive. You're a good sport."

"It's not so bad now, but I'm just imagining how it's going to be when we have kids," Karen continued.

"Yeah, kids can certainly complicate things. My wife and I used to do a lot of hiking together, but that pretty much ended after we adopted Jason. She's ended up staying home with him, and I've had to figure out ways to get back to my starting point without relying on her."

"I thought yesterday you mentioned that you and your wife had decided to hike the trail together."

"Sorry for the confusion. That was my first wife, Aimee. I had already been hiking the trail a few years when I met Donna."

"Oh, I'm sorry," Karen said, concerned that she had stumbled onto a sore subject.

"That's OK. I don't mind talking about it. My life's had its ups and downs, just like everyone's. Unfortunately, things didn't work out with Aimee and me. About a year after we started hiking the trail together, we ended up separating. That's when I began hiking sections of the trail by myself. Then I met Donna a couple of years later. We hit it off pretty quickly. I think we'd only been dating for six weeks or so when we did our first overnight hike together."

"Wow, that was quick. Is Donna much of a hiker?"

"Donna is certainly a far superior athlete to me," I responded, not quite answering her question. "She was a really good runner in high school and college. She has a lot of natural ability that I'll never have. But when Donna is on the trail, what she really loves to do is take pictures. She's a really good photographer, and she has a great eye for things on the trail that I don't see."

"What do you mean?"

"Well, when I'm on the trail I tend to want to get to the top of a mountain where there's a great view. And when it comes to taking pictures, I want to capture the view I'm seeing at the summit. But when Donna is hiking, she might see a little flower poking out from between two rocks, and she wants to take a picture of that. And then when we get home and develop the photos, hers are beautiful and mine are horrible. When Donna and I were hiking together, I got a much better appreciation for some of the minutiae along the trail. But after we adopted Jason, all of that changed."

"How so?"

"Well, by the time you've driven to the crossings and parked your cars and then hiked and then retrieved your cars and driven back home—it takes a lot of time. And that was a lot of time to be away from Jason. I'll never forget one hike that I had planned in Maine fairly close to where my mother lives. Jason was about eighteen months old, and I had arranged to have my mom take care of him so Donna and I could spend a day together by ourselves. The hike was only about eight miles. It's about the shortest section you can do in Maine. It was a really beautiful late-summer day, and we were climbing Crocker Mountain. Crocker's a four-thousand-footer, and the summit has two separate peaks with a really great view from one of them. We were practically surrounded by other mountains like Sugarloaf and Saddleback and Bigelow. It was, you know, one of those days when there were white fluffy clouds drifting by."

Karen drove in silence while I reminisced about a place she had never seen. I didn't want to bore her to sleep. It was time to cut to the chase.

"As the afternoon wore on, it became obvious that Donna just wanted to get back to Jason. She wasn't taking any pictures. So we finished the hike as quickly as we could, and we drove back to my mom's without stopping. We realized that the situation had changed and that some of the things we'd done as a couple weren't going to happen anymore now that we had a baby."

"That's kind of sad," Karen noted.

"I wouldn't say that. I wouldn't give up being Jason's dad for anything in the world. Donna and I have worked things out. But kids certainly do change things. That's for sure."

Karen was quiet for a couple of minutes, perhaps because she was beginning to understand that being married to a hiker might be more of a challenge than she had anticipated.

"You know, maybe I shouldn't be telling you this stuff, considering you're going to marry a hiker," I added. "I don't want to discourage you or anything like that."

"Oh, that's all right. Rex and I realize we'll have to be flexible, especially when we start raising a family," Karen countered.

"So you've been hiking the trail by yourself since that last hike with Donna?" she asked, shifting the focus back to me.

"Not all of it. Some of the time I've had a hiking partner. Usually my niece Erin. You remember me telling you how I got my trail name?"

"Oh, yeah. I remember."

"But, yes, I've hiked most of the trail by myself. Actually, I kind of prefer doing some of my hikes alone. There's just something about being out in the woods alone with your thoughts."

"I think that being out there alone would scare me the most."

Karen had hit on the major difference between hikers and non-hikers. It's not so much that hiking is physically challenging or especially dangerous. It's that some people thirst for solitude while others don't.

"Well, it's not everybody's cup of tea, but I think it's the main reason why hikers hike," I said. "It's kind of hard to explain."

"I'm curious," Karen said, changing the subject. "Aren't you really tired when you're biking back to your car after you've been hiking all day?"

"I don't do it that way very often. Usually I park my car where I'm going to finish and ride my bike back to where I'm going to start. That way I'm biking on fresh legs. Then I drive my car to where I've hidden my bike after I finish my hike."

"Except for yesterday," Karen interjected.

"You're right. Except for yesterday when I decided I'd bike after the hike because the weather was supposed to clear as the day went on."

"So, you've said you've had to hitchhike sometimes?"

"Well, I avoid it as much as I can. But, yes, I've had to hitchhike on occasion," I replied.

"If being out in the woods alone scares me, what really scares me are the crazies who are out there on the road," Karen said. "I wouldn't want Rex to get picked up by some nutcase." Her shoulders tensed as she gripped the wheel tighter. I had to give her some assurances that everything would be all right.

"Well, I've had my share of experiences with people you might call slightly eccentric, but, fortunately, I've never encountered anyone who really scared me."

"You don't mind hitchhiking?" Karen asked.

"No, I didn't say that."

*Haskell, you are such a goddamned idiot!* I chastised myself. *You can't walk back to your car. Stick out your thumb. Hitchhike, you fool!*

The third car I had seen within the past half hour was approaching me on a rural New Hampshire highway, about thirty miles from where my car was parked at Franconia Notch. Getting someone to give me a ride was my only option if I didn't want to walk. For the first time in my life, I had to hitchhike. I tried to force my arm out, with my thumb pointing skyward, but I just couldn't do it. The car passed me without slowing down.

The fourth car approached a few minutes later. Same thing. No thumb. No stop.

The fifth car—same thing.

I had just finished my first long hike by myself: five days of lugging a fifty-pound pack over the rugged terrain of the White Mountains. I had accomplished my goal, and I was really proud of myself. I had completed a significant section of the trail on my own. That meant I could probably finish the entire trail alone if I had to. I no longer felt that I had to hike it with someone else. The goal of hiking the entire Appalachian Trail with Aimee was history, just like Aimee and I were history. Now, hiking the AT was just my goal.

In planning this hike, I had decided to hitchhike back to my car after I had gotten off the trail. After getting to the road, however, I realized that it's one thing to think you're going to do something and quite another to actually do it. I couldn't bring myself to hitch a ride.

I had never hitchhiked during my thirty-plus years on the planet. My brother, Bob, on the other hand, was a veteran hitchhiker. Sticking his thumb out and getting someone to give him a ride had been his primary mode of transportation when he was a teenager. My parents had only one car then, so if he wanted to go somewhere he had to get someone else to stop and pick him up.

By the time my sisters were in high school, which was about ten miles from our home, my family had acquired a second car. Since my father refused to let his daughters hitchhike or accept rides from strangers, my mother spent a lot of time driving the girls back and forth to school until Elaine got her license and could drive herself and Patti with her. By the time I was a teenager, being driven to school had become the accepted way of doing things. And by the time I got my license, my siblings had finished school and I had the second car pretty much to myself unless my mother needed it.

So now here I was in the middle of New Hampshire, which has a lot more woods than people. I was in my early thirties. I had to hitchhike back to my car. And suddenly I was so overcome with shyness that I couldn't have asked for a drink of water had I been stranded in the Mojave Desert.

I'm sure that part of my problem was picturing myself in Jeffrey Dahmer's refrigerator—my body parts neatly cut up to eat. Since his arrest a few weeks earlier, the descriptions of what he had done to his victims had been splashed all over the world. Logic told me that the chances of someone picking me up and then hacking me to pieces were not very high. But logic does not always overcome fear. I couldn't shake those images.

This road was sparsely traveled, so there weren't many cars to hail in the first place. When the first car approached, I tried to force my arm out, but it wouldn't go. The car drove past without slowing down. A second car passed me a couple of minutes later.

I let the third, fourth, and fifth cars go by. Then there was nothing. The road was empty for five, maybe ten minutes, and I was seething at myself the entire time. Finally I heard and then saw the sixth car approaching.

The car slowed down and stopped a few feet beyond me. Two women were inside—a middle-aged driver and her elderly passenger.

The elderly woman rolled down her window. "Do you know how to get to North Woodstock?" she asked.

"Yup, I certainly do." Since North Woodstock was just a few miles south of where my car was parked, I knew exactly how to get there. I pulled out my map and showed them the routes they had to follow and in which towns they would find them. I was a freakin' encyclopedia. But what I neglected to tell them was that I needed a ride to the place they were going.

"Thank you," she said as she rolled up her window. The car drove away.

"Haskell, you are the biggest goddamned idiot on the face of the planet!" I scolded myself again. "Get over this. It's not a big deal. A million people have hitchhiked before. You can do it. I know you can!"

A couple of more cars cruised by. Finally, after spending an hour on the side of this road, and feeling pretty stupid, I got up my nerve. I stuck out my arm as the ninth car approached me. It didn't stop, but no one gave me the finger as it went by. Lightning didn't strike me. The earth didn't stop spinning. I'd be OK.

Another car passed me, and then another. But the next car slowed as it passed and stopped several yards away. I ran to the car, and the driver lowered the passenger side window. "Where you going?" asked the man who appeared to be in his forties.

"I need to go to Franconia Notch," I replied.

"Well, I'm not going that way, but I can give you a ride to Warren."

"That'd be great." I threw my pack in his backseat, hopped in front, and we took off.

We had a pleasant conversation for the few miles we spent together. He would be turning south on Route 25, and I needed to go north, so I got out in Warren. Newly emboldened by my success, I stuck out my thumb and the first car stopped. The young couple happened to be going to North Woodstock, so I rode with them for most of the remaining miles I had to cover.

When they let me out at the intersection of Routes 118 and 3 in the heart of North Woodstock, I was in a relatively congested downtown area—by northern New Hampshire standards. I stuck out my thumb at the first few cars that went by, but no one stopped. This went on for about ten minutes. There were a lot of cars, but no one was interested in giving me a ride.

It finally occurred to me that drivers tend not to pick up hitchhikers in the middle of town—that hitchhiking is done on the outskirts. I walked north on Route 3 through the main part of North Woodstock, and when I finally got beyond the built-up area, I began hitchhiking again.

The fifth car stopped. It was a small Datsun hatchback—probably a mid-seventies model. The driver was a rather large man, perhaps a few years younger than me. The backseat was down, and the back of the car was filled with cages, each containing several live chickens. This guy was driving around in a small, confined car with several dozen fully-grown chickens.

"Where ya headed?" he asked.

"Just up the road to Franconia Notch," I answered.

"OK, hop in."

I realized that when it comes to hitchhiking, beggars can't be choosers. I suppose I could have taken one look at those chickens crammed into that car and said, "Thanks, but no thanks." But then I'd still be standing by the road. So I kept my mouth shut and got in the car.

"Why are you carrying all these chickens?" I asked.

"I breed hens and raise them until they're old enough to lay," the man told me. "Then I sell them. I'm driving these hens to a farm up north."

"That sounds interesting," I replied.

The guy told me quite a lot about the business of raising chickens during the next few minutes. The cackling from the birds was a bit distracting, and the air was filled with feathers even though the windows were open, or perhaps because of it. I sneezed a half-dozen times, but the driver did not seem to be adversely affected by the feathers or the noise. Fortunately, it was only a few miles to Franconia Notch, where he dropped me off beside my car.

Hitchhiking, it occurred to me, is a lot like what a friend of mine told me about being a good bartender. You have to be a good listener and able to talk about anything with whomever picks you up. And if the driver doesn't want to talk, you leave him alone.

I told Karen to take the exit off the Blue Ridge Parkway onto Virginia Route 56. Rex was following closely behind. While the drive along the meandering ridgeline had been very pleasant and picturesque, the drive off the ridge was anything but. Route 56 is a combination of obscenely steep hills and sharp turns as it descends to the Tye River and the valley floor. While we had been cruising along at about forty-five on the parkway, it was now difficult and dangerous to go much over twenty-five. Our conversation ended abruptly because Karen had to focus on driving.

The time had flown by as we had talked and ridden along the parkway. Now it stood still as we made our way down to where the Appalachian Trail crosses Route 56 next to the Tye River. It had taken us two and a half hours to travel a little under a hundred miles.

Rex parked and locked his car in a small dirt lot beside the trail crossing. The lot was vacant on this November morning except for our vehicles. I got into the backseat, beside his brother's pack, so Rex could sit next to Karen as we retraced the route back to Skyland. We got there a bit before noon. The resort was considerably busier than when we had left at six thirty.

It was time for Rex and me to start hiking. I took my time rebalancing the load in my borrowed pack before hoisting it on. I adjusted the straps so it would rest comfortably on my back while the young couple said their good-byes. Rex strapped on his pack as Karen drove away. We stepped off the pavement and onto the trail.

# 5

# Looking For Love

A little over one hundred miles of the Appalachian Trail runs through Shenandoah National Park, cutting a north-south swath through western Virginia. The trail frequently crosses Skyline Drive, a two-lane highway that runs the length of the park. Hikers are never far from that road. As a result, the trail is heavily used and is quite broad and easy to follow in most places. Because the trail follows the ridge crest, it doesn't have the steep inclines or descents that hikers encounter elsewhere along the trail. The Shenandoahs are the easiest sections of the AT. While easy is good, it can also be a bit boring. It was good to have someone to talk with as I retraced my way southward on the trail.

Rex took the lead. He maintained a reasonably fast pace that was comparable to mine. I could tell we'd be compatible hiking partners for the next couple of days.

"I'm assuming the trail is like this the rest of the way," Rex said after we were a few steps into the woods.

"Yeah, pretty much what you see is what you get. The ups and downs are pretty gradual, not a lot of rocks, and the trail is pretty wide."

"After all those rocks in Pennsylvania, I was really happy when my brother Tom and I got into the park last year."

"This is probably the easiest section of the trail," I told him. "Enjoy it while you can. It gets considerably tougher south of here, and then, of course, there are a lot more mountains and rocks when you get above New York."

It was easy to carry on a conversation even though Rex remained in front of me. The air was crisp, the woods were still, and Rex's words came back to me as clearly as if we were sitting face-to-face in a small room.

"So, I had a great conversation with that fiancée of yours," I said, changing the subject.

"What did you guys talk about?" Rex asked.

"Oh, you know, a lot of stuff. Mostly about hiking. It's really great you've found someone who's supporting you like Karen is."

"I know. Sometimes I wonder why she puts up with all of this. Maybe it's because she thinks I'm going to find another woman while I'm out on the trail," Rex joked.

"Like that's going to happen," I said. "My experience has been that there's remarkably little sex out here."

"Mine, too."

"There was one time when I spent several nights with this newlywed couple while I was doing the Hundred Mile Wilderness in Maine. They'd been married for about a month. So I figured they'd pitch a tent and go at it like rabbits. Instead, they slept in the shelters every night. As far as I could tell they didn't do it at all. That kind of told me that this probably isn't the best place to find romance."

"Of course, it doesn't help that it's mainly guys out here," Rex responded. "My brother and I hiked for a couple of years before I got serious about Karen, before we got engaged. So I was on the trail, foot-loose and fancy free, and there was nothing."

"Yeah, I think some people have this idea that the AT is something like a brothel. I have heard hikers refer to two tents, my trail name, as the, ah, situation when a couple camps out with the express purpose of doing—well, you know, what couples do. But I've never encountered anything like that myself. The trail is probably closer to a monastery. I'm thinking that Mark Sanford thought he'd find love on the AT but realized he had to go to Argentina instead."

"Who?"

"You know, Mark Sanford, the South Carolina governor. It's been in the news recently. He said he was hiking the AT, but instead he went to Argentina to be with his mistress."

"Oh yeah, I heard something about that," Rex laughed. "What a loser. Anyway, aren't you a married guy? Why would any of this interest you?"

"You're right. I've been married most of the time I've been doing this, so I've just been an observer and not a participant. But, like you, there were a couple of years when I was single."

"And you didn't find the love of your life out on the trail?"

"No, I didn't. But there was one trip when I thought I had."

"Hi. How are you doing?" I called out as I approached Stover Creek Shelter, just a few miles north of the AT's southern terminus at Springer Mountain in Georgia. I had seen a woman standing inside the shelter as I had come down the short side trail, and I wanted to make my presence known before I got too close.

Despite my best intentions, I startled her. She turned around quickly, realizing she was no longer alone.

"Oh, I didn't see you there," she said a little anxiously. "I thought I was going to be the only one here tonight. Do you know how to put up this kind of tent? I've never put one up before."

I could see her better as she stepped out from the shadow of the shelter. She did not have a body that immediately said "hiker." Although she was not morbidly obese, she was carrying a substantial amount of weight—the pudgy versus the "built like an ox" variety. She had long blonde hair and a fair complexion. In general, she looked girly-girlish. The woods didn't seem to be her natural environment.

"Well, it depends on what kind of tent it is. But, yeah, I can probably help you. And I wouldn't be so sure that we'll be the only ones here tonight. It's still pretty early, you know."

"Oh, well, then maybe I should wait and see." She started folding up the tent poles that she had been putting together as I was approaching the camp. She refolded the tent and tried to stuff it back into the bag she had just pulled it from. It was obvious that the tent was brand new. It had never been outside of the bag. In fact, everything that she had was new—new backpack, new stove, and new boots.

"So, what's your name?" she asked.

"Jim. What's yours?"

"Amy."

*Oh, shit!* I thought.

I was getting this very strong "damsel in distress" vibe from her, and the last thing I needed now was a woman with my ex-wife's name looking to me for advice and guidance. Aimee and I had finally separated the previous fall after being married for seven years. It had taken me a while to begin to feel like I was ready to face the world again, but by the spring I was liking the idea of being single. I hoped I would be a better Casanova during my thirties than I had been during my school years. But dealing with another Amy, regardless of how she spelled her name, was a little more déjà-vu than I was prepared for.

However, one of the things about the trail is that it's difficult to change the company you wind up with at a shelter unless you're willing to hike a long way to the next one. I was going to be stuck here with Amy for the evening, so I decided to make the situation as pleasant as I could.

Amy and I began talking. It turned out that she had been discharged from the army several months earlier after serving her initial enlistment. She'd moved back with her family, fell into a pretty deep funk, and gained about thirty pounds. She had been driving around Georgia a few weeks earlier and stopped at the Walasi-Yi Inn in Neel's Gap. There she met several people who told her they were about to start thru-hiking the AT. From that conversation she had become inspired to hike it herself.

Amy had bought all of the equipment she thought she'd need. But she couldn't buy experience. She had never actually spent a night in the woods by herself. She had decided to set up the tent inside the shelter because she didn't want to sleep in the open, nor did she want to sleep in the tent outside the shelter. She was off to a bad start.

Amy needed help with everything. Lighting her stove. Treating her water. Preparing her meals. She kept asking me how to do things, and I became more and more annoyed. I put great stock in being self-reliant on the trail unless you are confronted by an emergency such as a broken leg. We're all adults, and the first rule of the AT is to take care of yourself and not be a burden to others. Amy was leaning on me a lot more than I liked. It made me uncomfortable. Besides, I had my own stuff to do. The fact that she had the same name as my ex-wife just made it worse.

As more and more hikers arrived during the afternoon, it became obvious that Amy would not be able to set up her tent in the shelter. She decided to sleep in the shelter with the others. I, on the other hand, preferred to sleep in my tent away from the shelter so I wouldn't have to listen to other people snoring. I also figured that might help distance me from Amy and her constant requests for help.

As the night settled in, all of us sat around the campfire telling our life stories and why we were on the trail. The one thing I didn't share with the others was that I was recently separated and getting a divorce. I was trying to put that part of my life behind me.

The next morning was clear, and I got up early, intending to get on the trail quickly. Maybe if I moved fast enough, Amy wouldn't be ready to leave when I did. Amy got up as I was boiling water for my standard breakfast of coffee and oatmeal.

"Hey, good morning," she greeted me.

"Good morning," I replied.

"Say, would you mind if we hiked together today?"

So, here it was. There was no chance that I could dodge the situation by getting ready quickly and going on my own. I could either be really rude and flat-out refuse, or I could agree to be her hiking partner. If I had thought quickly enough, maybe I could have made some clever excuse about why we should hike separately. But I've never been good at thinking of things like that on the spur of the moment.

"Sure, that'd be great," I answered.

I was afraid I would be stuck with Amy for the entire trip. Fortunately, Amy's neediness that had so irked me the day before was not nearly so evident this morning. Once she was away from the camp, and all we had to do was hike, she was a much more pleasant person. We struck up the typical hikers' conversation. We talked about our childhoods and the experiences that made us who we are. I told her about my past hikes. We also commented about our immediate concerns—how our shoulders and feet were feeling and our thoughts about this part of the trail. Amy thought it was more difficult than I did because this was where she was starting. She had never hiked in the White Mountains.

Amy was an easy conversationalist, and our banter made the time go by quickly. Since we were hiking only five miles, we got to our next shelter about noon. We rested for a few minutes and prepared our lunches. We had the entire afternoon to ourselves. I took a nap. It was four o'clock when I woke up. Two other women, Leigh and Ellen, had arrived while I was sleeping. Amy introduced me.

"Hey, this is Jim, who I was telling you about. He's from Massachusetts like you are."

"Oh, where are you guys from?" I asked.

"We're from the Plymouth area. Where do you live?"

"Amesbury, almost up into New Hampshire. But I used to work in

Plymouth. I was a pilgrim at one time."

The first full-time job I landed after quitting law school was at Plimoth Plantation. I was a cultural informant who dressed in period clothing and assumed the role of a Plimoth resident in 1627. The job was a lot of fun, but the pay was horrible.

Being from the Plymouth area, both Leigh and Ellen knew a lot about Plimoth Plantation. They were hiking the trail together. Ellen was starting her thru-hike, and Leigh was hiking with her for the first couple of weeks. They worked together and were close friends.

Ellen seemed suited for an AT thru-hike. She was about five feet three, broad-shouldered, and muscular. Leigh, on the other hand, did not have an ideal hiker's physique. She was about five feet tall with a small, almost waif-like frame. Both women were obviously very intelligent. Ellen tended to be quiet, and interjected comments only from time to time. Leigh was the exact opposite—gregarious, sassy, and flirty.

I was immediately attracted to her.

We talked well into the night. When it came time for bed, Leigh and Ellen crawled into their tent, Amy stayed in the shelter, and I slept in my tent.

When we got up the next morning and started to break camp, Amy assumed she and I would again hike together. Leigh and Ellen took off before Amy or I were ready to leave. Leigh struggled a bit with her pack, which seemed to be as heavy as she was. Amy and I struck out a few minutes later. As much as I had appreciated hiking with Amy the previous day, I really wanted to hike with Leigh today. I was totally smitten by her.

The section we were doing that day is where many northbound thru-hikers begin to find out how difficult the AT can be. While the trail is devoid of the boulders that I knew so well in New Hampshire and Maine, it is not easy going. It's where hikers encounter switchbacks. Instead of going straight up a mountain, as it generally does in New England, the trail is cut into the side of a mountain so that it zigzags its way up with a series of hairpin turns—called switchbacks. That way, the trail is never very steep, but it makes the climb a lot longer. Georgia is filled with switchbacks. Mountain summits will appear tantalizingly close, but it seems as if it takes forever to get there. Then, after hikers reach the summit, they follow switchbacks down the mountain until they get to the gap, where they begin climbing the next mountain—again by switchbacks.

It felt like we were on a roller coaster all day. We were either hiking up or hiking down, climbing named and unnamed mountains.

Amy and I saw Leigh and Ellen several times. We passed them while they were resting, and they passed us while we were taking a break. That night, we all camped at Woody Gap where Georgia Route 60 crosses the AT—the first major road that crosses the trail.

The four of us decided to hike together the next day. The next shelter, on Blood Mountain, was a little over eight miles away. Even more enticing was the prospect of ending up at Neel's Gap—two miles beyond Blood. Neel's is where the Walasi-Yi Inn is located. It's a private establishment that has a hostel, showers, and a washer and dryer as well as a store where hikers can buy food and other supplies.

Walasi-Yi is probably the most strategically located store on the trail. By the time hikers get there, they have carried their packs for three or four days. They have discovered that their packs are too heavy with stuff they don't need and that they lack certain items they can't do without. The folks at Walasi-Yi will ship back home the items that hikers wish to discard, and they are happy to sell the items that hikers need.

It was obvious as the day wore on that the climb up Blood Mountain was taking its toll on Amy. Ellen and Leigh kept moving ahead, while Amy and I steadily fell back. A blue-blazed side trail about a mile and a half below the summit would have enabled us to skirt around the mountain and avoid the climb to the top. Amy tried to convince me to take the side trail with her. I told her, as gently as I could, that following that trail would kind of defeat the purpose of hiking the AT in the first place. She considered venturing onto the side trail by herself but reluctantly decided to stay on the main trail with someone she knew. She wasn't any too happy that I was, in effect, forcing her to climb the mountain.

A soaking rain from a thunderstorm darkened her mood even more. It made the trail soft and, in some spots, slippery underfoot. The rain made our boots and packs heavier. Branches dripping with water and hitting her in the face made the climb to the top even more torturous. Amy was not a happy hiker.

By midafternoon, in the middle of the storm, she and I opened the door of the stone shelter on top of Blood Mountain. The rest of our hiking group was already inside. Ellen and Leigh had built a fire in the fireplace, and the smell of burning wood and the heat coming from the hearth was a welcome respite from the rain. We waited for the storm to pass and began the descent into Neel's Gap. We reached Walasi-Yi Inn around five o'clock.

You don't know how dirty you are and how wonderful "civilization" feels until you've been in the woods for several days and then find yourself in a place with modern conveniences.

We were all very wet, very sweaty, very muddy, and very hungry. Walasi-Yi had all of the luxuries that hikers could ask for—including beds with mattresses and flush toilets. We were in heaven.

I suspected that Amy was losing her motivation for hiking the trail. She had been exceedingly upbeat and enthusiastic until today. But her stamina had evaporated and her mood had turned sour during the seemingly endless climb up Blood Mountain's switchbacks in the pouring rain. Amy was confronting the dilemma that all hikers face sooner or later: Is this what I really want to be doing?

A small sign posted on a bulletin board in the hostel said it all:

No Rain
No Pain
No Maine

Amy now had to decide if she was willing to withstand lots of the first two in order to accomplish the third.

Leigh and I shared a washing machine and a dryer because we each had only a few clothes to launder. We were sorting through the clean and dried clothes, separating my underwear from hers, when she nonchalantly said, "Hey, we should get together sometime when we're back in Mass."

Wow! I was immediately flying high. As much as we had talked during the past couple of days, the conversations had always been in the context of our trail selves and not our real selves.

For those on the trail, especially for hikers who are out for a long time, it is easy to think of the trail as a place unto itself. The rest of the world does not exist. Your focus becomes the trail ahead of you. The road crossings become landmarks that define how far you've hiked. You forget that those roads actually lead to somewhere. Personal relationships become part of the trail's twilight zone. The people you meet only exist in that dimension. They have no jobs, no relationships, no families, no homes. They're hikers. That is all that defines them, and that is all the camaraderie you need.

Now here we were, Leigh and I, sorting our undies, and she was talking about us getting together, perhaps for dinner, after we got home.

It wasn't as if the thought hadn't already occurred to me. I had found her to be very attractive the first afternoon we met. She was vivacious and flirty and exceedingly intelligent. Furthermore, the sacrifices she was making to help her friend told me she had a good heart. I had been concerned that Leigh might think Amy and I were an "item" since Amy was constantly with me. While I wasn't interested in Amy, I suspected that Amy was interested in me. But if I was rude to Amy, that might turn off Leigh. It was like being in junior high school again. So for the past two days I had been trying to find a way to suggest that we go on a date when we got home, and here she was bringing it up herself.

"That would be great!" I said, trying not to appear too enthusiastic, but also wanting to make sure she knew I was very receptive to the idea.

That night as I lay on my bed, Leigh only a few feet from me in the open bunkroom, my mind was racing, thinking how wonderful it would be to be with her, envisioning my life with her, and then feeling foolish that I was already picking out the china patterns. We hadn't even had a date yet.

Come morning, Leigh, Ellen, and I got busy packing for another few days on the trail. Amy, however, was slow to get ready. Her heart clearly wasn't in it.

"My feet are really killing me. I think I'm going to take a day off," she said in that needful voice that had so irritated me the day we met. I sensed she hoped I would stay and keep her company.

I wasn't interested. "OK," I said. "I think I'll keep going."

"All right. Well, you have a great hike," she replied with a hint of disappointment.

"You, too."

With that, the friendship that Amy and I had developed during the past four days abruptly ended. As I took off with Leigh and Ellen, I wondered if Amy would keep hiking or call it quits. Would she simply rest up and hike again the following day? Would she drop her excess weight, lighten her pack, become a hiking machine, and stand on the top of Katahdin sometime in October? Or would she become another of the 75 percent of those who start their thru-hikes and never finish? I suspect she was among the latter group. To me, she didn't have the desire or the drive to complete the AT. She had decided to hike the trail on a lark, and when the going got tough while climbing Blood Mountain in a thunderstorm, she was ready to pack it in.

Maybe she took that day off, read the sign on the bulletin board, re-gathered her resolve, picked up her pack, and resumed her hike the next morning. Or maybe she used the pay phone at Walasi-Yi to call home and get a ride.

I'll never know.

Ellen, Leigh, and I hiked ten and a half difficult miles from Neel's Gap to the Low Gap Shelter that day. It was Thursday night. I had already decided that I would end this hike the next day. As much as I'd been in my own little world for the past several days, I realized I had to get back to reality. After all, I did have a mortgage to pay. If I spent Friday night with my college friend in Atlanta, I could be back in Massachusetts by Sunday night and back to work Monday.

"How do you plan on getting off the trail?" Leigh asked me as we sat around the campfire that evening at Low Gap.

"I'm planning on getting off at Unicoi Gap tomorrow. There's a major road there, Route 75, and I'm going to hitchhike from there back to Amicalola. My truck's parked there, and then I'll probably go down to Atlanta to stay with a friend of mine for a night. Then I'll drive back to Mass. Why do you ask?"

"Well, as you know, I'd planned to hike all the way to Wesser with Ellen," Leigh said. "Wesser is over ninety miles from here, and in four days we've only traveled a little over forty. I still have another week off from work, but I'm getting really tired and I don't want to slow her down. If I go out with you, could you give me a ride to the airport?"

"I'll do you one better. I'll give you a ride back to Mass."

"I don't want to inconvenience you."

"It's no problem at all. I'd love to have the company."

Oh my God, my dreams were coming true. I was going to be with Leigh, alone, for two or three days. Just her and me in the truck, driving up the Eastern seaboard. Oh my God. Oh my God. Oh my God. This was going to be great!

For the second night in a row, visions of me with Leigh kept me awake for several hours. Was I on the verge of having a relationship with another woman? I could only hope.

Morning finally came after some light, fitful sleep. We ate breakfast, packed our bags, and broke camp. The trail today was relatively flat, a welcome change from the ups and downs we'd been experiencing. Ellen decided to take it easy and hike just the seven and a half miles to Blue

Mountain Shelter. Leigh and I would continue for another couple of miles and descend into Unicoi Gap where we'd hitchhike out. We made good time and reached the shelter by noon. The shelter overlooked a scenic mountain vista and would be a great place for Ellen to spend the night. We ate lunch, then it was time for Leigh and me to leave. The women said their good-byes, and Leigh and I were soon descending to the gap. We reached the road around two o'clock.

Hitchhiking to Amicalola was a snap, probably because Leigh was with me. Although we undoubtedly looked like a couple of bums, our packs immediately identified us a hikers, and her dirty clothes and kerchief did not conceal Leigh's feminine qualities. We needed three rides to get to my truck. Each time, the first car to come along picked us up. It seemed that people were more inclined to pick up a man and a woman hitching a ride than they were a man by himself. We got to my truck in a little more than an hour and headed for Atlanta.

My friend, Doug, offered to take Leigh and me on a top-down tour of the city in his classic convertible as soon as we got to his house. But we were both tired to the bone. All we wanted was to shower and sleep.

We were well-rested and clean the next morning. Doug, ever the gracious host, made us a magnificent breakfast of bacon, eggs, pastries, freshly-squeezed orange juice, and brewed coffee. After eating freeze-dried food for six straight days, Leigh and I devoured Doug's home cooking.

For the first time since I had known her, Leigh's hair was not enclosed in a kerchief. It was shampooed and blown dry, hanging almost to her shoulders. She was even more attractive than I had originally thought.

"She cleans up really nice," Doug told me when she temporarily left the dining room.

"Yeah, I know!" I could now see what Leigh looked like in real life, and I was impressed.

"Something going on between the two of you?" he asked. Doug had been good friends with both Aimee and me in college, and I had never asked him what he thought about our splitting up.

"I sure hope so," I replied. "We're going to be traveling together up to Boston, so hopefully something will happen. I really do like her."

Leigh and I packed our belongings after breakfast. I had brought some non-trail clothes in a suitcase, but Leigh was still living out of her backpack. However, clean clothes, clean hair, and a clean body can make someone look entirely different. We said "So long" to Doug and began driving north.

Now that we were away from the trail, Leigh and I discussed our lives in detail. She had recently ended a relationship with a longtime boyfriend she had met at work. For years she had wanted him to propose, but he hadn't. When he finally did, she decided that she no longer wanted to marry him. While at some point during our hike I had casually mentioned that I had been married, I now talked at much greater length about my relationship with Aimee and the end of our marriage.

We drove until dark. We had reached the Richmond area. I was getting very weary and knew we had to find a place to spend the night.

"Hey, I'm getting really tired. Why don't we get a motel after another few miles?" I suggested.

"Sure, I'm getting tired, too."

For the past several hours I had been deliberating about what to say next. What I really wanted to say was, "Hey, we've been spending a lot of time together. We get along really well. What do you say we hop into bed and move this thing to the next level?" But something told me that might not work so well.

I figured the best thing to do was to make an innocuous suggestion, one that could be interpreted as an interest in having a sexual relationship with her, if she was so inclined, but that could also be taken as an innocent comment if she wasn't.

"I know this trip is costing you a lot," I said. "If you want, we can either share a room or we can get separate rooms. It's up to you."

OK, it wasn't the smoothest approach I'd ever made, but it probably wasn't the most callous comment I'd ever made either.

"It's probably best if we get separate rooms," Leigh replied.

With that said, we found a motel and stayed the night—separately.

We met at the continental breakfast room the next morning. Back on the road, our conversation continued much as it had the previous day. We stopped for lunch at one of the rest areas on the New Jersey Turnpike, not far from where Aimee had grown up. The irony was not lost on me.

After we crossed the George Washington Bridge into New York, however, our conversation became increasingly labored. We'd talk for a while. Then there would be a long silence. Then we'd find another topic to discuss for a little while. Then a longer silence would follow. We had spent the past week talking with each other almost nonstop. Now it was as if we had covered every topic that we could, and there simply was nothing more to say.

Maybe, after crossing the Hudson River, Leigh realized she had a life that transcended the Appalachian Trail and she was beginning to question whether I would be part of it.

The silences grew longer and more awkward as we drove through Connecticut and Rhode Island and then finally to the South Shore of Massachusetts where she lived. When we got to her place, I carried her pack up the stairs and into her apartment. She offered me a soda, and we sat and drank in near silence. After a few minutes, it was time for me to say good-bye. She gave me a halfhearted hug, and I drove to my house in Amesbury. I called her later that week and left a message on her answering machine. She never called back. I was disappointed but not terribly surprised.

I've often wondered why the promise of a relationship with Leigh did not turn out as I had hoped it would. Had she decided at some point that she really wanted to get back with her ex-boyfriend? Did she call him after we got back? Did they get married? Do they have a house and kids? I hope that's what happened to her.

My worst fear is that Leigh thought I was just too creepy or that I came on too strong. Did my suggestion about sharing a motel room backfire on me? If I hadn't suggested that, could we have had a future together? That's also a distinct possibility.

I'll never know.

# 6

# Feuding Founders

Rex and I had hiked for a little over an hour when we found ourselves at a trail junction—a good place to take a break. We had no interest in exploring the side trails. One led uphill to the Hawksbill Gap parking area, which wouldn't be very interesting. The other led downhill to a spring, and we both had plenty of water. We settled our butts onto a couple of flat rocks.

So far, this hike had been a breeze. The temperature had risen to the mid-fifties, and there was no wind. It was a perfect day for hiking. The trail was wide and flat and well-traveled. We had hiked nearly three and a half miles, but we had lost only four hundred feet in elevation. While we had not actually crossed Skyline Drive, the road was ever present, as the trail ran right beside it, sometimes as close as a few feet. Civilization was never far away. If the entire Appalachian Trail was this easy, a lot more people would hike the whole thing.

But backpacking is hard work under the best of conditions, so it felt good to drop our packs and sit on rocks and savor the fall air on this sunny day. I dug out my standard snacks: a small box of raisins, a mini-candy bar—the kind you give to kids on Halloween—and Gatorade. Rex brought out a plastic bag filled with gorp—a mixture of peanuts, raisins, and M&Ms.

I pulled out my trail maps to check my bearings, just as I had done during hundreds of other breaks on the trail. Where am I? How far have I gone? How much farther is the road or campsite or water supply or vista that is my next destination? I suppose this might mean I'm not entirely comfortable about being out in the wilderness; that, deep down, I have to know how far I am from civilization. But this ritual has also served me well many times when I have picked up some detail in a trail guide or on a map that enabled me to find water where I wasn't expecting it or to make it to a campsite before dark.

The trail guides are an excellent odometer. If I had hiked a mile in half an hour, then I knew I was hiking at a two-mile-per-hour pace. Knowing my speed, I could determine if I had time to get to my destination by sundown or if I had to find someplace else to sleep. No matter how thoroughly I had planned the hike beforehand, I was always prepared to alter my plans if circumstances—a late start, a heavy rain, or a sprained ankle—dictated. The trail guides helped me be flexible.

"We've gone three point three miles so far, and we have seven point five to go to get to Big Meadows Campground," I informed Rex. "Sundown is around five, and it's almost one thirty. We're traveling at about two and a half miles an hour, so at this pace we should get there just about sundown."

"Sounds good," Rex replied. "I'm doing fine. I don't need much of a rest. Let's get going." We threw on our packs and resumed hiking, Rex leading the way.

"Jeesh, on this section we might as well have walked down Skyline Drive," Rex said. "It seems like every other minute we're hiking next to it."

"Well, according to the map we're going to be getting away from the road just a little on this next section. But you're right. Skyline is really close by. A little farther south from here, you begin crossing the road a lot, too."

"It must have been really easy to lay out the trail with Skyline Drive so close by."

"Well, actually the trail was here before the road," I replied.

"Huh? That doesn't seem possible."

"I know it doesn't look that way, but it's true. In fact, you could say that building Skyline Drive was one of the AT's defining moments."

"How so?"

"Well, are you sure you want to hear this story? I'm kind of a history geek, and this stuff really intrigues me. But I know some people would rather stick needles in their eyeballs than hear about the history of something."

"No, no, I'd like to hear it," Rex replied. "Besides, we got plenty of time to kill."

"OK. But don't say I didn't warn you. If you're about to commit suicide or something, just tell me and I'll stop. OK?"

"OK."

"So, what do you know about the creation of the Appalachian Trail?" I asked. If Rex already knew a lot of the background, I didn't need to bore him with the basics.

"I think there was a guy named McKay or something like that, but I don't really know much about it, to be honest," Rex replied, turning his head sideways so his words would drift back to me.

"His name was MacKaye, pronounced with a long 'i' instead of a long 'a,' but you've got the guy right. So there was this guy named Benton MacKaye, and in nineteen-twenty-one he published an article that basically said: 'Hey, why don't we create a trail that will run from Mount Mitchell in North Carolina, which is the highest point east of the Mississippi, to Mount Washington in New Hampshire, which is the highest point in New England.' But actually, the article said a lot more than that."

"Wait a second. The AT runs between Springer in Georgia and Katahdin in Maine," Rex interrupted.

"You're right. Where the trailheads were ultimately located is just one of many twists and turns this story is going to take." We resumed walking.

"Anyway, MacKaye's article gets published, and a lot of people grab onto the idea and become really excited about it. Of course, it didn't hurt that there was already a lot of infrastructure for the trail in the first place. There had been trails in places like the White Mountains since the nineteenth century, and the Long Trail in Vermont was nearly complete. So it wasn't too much of a stretch for people to realize that they could connect the trails that had already been built in the Northeast into one trail and then extend it down South.

"But what was even more vital," I continued, "was that there were already several trail clubs that could maintain the trail. The Appalachian Mountain Club in New England had been around for some time, and there was a club in New York and New Jersey, and, of course, the Green Mountain Club was busy building the Long Trail."

"Who was this MacKaye guy, anyway?"

"Well, to say the least, he was an interesting character. He's been described as a Yankee's Yankee. He was born in Connecticut, attended Harvard, and got a job working for the Forest Service. Remember that the feds were creating national forests at that time, and the AT basically goes from one national forest to the next. So it was no coincidence that someone with a lot of knowledge about the Forest Service would be writing an article about creating the Appalachian Trail. But what MacKaye envisioned was something much more than just a trail."

"How so?"

"What MacKaye saw was a trail that would connect a series of communities together. He called them camp communities, and each community would be self-supporting and cooperatively owned. The people living in the communities would be more or less living off the land and forests, and the people hiking the trail would help support those communities by staying there and doing some of the work."

"That sounds almost like a sixties commune," Rex said, flashing me a peace sign.

"Yeah, I would say very close to it. Except this is something like forty years beforehand."

"Why did he want to create all of those communities?"

"Well, MacKaye thought those communities would essentially create a counterculture to offset the urbanization and industrialization that was taking over the East Coast. So, pretty much, he was a social revolutionary."

"Was the trail going to be just for the people living in those camps?"

"No, the trail was supposed to be for everyone. Of course, there would be people living in the camps. But there was also the general population who would venture onto the trail and spend a couple of weeks a year living in those communities and helping with the work.

"MacKaye's article was published in 'twenty-one, and, like I said, the idea really took off. The trail clubs got really excited about it, and MacKaye was traveling up and down the East Coast talking about his idea. The trail clubs began blazing more trail to make the AT a reality. They were connecting trails that already existed in the Northeast. At the same time, some of the trail was being developed in the South. Finally, in nineteen-twenty-five, all of these groups got together and formed the Appalachian Trail Conference, the ATC. Everything seemed to be going great, except that after the ATC was formed, they forgot to do one thing."

"What was that?" Rex asked.

"They kind of forgot to make any more trail," I answered.

Rex again stopped in his tracks and gave me a quizzical look.

"While there had been a lot of trail-building between 'twenty-one and 'twenty-five, the amount of trail developed after 'twenty-five dropped off a lot," I explained as we resumed walking. "It was almost as if they had put all of their efforts into creating the organization, and forgot about the trail in the process. So now, enter Myron Avery."

"Who's he?"

"Well, if Benton MacKaye was the guy who envisioned the AT, Myron Avery was the one who made it happen. And Avery was just as interesting, if not more so, than MacKaye."

"Really?"

"Oh yeah. When you look up 'Type A personality' in the dictionary, you find a picture of Myron Avery. This guy was driven. He grew up in Lubec, Maine, which is on the easternmost point of the state. In fact, he practically grew up in Canada."

We reached a trail junction and quickly read the sign posted there. The trail to the right descended to some kind of cabin, while the one to the left led up to the summit of Hawksbill. That might have been interesting, but it was almost a mile to the summit. It was much more of a detour than we wanted to take, so we stayed on the AT.

"You grew up in Maine, right?"

"That's right, in the central part of the state. Where Avery grew up is about a three-hour drive to the east. It's a whole different world. Maine's a lot bigger than most people realize. Even now, there's a lot of woods between the two regions. Myron's dad was the manager of a sardine factory, so I get the idea that the Averys were big fish in a really small pond. I'd guess that Myron Avery's upbringing was a lot different from the way MacKaye grew up in Connecticut. The cultures were totally different. Still, Avery was very smart, and he did what lots of intelligent Maine boys did back then. He went to Bowdoin College in Brunswick. Then he went to law school at Harvard. While he was in law school, he worked at a Hartford law firm during the summer, then he landed a job in DC with the Maritime Commission after he graduated."

Rex tripped on a root and almost fell flat on his face before he caught himself. "Better concentrate on what I'm doing," he said.

"You OK?" I asked.

"Yeah, I'm fine."

"From all accounts, Avery was a workaholic, but in his free time he liked to go into the woods and do some hiking. He was on one of these hikes in nineteen-twenty-seven when he ran into another hiker. They began talking about hiking and the trail they were on—you know, the usual stuff—and the hiker mentioned that there was this movement afoot to create a trail along the crest of the Appalachian Mountains. Now, remember, the ATC had been formed a couple of years earlier. Avery remembered that one of the partners in the Hartford law firm had done some hiking, so when he got back to Washington, he sent this guy a letter asking if he knew anything about this trail idea.

"This partner, Judge Perkins, had retired from the firm. But he had become very involved in hiking. He had attended one of the presentations that MacKaye had given, and became so inspired that he had joined the board of the ATC. So Perkins told Avery all about MacKaye's vision for the AT, and pointed out that the trail was going to be constructed and maintained by local trail clubs.

"Avery asked him which trail club was working in the DC area. Perkins told him there wasn't any. No problem. Avery organized the Potomac Appalachian Trail Club within a few weeks, and that club began blazing trail in this area. Then he found out the ATC hadn't had a meeting since nineteen-twenty-five. Again, no problem. He and Perkins organized a meeting in nineteen-twenty-eight, and they made sure it was held in Washington. They also saw to it that the ATC's bylaws were to their liking and that Perkins was elected chairman. So within a year or so of first learning about something called the Appalachian Trail, Avery had basically engineered the takeover of the organization and was leading one of the trail clubs that was creating hundreds of miles of the trail in this area. Then Perkins suffered a stroke in nineteen-thirty, so Avery became the head of the ATC. And remember, this guy was only in his late twenties and early thirties at the time. He was a real go-getter."

"Did he have a day job all this time?" Rex asked.

"Yes, he did. In fact, from every account I've read it sounds like he worked very long hours at his job, so he did all of this AT stuff during weekends and any other spare time he had. And, oh by the way, he was also married, and he and his wife were beginning to have kids.

"Now that Avery was involved in the ATC, he realized that it was imperative that trail clubs be formed wherever the trail still needed to be built. Once again, no problem. He and other members of the PATC went down South and up to Maine, and they began working with the locals in those areas to form clubs. Pretty soon, there were clubs working on the trail all over the place. Oh, and remember how I mentioned that MacKaye had originally said the trail was going to go from Mount Mitchell in North Carolina to Mount Washington in New Hampshire?"

"Yeah?"

"Well, Avery basically said this puppy is going to end up in Maine if I have anything to say about it. So that's why the AT ends at Katahdin and not at Washington."

"So what about the southern end?" Rex asked. "Why does the trail end in Georgia and not on Mitchell?"

"My understanding is that a group from the South got involved, and they wanted the trail to end at Lookout Mountain in Tennessee. But they couldn't make that happen, so they decided to end it at Oglethorpe in Georgia. But there was too much development in that area to suit them, so they ultimately ended it on Springer. In fact, what's even more curious is that the trail doesn't even go over Mitchell, even though it comes pretty close."

We hiked in silence for a few minutes while Rex processed what I had told him.

"Where was MacKaye during all of this?" he asked, because I hadn't mentioned MacKaye for quite a while.

"Well, it seems pretty obvious to me that MacKaye and Avery weren't exactly bosom buddies. I think both of them were very ambitious and articulate, but they had different ideas about how the trail would be used and how it should be developed. MacKaye was the true visionary, so he spent a lot of time going around and talking about the trail and this utopian society.

"Avery was more pragmatic. Creating the utopian communities was secondary to him. He wanted to focus on building the trail, because if you didn't have the trail then you wouldn't have the communities. He also spent a lot of time going around promoting it and organizing the groups that would actually go out and build the thing. I think MacKaye saw Avery as some Johnny-come-lately who wasn't making the trail everything he had envisioned, and I think Avery thought MacKaye was some pie-in-the-sky dreamer who couldn't build the trail if his life depended on it. I'm sure that each of them just wanted the other to shut up and go away.

"Finally, the whole thing came to a head in nineteen-thirty-five during the ATC's meeting, which was held at Skyland Resort. The topic of discussion was the construction of Skyline Drive."

"You mean the place where we met yesterday?" Rex asked.

"Yup, right there. It's a different building, but the resort was there at the time. Remember, the country was in the midst of the Great Depression, and the federal government wanted to make this area into a national park, and they wanted to build a road over the top of the ridge. So they went to the ATC and said, 'Hey, you wouldn't mind moving your trail so we can build a road, would you?' Now the ATC had to make a choice. Would they move the trail or would they fight?"

We stopped for a moment at Spitler Knoll Overlook to take in the view of the Shenandoah Valley.

"Do you think they called it Spitler Knoll because someone could spit off it and have it reach the valley?" I asked Rex in jest.

"With a favorable breeze, a good wad of chewing terbacky would travel a couple of miles," he replied, not to be outdone.

"So what happened during the meeting?" Rex asked.

"Well, there were two factions at the meeting. The faction led by MacKaye said the ATC should fight it. If they allowed the feds to build the road, then the wilderness experience would be lost, and it would be impossible to ever fulfill his vision of creating a camp culture. The faction led by Avery said, 'Hey, we don't like it, but we realize we need the feds to support this trail in the long run, so we might as well give in.'

"MacKaye's faction argued that Avery's people were traitors to the cause. Avery basically said, 'Screw you. It was my group that built the damned trail in the first place, so if we have to rebuild it, we will.' You have to remember that it was Avery's Potomac club that had constructed that section of the trail in the first place, so MacKaye was fighting over a piece of turf that Avery figured belonged to him. Anyway, Avery's side won. The meeting ended with several members leaving the ATC. MacKaye went off to form the Wilderness Society with a number of them, and I don't believe the two men, MacKaye and Avery, ever spoke to one another again."

"So they moved the trail?" Rex asked, looking at me in surprise.

"Yup, they moved the trail, and Skyline Drive was built," I confirmed. "But in doing so, they got the feds to agree to never build another road running parallel with the Appalachian Trail. So, yes, they agreed to let the feds build Skyline, provided that kind of thing would never happen again."

"Wait a minute," Rex interjected. "Why would the feds, the federal government, give a damn about what the Appalachian Trail people thought? If they wanted to turn this area into a national park and build a highway, why didn't they just go ahead and do it? Why should they be concerned about relocating the trail?"

"Damned good question. Technically, I suppose, the feds didn't have to ask the ATC to do anything. But those were different times. The federal government was a lot smaller in the thirties and, let us say, more user-friendly. After all, we're not talking about the Bush administration."

"Not so sure Obama is doing any better," Rex said, resuming the hike.

"You've got a point," I replied. "Anyway, we're talking about FDR. He was the consummate politician, and he knew better than to piss off any group of people who might be able to help him later on. That's how he got the New Deal off the ground.

"And the ATC may have been young, but it already had some pretty powerful allies. Herbert Hoover had attended the first meeting in 'twenty-five when he was secretary of commerce. Then there was FDR himself. He was a Harvard man. So were MacKaye and Avery. I'm not sure they knew the president, but they certainly knew people who knew him.

"Also, both MacKaye and Avery either had worked or were still working for the government, and they knew how to work the system. So the ATC was not a group to be taken lightly. The feds probably knew that and decided it would be better to stay on the ATC's good side by asking them to move the trail."

"So Skyline got built and the trail got moved," Rex said.

"That's right. It took them a couple more years to finish the entire trail. The last section in Maine was completed in 'thirty-seven, and the trail was finally finished." I waited a couple of seconds for dramatic effect and then continued, "For about a year."

"What?!" Rex exclaimed, looking back at me in disbelief.

"Well, the trail was completed in nineteen-thirty-seven, but two things happened in 'thirty-eight that closed it again."

"The trail was only open for a year?"

"That's right."

"Oh my God. After all that work. How did that happen?"

"Well, the first thing that happened was the Hurricane of Nineteen-thirty-eight. A lot of the trail in New England was closed because of all the blowdowns."

"I think I've heard about that one. What was the name of that storm again?" Rex asked.

"The Hurricane of Nineteen-thirty-eight. It was before they gave hurricanes names."

"OK. So what else happened?"

"Do you remember that I told you that one of the ATC's conditions for agreeing to Skyline Drive was that the feds would never build another road beside the trail?"

"Yeah?"

"Well, in nineteen-thirty-eight the feds went back to the ATC and said, 'You know, we liked building Skyline so much, we'd just like to continue that whole project and call it the Blue Ridge Parkway. By the way, you wouldn't mind if we moved a hundred and twenty-five miles of your trail, would you?'"

"But hadn't the feds said they wouldn't do that again?"

"Yeah, but I guess they had a really short memory," I replied. "Of course, this totally pissed off Avery, but there really wasn't a lot he could do about it, so the feds relocated the trail to build the parkway. But before the trail could be reopened, this little thing called World War Two came along. For several years the guys who would normally be working on the trail were doing other things like saving the world. It wasn't until nineteen-fifty-one that the entire trail was finally reopened.

"All the while, Avery had been chair of the ATC. In 'fifty-one he said it was time for him to step down now that the trail was open again. He died of a heart attack eight weeks later. He was only fifty-two. Supposedly, MacKaye didn't even send a condolence card."

We stopped again to take in the view to the west. We seemed to be practically hovering over the valley from our perch on Franklin Cliffs. I was really enjoying these views because I had been in a rainy soup while hiking this section the day before.

"You know, I never realized there was so much drama involved with creating the AT," Rex responded. "I kind of just figured that they decided to make the trail, and then a few years later the trail was finished, and that was it."

"Yeah, the history of the trail is not very well known. I'm kind of a history nut, if you hadn't already noticed. I'm more interested in the trail than a lot of people, and it's taken me years to get even a basic understanding of everything that happened. What I find most fascinating is that the AT probably wouldn't have been possible had it not been for MacKaye, Avery, and the federal government. And yet, by the time the trail was finished, all three were totally disgusted with each other."

"What do you mean?"

"Well, first you needed someone like MacKaye to have the vision," I replied. "I don't think either Avery or the feds would have ever thought about creating an Appalachian Trail. Someone might have gotten the idea to connect some of the trails in the Northeast, but the trail certainly wouldn't have gone as far as Georgia.

"But once that vision became public, you needed someone like Avery to motivate folks to go out and make the trail. Not only did Avery organize the Potomac Appalachian Trail Club and have them blaze something like three hundred miles of the trail, he also organized many of the clubs that blazed other parts of it. And those clubs have maintained those sections ever since. I don't think MacKaye had the temperament to do that.

"And the backdrop to all of this," I concluded, "was the fact that the federal government was creating a string of national forests and parks that most of the trail goes through. So if the feds hadn't acquired the land in the first place, it wouldn't have been possible to create the AT."

Rex took a couple of seconds to let all of this sink in. "OK, so then I've heard about this guy named Earl Shaffer who was the first person to hike the entire AT. How does he fit into this?"

"Well, that's a bit of a misconception. Actually, Avery was the first person to hike the entire trail, and there were several others who did it before Shaffer. But Shaffer was the first thru-hiker. He did the entire trail in 'forty-eight."

"Wait a second," Rex countered. "Didn't you say the trail wasn't reopened until sometime in the fifties?"

"You're right. Shaffer had to bypass some sections because the trail was still closed, officially. But he did do the hike from Georgia to Maine, so it counted as a thru-hike. What's interesting about Shaffer's hike was that the ATC didn't think it was possible for anyone to complete the trail in a year, so at first they didn't believe him. However, he convinced them that he had. What's even more amazing is that he hiked it all in about four months. That's a hell of a thru-hike by today's standards, considering most thru-hikers take anywhere from five to seven months."

"OK, so Shaffer was the first thru-hiker," Rex said. "But there were others who had section-hiked the entire trail before him?"

"That's exactly right," I confirmed as we resumed following the white blazes. I then changed the subject slightly. "Of course it's impossible to prove, but I think that the reason the trail still exists today is because of the thru-hikers."

"Why do you say that?"

"Well, I remember first hearing about the Appalachian Trail when I was nine, so that was nineteen-sixty-nine. And I distinctly remember my brother talking about thru-hikers at the time. What's curious is that at that point, fewer than one hundred thru-hikes had been completed. Yet, that was the thing that fascinated people. It certainly fascinated me. Now, of course, a lot more people have completed thru-hikes. But I believe that if it hadn't been for the lore of the thru-hike—the idea that someone could start out in Georgia in the spring, walk over two thousand miles, and wind up in Maine by the fall—I don't think this trail would have captured the imaginations of so many people. The more popular sections would still be there, like the ones over the mountains in the national parks and forests. But I think some of the trails connecting those sections would have been lost over time."

"But as a section hiker, don't you sometimes feel like you're a second-class citizen out here?" Rex asked. "That the only 'true' hikers are the ones doing the thru-hikes?"

"Of course I feel that way at times," I answered. "But I'm not so sure that idea is coming from the thru-hikers. Maybe it's just my own conscience asking me if I'd have the guts to actually do a thru-hike. It's funny, but the thru-hiker who originally inspired me and my first wife to do this section hike said he would have section-hiked the trail if he could do it again. He also said that many of the thru-hikers he had met were so depressed toward the end of the trail that they just wanted to get it over and done with. I think I would wind up feeling exactly like that if I were to try a thru-hike. I'm afraid I'm too hyperactive to do the same thing day in and day out for six months in a row. So, for me, these section hikes every year have been a great diversion from the rest of my life. But I still wonder if I could do a thru-hike. I don't think you can be out here for very long without wondering the same thing."

"Is that the difference between thru-hikers and section hikers like you and me?" Rex asked.

"Exactly. Every year you get the thru-hikers who become totally consumed by the trail and its culture, at least for the year they're hiking it. Then you have the schleps like you and me who really appreciate the trail but aren't quite willing to give up their day jobs to do it. MacKaye's vision was that both of those cultures would come together on this trail, and that is what has happened. In effect, the camp culture that MacKaye originally envisioned has been created. It's just that the culture exists within the thru-hiker community. The only difference was that MacKaye envisioned that culture being stationary, but instead the camp culture is very mobile."

"Does that mean that MacKaye won the battle?"

"Well, in a way I guess everyone won the battle. MacKaye's vision of a trail culture became a reality, and Avery got his trail. What's ironic is that Avery and MacKaye weren't really that far apart on their visions of the trail. It's just that neither of them could compromise even a little bit to accommodate the other guy's perspective. Of course, given how much they accomplished even though they hated each other, one of the big questions that will never be answered is how much they could have done if they had worked together."

Rex and I had been so engrossed in our conversation that the afternoon had slipped away as we hiked the easy miles. We were both surprised when we came upon the unmistakable signs of civilization as we rounded a bend in the trail. Up ahead, the forest had been thinned out, and we could make out a scattering of tents and RVs through the trees. We were approaching the back side of Big Meadows Campground.

The smell of smoke mixed with the aromas of hamburgers and hot dogs being cooked over open fires quickly made us hungry for something more substantial than trail snacks. We hiked along the back of the campground for a couple of minutes and found an empty campsite that looked ideal. The site had the standard picnic table and fire ring next to the camp road; a separate lower section would be a perfect place to pitch the tent. After a pleasant afternoon on the trail, we had arrived at our destination in time to enjoy the evening.

# 7

# Dating Donna

"How'd it go?" Rex asked when I returned to the campsite we had claimed for that mid-November Sunday night at Big Meadows Campground.

"Oh, all right, I guess," I replied, a little deflated. "I'm still recovering from sticker shock."

"Why's that?"

"Well, the cost for this campsite is seventeen bucks."

"What?!" Rex exclaimed.

"Yeah. I didn't think we'd have to pay, considering it's so late in the season. Believe it or not, seventeen dollars is the off-season rate."

"Holy shit. Well, at least let me chip in half."

"No, that's OK. After all, I'm using your equipment and eating your food. The least I can do is pay for the campsite," I said.

"You sure?"

"I'm sure. This one's on me."

After Rex and I had selected this campsite, we'd begun unpacking our gear to settle in for the night. It's like checking into a Holiday Inn after a long day of driving—it's comforting to know that you have a place you can call your own even if it's only for ten or twelve hours.

This is when I normally get busy—setting up my tent, unrolling my mattress pad and sleeping bag, getting water, lighting my stove, and cooking my evening meal. I've followed that routine for so long I don't even think about it. But tonight the tables were turned. Rex was in charge. All of the equipment we were backpacking belonged to him or his brother. I owned only my clothing. Rex knew how to set up his tent and fire up his stove and cook the meal.

I tried to help and only managed to get in his way. I was feeling about as useless as a flat tire. So it made more sense for me to get us registered for the evening—to do something useful—than it did to keep getting in Rex's way or to do absolutely nothing at the campsite. I grabbed my wallet and set out for the office, confident that the tent would be set up and dinner would be cooking when I returned.

Money is rarely needed on the Appalachian Trail. Although hikers certainly have to buy food and other supplies before they set out, it doesn't cost anything to stay in the AT shelters. I have been on the trail for days at a time without having to engage in a single financial transaction. That's why I was so surprised about the seventeen-dollar campground fee at Big Meadows. It seemed like a foreign concept.

"That's our policy. Everyone pays," shrugged the man at the office when my eyes nearly popped out of my head after he told me the price. I was glad I had brought my wallet, which I always carry in my pack. Otherwise, I'd have had to walk back to the campsite and then back to the office to pay the man—which would have totally pissed me off.

Back at the campsite, I looked for things to do to get the camp completely set up by dark. Rex had already put up the tent. He had drawn water from a camp spigot, and it was heating on his stove. About the only thing left for me to do was to see to our sleeping accommodations. So, with Rex's approval, I began pulling the pads and bags from the packs.

That's when I learned a thing or two about advanced camping technology.

I began comparing the equipment that Rex and his brother use with the gear I carry. At first glance, the plastic, one-liter water bottles and the sleeping bags would be familiar to anyone who had done any camping at all. But these sleeping bags were considerably lighter than the one I pack. As I opened them up to air them out, I could also tell they were warmer than mine. I would be very comfortable tonight.

Rex had also packed self-inflating mattress pads that were newer and a little lighter than mine. These pads don't actually expand very much when filled with air. Yet, they are just thick enough to keep your body off the hard ground; to make the difference between having a relatively comfortable night's sleep and no sleep at all. I rolled out the pads and opened the valves so air could seep in. We would add a couple of final breaths and seal the valves just before bedding down to give ourselves comfortable cushions.

His three-person tent was similar in size to mine, but the fabric and poles were made of lighter materials. I could have easily picked up his tent with one finger. A three-person tent is something of a misnomer. The tent is designed so that two people can sleep with their heads and feet pointed in the same direction and for a third person to lie between them the opposite way. You're packed together like sardines in a can—without the oil. If one of the three is a restless sleeper or snores or talks in his sleep, it is hell to pay for the other two. In reality, a three-person tent is cramped even for two. I've never known anyone to be happy about sleeping with two other people that way. Still, Rex's tent was lighter than mine, so, psychologically, that made it better.

By the time I had set out our bags, Rex had poured boiling water into two pouches containing prepackaged, freeze-dried meals—beef stroganoff and chicken teriyaki. Store-bought, freeze-dried meals are gourmet fare on the trail. On the downside, they are very pricey and they have a lot of excess packaging that makes them too cumbersome to suit many thru-hikers. On the other hand, they are pretty tasty and have the perfect nutritional balance a hiker needs—a little protein and a lot of carbohydrates. They are a luxury I am more than willing to pay for and carry, and I was glad that Rex felt the same way. We'd eat well. Now we had to wait ten minutes for the water to cook the food inside the pouch.

"I'm really pissed at myself," Rex started. "No matter how much I plan, there's always something I forget."

"Been there. Done that. What'd you forget?" I replied knowingly.

"Coffee. Had it on the counter and just didn't put it in my pack."

"Yup, done that, too. We can get by without it. Do you normally bring instant or bags?"

"Bags."

"Me, too. Hate instant. Coffee bags have pretty much saved me. I think we'll probably be able to get a cup of joe at the store, if it's still open. Otherwise, I guess we'll be going cold turkey. No problem. I just hope we can get a cup in the morning."

If I'm addicted to anything, it's my morning coffee. But one of the first things you learn about hiking is that if you forget something, you do without. There isn't a 7-Eleven around every corner.

"You forget much on your hikes?" Rex asked.

"Yeah, sure have. Coffee is pretty far down the list of important things I've forgotten."

"Like what?"

"Well, one time I forgot my raingear, and of course it rained cats and dogs. Then another time I forgot toilet paper. But, fortunately, my brother had given me a small package of goodies from one of his National Guard rations, and in it was this tiny roll of toilet paper. I had to ration the TP during a five-day hike. I think I had like five sheets a day."

"That's pretty gross," Rex laughed.

"But that doesn't come close to the most important thing I've forgotten."

"DONNA!!!!!!

"DONNAAAAAA!!!!!!!!

"STOP!!!!! PLEASE STOP!!!!!!"

I stood in the middle of the road, yelling my lungs out, waving my arms over my head, jumping up and down, doing everything I could to get my wife's attention as she drove away. Maybe she'd hear me over the noise of her engine. Maybe, just maybe, she'd see me in her rearview mirror or she'd look back one last time before driving out of sight.

But she didn't.

I watched her little red Escort crest the top of a small hill and disappear down the other side, leaving me alone in the silence of the Vermont countryside.

"Oh shit! This just sucks!" I mumbled to myself after I had stopped jumping and screaming loudly enough to awaken a hibernating bear. "What the hell are you going to do now, Haskell?"

I sat on a boulder by the road to consider my options.

Until now, this trip had been going very well. Donna and I had escaped Massachusetts in late September for a long weekend in Vermont after a summer filled with anxiety over the adoption of our son.

We had driven to Vermont in separate vehicles on Thursday and stayed in a motel that night. The plan was for me to park my truck at one trail crossing on Friday morning and for Donna to drop me off at another. So far, so good. Then I would begin a four-day hike back to my truck, and Donna would drive to Waitsfield to ride Icelandic horses for a couple of days. She would drive home on Saturday, and I'd get back on Monday.

But the plan began to unravel the moment I realized I had left something very important in my wife's car….

Although I was disappointed that a relationship had not developed with Leigh after our hike was over, I had gotten a taste for being back in "the hunt" after my divorce. I realized it was time to take the bull by the horns—to actually start dating women. Even though I knew that the male of the species traditionally initiates that sort of thing, I really would have preferred to have the women take the first step. However, I resigned myself to the idea that I had to take charge of my own destiny. So I took the plunge.

In mid-June, a couple of months after returning from Georgia, I went on a blind date. I met Donna at a waterfront park in Salem. I could tell immediately that she was very athletic—the human equivalent of a cheetah—thin, sleek, built for speed. We sat on a bench and talked for a few minutes. Donna had put the gifts that God had given her to good use. She had run track—the middle distances—in high school and college, and she still ran in some road races. She still held her high school's record for the half-mile after fifteen years. While I had been running since high school, there was too much Maine farm boy in my DNA to be anywhere nearly as competitive as Donna had been. I was built much more for endurance than speed.

While we talked, I became intrigued by her sunglasses. Each lens was imprinted with a silhouette of a palm tree. I had never seen anything quite like them before; they were just cool to look at. Anyone who would wear something like that must be OK.

After several minutes of "getting to know you" conversation, we decided to have dinner at a nearby restaurant. For reasons that I still do not understand, I turned into a total idiot after we walked through that restaurant's door. We were seated, chatted for a few minutes, and then proceeded to the restaurant's generously-stocked salad bar to get our first course. Rather than handing a plate to Donna, which would have been the gentlemanly thing to do, I grabbed a plate for myself, cut in front of her, filled it with lettuce and tomatoes and blue cheese dressing and returned to the table, leaving Donna behind at the salad bar. She followed me back to the table a couple of minutes later. When the bread was served, I cut off a hunk for myself and didn't offer any to her. For some reason, I totally forgot all of the good manners that I had learned from the time I was five. It was as if I had grown up in a cave.

Still, we talked about our interests as we ate dinner. Donna was into horseback riding and photography. She especially liked to photograph flowers and scenery. "Taking pictures really gets my mind off my job," she explained. Her light brown hair, bleached almost blonde by the sun, told me that she indeed did spend a lot of her spare time outdoors.

"Oh, really," I replied. "Maybe I could see some of your photos some time."

"We'll see," she said without any hint of a commitment. "So how do you spend your spare time?"

"Well, I like to run. I've done a couple of marathons. But what I'm really into right now is section-hiking the Appalachian Trail."

"Oh, that's interesting," Donna said after pausing just long enough for my words to sink in. She didn't know if I was serious or just pulling her leg. "You mean THE Appalachian Trail? The one that people stay out on for, what, a whole year? How do you find the time to do that and hold down your job?"

I told her I had hiked about a hundred miles of the AT in the past two years, and that I hoped to hike the entire trail in about twenty years.

"You mean you go out and hike with a heavy pack for days at a time, and get all dirty and smelly? And you call that fun?" she asked.

"Well, I suppose that's one way of putting it," I answered.

"Haven't you ever heard of golf? Or bicycling?" she asked. "I've never met anyone who was hiking the entire Appalachian Trail."

Our date ended with the arrival of the check. I offered to pay, but Donna insisted we go Dutch. I assumed she didn't want to feel obligated to me in any way. I also got the idea, after we parted, that I would never see her again. I had enjoyed her company, but I figured I had not scored many points because of my Neanderthal behavior and because she thought I was some kind of a nutcase because I was hiking the AT.

"Oh well," I told myself. "Nothing ventured, nothing gained. I wonder when I can meet someone else."

I got home from work a little earlier than usual the following Tuesday, and went for a five-mile run. The phone was ringing when I returned. I was still breathing heavily and soaked with sweat because of the heat and humidity.

"Hi, it's Donna. From last Saturday?"

"Oh, hi!" I was thoroughly surprised to hear her voice. Nervously, I tried to switch the phone from my left hand to my right. But the phone slipped through my sweaty fingers. It hit the side of the counter with a THUD and bounced up. I reached to catch it, but I missed and it hit the counter again, THUD, before it landed on the floor, THUD, bounced, and came to rest with a softer thud.

*Oh, great,* I thought. *She's either deaf or she thinks I'm the biggest klutz since Laurel and Hardy. It'll be a miracle if she hasn't hung up.*

I picked the phone off the floor. "Hello?" I asked. "You still there?"

"Yeah, I'm here."

"I'm really sorry. The phone slipped out of my hand, did this little dance, and finally landed on the floor. So, how are you doing?"

"Well, as soon as I get my hearing back I should be OK."

Fortunately for me, she sounded amused. She apparently had a good sense of humor. Maybe I was still OK.

"Sorry."

"No problem. I was just kidding. Hey, I have to drive up to Amesbury in a little while. Do you want to grab an ice cream?"

"Sure, that'd be great!" I was amazed, and very happy, that Donna wanted to see me again considering I had not exactly been Mr. Wonderful during our dinner or with the phone. Maybe she was taking pity on me.

"I just got done with a jump, so I need to run in the shower," I added, my tongue tied in a giant knot. "No, no, no. I mean, I just got done with a run, so I need to…"

"Yeah, I know what you mean. Go take your shower. You obviously need to get the blood running back into your brain from your run."

"You've got that right."

"OK, I'll be there in about two hours. That OK?"

"Yeah, that would be great."

I hung up the phone after making sure she knew where I lived. *Wow. I've been this total idiot, and she's still interested in me,* was all I could think.

I showered, dressed, and waited. She drove into my driveway, I hopped into her car, and we went to the local ice cream parlor. We each ordered a sundae, and then we sat in the parking lot for the next couple of hours—talking about our lives, our families, our previous spouses, and our aspirations, including hiking the Appalachian Trail.

I was smitten. For the next several weeks, every waking moment that I wasn't with Donna I was thinking about her. We spent as much time together during weekends as we possibly could. We talked on the phone two or three times a day. And even though both of us had full-time jobs, we got together one or two nights during the week, usually at her apartment in Salem. I'd typically leave her place at one or two in the morning, drive for an hour back to Amesbury, grab a couple of hours of sleep, and then drag myself into work in Gloucester by eight.

The more I learned about Donna, the more it seemed we had lived parallel lives. Like me, she had grown up in a family of four children, two boys and two girls, who were spaced over twelve years. While I am the youngest, Donna is the third child. In both of our families, three of the four children are left-handed.

We came from working class families. In fact, our mothers had worked for the lunch programs at our schools. Both of our fathers had been larger-than-life figures in our respective lives, and both had died suddenly at about the same age.

Donna had gone to Brandeis University in Massachusetts and had run cross-country and track. I had gone to Boston University. We had each gotten married when we were fresh out of college, and both marriages had ended after about seven years. Since Donna is three years older than me, she had been out of her marriage for four years and I had been out of mine for a little less than one.

Although I had never expected to fall in love again this quickly, I realized I was falling head over heels for Donna.

We had known each other for only six weeks when Donna agreed to spend a weekend hiking with me over the Franconia Range of the White Mountains in New Hampshire.

"I'm just going to set up another shot from this angle, and then I should be done."

"OK," I replied. "You know, that's something I wouldn't have even noticed before."

Donna was on her knees, her camera attached to a small tripod. She was kneeling before a delicate flower, a lady slipper. The light was illuminating the flower amidst the darkness of its surroundings. Donna had spotted the flower as we were walking past it. She just had to get the picture. She had taken her camera from her bag, screwed the tripod to it, set up one shot, and then snapped several frames, each time readjusting the settings on her camera to "play with the exposures," as she put it. Then she moved her tripod and camera to photograph the flower from a completely different angle.

"The light is only going to last for a couple of minutes, so I have to get this shot quickly," she explained as she worked.

I stood there, somewhat amazed that she had seen this flower in the first place. I would have walked by it without a second glance. For me, the only reason to bring a camera on a hike is to take a picture at the top of a mountain I have just climbed—one of those "Yup, I made it" photos.

I tend to focus on the big picture. I want to climb to a summit and see a sweeping vista of mountains all around me. Donna approached hiking from a totally different perspective. She saw the beauty in nature's minutiae: a single flower, a small reptile, a rock partially covered by moss.

I was seeing the trail in a very different way through her eyes. And her photos were incredible.

Donna was thirty-six and I was thirty-three when we got married. We both wanted children. We agreed we'd have one naturally and then adopt another. Doing the math, if we had our first child when Donna was thirty-seven or thirty-eight, and then waited a couple of years, the second child wouldn't come until she was in her forties. Although many women have had healthy babies at that age, we didn't think it was necessary to risk any complications. Furthermore, we felt strongly that adoption was perfectly acceptable.

However, after a couple of years, the natural option wasn't working for us, so we started exploring the possibilities of adopting a baby. Donna and I were deeply involved in that process by the fall of 1996, and we sent our application to our adoption agency the following January. Our phone rang at ten thirty on the night of February second.

"Hello?" I answered, knowing that a call at that time of night was probably not good news.

It was the head of the adoption agency. As we sat up on our bed,

Donna and I held the receiver so we could both hear what the woman was saying.

"I just came back from Guatemala, and there's a five-day-old, very healthy boy there who is available for international adoption. Would you be interested in adopting him?"

We looked at each other for a couple of seconds, barely believing what we had just heard. "Yes! We will!" we answered together.

"OK, fine," said the woman. She spent the next few minutes giving us a crash course in the Guatemalan adoption process. We got off the phone, too excited to sleep. We jumped and hugged and talked nonstop for the next hour. We were going to be parents! We wanted to share this wonderful news with our families and friends, but we realized they probably wouldn't appreciate a call from us after midnight. We'd tell the world later. But Donna and I didn't get much sleep that night.

A thick envelope arrived from the agency a few days later. It contained the documents we would have to fill out to begin the adoption process. However, the most important items in that envelope were two small photographs showing a newborn boy in yellow fleece pajamas lying on a pillow. He had scowling eyes and a full head of jet-black hair. I know that millions and millions of pictures like these have been taken of newborn babies. But these were special. They were pictures of our new son Jason.

We couldn't wait to bring him home. But the bureaucracy was beyond belief, and the adoption process proved to be agonizingly slow. Saying that it moved at glacial speed would be an insult to glaciers. We were told we'd probably be able to fly to Guatemala and adopt Jason in September. But that was delayed because of a snafu with the paperwork, and no one seemed to know how long it would take to fix it.

We needed a change to hopefully get our minds off the aggravation. Escaping to Vermont suddenly seemed like a good idea.

We spent Thursday night in Wilmington and, after breakfast, drove to the crossing on Route 9, just east of Bennington, the next morning.

I parked my truck, grabbed my pack and boots, and put them on the backseat of Donna's car. She drove us north to the crossing on Route 11, where I pulled out my pack. Donna gave me a hug and kiss as we stood on the side of the road. I watched as she got back into her car and drove away. I noticed my feet as I reached down to lift on my pack. Sneakers. I was still wearing my sneakers.

My boots! They were still in Donna's car! Oh shit!

"DONNA!!!!!!

"DONNAAAAAA!!!!!!!!

"STOP!!!!! PLEASE STOP!!!!!!"

All of my screaming and jumping were to no avail. Donna was gone—with my boots.

"What the hell do I do now?"

I propped my pack against a tree, sat on a boulder, and tried to think.

"All right, so your truck is four days away, and you don't have your boots. Do you give up now or do you give it a try?" I asked myself.

Hiking without boots isn't the end of the world. A lot of day hikers have never owned hiking boots, and even some thru-hikers don't use them. Hell, I've seen people hiking the trail barefoot.

This wasn't the first time I had forgotten, or nearly forgotten, something important. Usually, when I was getting ready for a hike, Donna would ask me the "Did you remember" questions. "Did you remember food?" "Yes." "Did you remember your pack?" "Yes, dear."

One time she asked, "Did you remember your stove?" I'd actually forgotten to pack it. I'd taken it out of my pack, tested it, and left it on the porch. It would have stayed there, and I would have eaten cold food for five days if she hadn't reminded me. "Did you remember your tent?" Whoops. I'd taken it out to air, and it was draped across the railing on the back porch. Once again, good thing she'd reminded me.

Donna wondered why I had never developed a list that I could refer to each time I packed. That would somehow take the sport out of it, I told her. So I didn't make a list, and I usually remembered everything that I needed—with a little help from my wife. And, hey, I hadn't actually forgotten my boots. I had just forgotten to take them out of Donna's car.

My biggest concern was my ankles. I usually wear ankle supports under my woolen socks. I also wear high-topped boots for additional support. Considering my history of sprained ankles, all of that support has helped me hike the trail. When I'm hiking, one of my feet will slip off a rock and I'll twist an ankle at least once a day. The combination of the ankle supports and my high-topped boots has frequently prevented a serious sprain that would force me to get off the trail or, worse yet, wait for another hiker to help me.

Now the question was whether I could hike without my boots for the next four days. I took out my trail guide and carefully analyzed my situation. By road, I was about five miles from Manchester, a sizeable town by Vermont standards that had motels and restaurants. Once I left this area, I wouldn't find much civilization until I reached the Bennington area. Fortunately, the AT paralleled Route 11 for the next couple of miles and brought me closer to Manchester. Old Rootville Road, a woods road, connected with the trail fairly close to town. If I decided I couldn't go on without my boots, I could hike out a couple of miles from that junction to Route 11. I remembered passing a couple of small mom-and-pop motels in that area. I could probably stay at one of them if I had to.

By now I was wishing that Donna and I had gotten cell phones. They had seemed like such a luxury in 1997, something owned by yuppies, a status that we did not desire. However, now, with a cell phone, I could have simply called Donna and had her turn around and bring me my boots. Oh well, I consoled myself, there probably wouldn't be any signal in this part of Vermont anyway. I'd just have to make do.

I decided to hike to the Old Rootville Road junction in my sneakers. Then I would decide whether to continue hiking or get off the trail and make my way to town. If I wound up doing the latter, I would have to figure out how to contact Donna so she could bring me my boots and take me to my truck if I decided to bag this hike. I'd cross that bridge when I got to it.

I set off, carefully placing each foot squarely on the trail with every step I took and avoiding every rock I could on this rocky trail. I quickly discovered that the difference between wearing boots and sneakers is profound. While my ankles feel securely encased in my ankle supports and boots, in sneakers I felt like my ankles were vulnerable to anything that could make them snap. I felt like an elephant walking on the legs of a gazelle. But what was even more troubling, and unexpected, was how much the rocks hurt my feet through the thin soles of my sneakers. I would barely have felt them under the thick soles of my boots. Every rock protruding from the ground felt like the tip of a spear, set there by some demonic trail-builder to rip open the bottoms of my feet and make me miserable. Furthermore, walking so carefully in my sneakers was slowing me down considerably. I just wasn't moving with the quickness and confidence that I did in my boots.

I knew I had to have my boots. All I wanted to do was get to Old Rootville Road, get off this damned trail, and get back to a smooth surface. As for what I thought of those who hike the trail in sneakers or flip-flops or barefoot: Part of me envied their intestinal fortitude. The other part thought they were just plain crazy.

Two hours later, a little after noon, I had rented a room at one of the motels on Route 11. The room was old but clean and functional. It had a telephone.

I had only a vague idea of the name of the stable where Donna was riding in Waitsfield, but the directory assistance operator found the right place within a couple of minutes, and the phone began to ring.

"Hello," a woman answered. Thankfully, I didn't have to leave this message on an answering machine.

"Hi. My wife is riding out of your stable today, and I need to get a message to her. It's not life threatening or anything like that, but it's very important that she gets this."

"OK, what's the message?"

"Tell her she has my boots, and I couldn't go on my hike. Please ask her to call me at the motel where I'm staying so she can bring my boots to me."

"OK, I can do that."

I gave the woman the motel's telephone number and my room number and hung up. Now all I could do was wait. I spent the afternoon watching TV and waiting for the phone to ring. I hoped that the woman at the stable had copied my message correctly. If she hadn't, if she had mixed up a number or two, Donna would not know how to reach me. And if she couldn't, I would have to find some other way to get to my truck.

Finally, at around three, the phone rang.

"Hey, honey. Missing something?"

"Ha, ha, ha. Very funny. Yup, I'm missing something. Where are you?"

"Well, I'm back at the stable office. I saw your boots on the backseat when I got out of the car up here, but I knew you'd be on the trail by then, so it didn't make sense for me to go back. I figured if you couldn't do the hike you'd find a way to find me. And you did."

"OK, well, I've got a room in a motel just outside Manchester. It's one of the ones we passed on our way to the crossing. Why don't you come here? We can spend the night and figure out what we'll do next. Maybe I'll do a shorter hike, but let's see."

Donna arrived about an hour later. We had a splendid dinner at a local restaurant and spent a nice evening together. Donna rode horses again on Saturday while I did a day hike—wearing my boots. We spent Sunday together hiking up Stratton Mountain, and then we drove our vehicles back to Massachusetts.

Even though we'd planned to do our own things during the weekend, it was really nice being alone with Donna away from the house. We had been consumed with the adoption for several months. Neither of us had taken any time off during the summer because we were saving our vacation time for the trip to Guatemala and to spend time with our new son. Even though we didn't know when we would get him, somehow, despite the delays, we still believed we would.

As much as we were looking forward to becoming parents, we knew our "couple time" would be drastically reduced after Jason came into our lives. So winding up together for the weekend was an unexpected surprise—made possible because I had forgotten my boots.

# 8

# Trail Technology

We had finished our dinner, and I started washing our two dishes and spoons.

"I might as well tell the rest of the world where we are," Rex said, half to himself, as he dug into his pack. He pulled out a piece of orange and black plastic about the size of a man's wallet. Although it wasn't quite the right shape, I figured it must be his cell phone. I watched as he fiddled with the device, looked up to survey the sky, and then walked a few feet from the campsite. He laid the gadget on a rock and came back to where I was sitting.

"What's that?" I asked, perplexed. "Is that your cell phone?" I couldn't imagine why anyone would leave a cell phone lying out in the open, but that seemed to be what Rex was doing.

"No, that's my satellite messenger. I just press a button, and it sends out a text message that says I'm OK. I can send it to as many as ten people, but I just sent it to Karen, my mom, and my brother. It also pinpoints where I am so people can track my progress along the trail. This version is brand new, so this is the first time I've used it. It's really, really cool."

It was yet another reminder of how much the technology available to hikers had changed over twenty years.

The steep climb up North Kinsman Mountain in New Hampshire's White Mountains was exhausting. But by midmorning of this August day in 1991, I had reached the summit and could cross off another four-thousand-footer.

I was standing on top of South Kinsman an hour later. Despite the elevation, the air was warm and humid.

A man was already on the summit when I got there. Beside him was a large metal contraption—the size of a small suitcase—with antennae protruding at different angles. It looked like something from Star Wars.

"Hi. How are you doing?" I asked.

"Fine. It's a great day, isn't it?" he replied.

"Sure is. Can I ask you what that thing is?"

"Yes, it's a global positioning unit. It's getting a signal from a satellite, and then it can tell me exactly where I am in the world within a second."

It took me a moment to realize that his use of the term "second" was a reference to place rather than time. I knew from my college geography classes that degrees of latitude and longitude are further broken down into minutes and seconds. If you know your degree, minute, and second of latitude and longitude, you can tell within about sixty feet where you are on the planet.

"Wow. That's something," I said. What I was really thinking was: *Wow. Why the hell would you lug that huge thing up this mountain just so you can know what latitude and longitude you're at? What practical use is there for something like that? Why do you need something like that to tell you exactly where you are? You're on the Appalachian Trail, and you're on South Kinsman Mountain for God's sake! You don't need to know anything besides that to orient yourself.*

Instead, I politely listened to his explanation about why his global positioning unit was the greatest thing since the sextant.

Hikers communicate a lot with one another. It's important to exchange vital information. Had a hiker not told Erin and me that there was no water on top of Chestnut Ridge, we would not have carried enough up that mountain to drink and to cook our meals. We could have been in serious trouble.

But helpfulness has its limits. Most hikers, me included, resent unsolicited advice. This is especially true about the gear we carry. The general consensus is that we're all reasonable, rational adults and that what we decide to carry in our packs and on our persons is our own damned business. If I don't mind carrying the load, then you shouldn't be bothered that I'm carrying it.

So as I continued talking with my new friend that morning, I didn't share with him my opinions about the dubious utility or the weight of his device. I just figured that if he wanted to carry it up the mountain, and if it gave him a little pleasure to know precisely where he was, more power to him. I started my trek down South Kinsman figuring I'd never again see a global positioning unit during a hike. Little did I know.

Rex laughed when I told him about my encounter with the man and his cumbersome GPS unit in New Hampshire and how I never dreamed I'd be hiking with someone who used the same kind of device—only a lot smaller and lighter—as a matter of course twenty years later.

"The computer age has changed everything," Rex acknowledged. "There's no way I'd have lugged that old GPS contraption with me on the trail, but my brother and I won't leave home for a hike without one of these smaller devices. It's just the way we do things. Karen especially wants to know where I am, and I'm OK with that. You could say it's one of the reasons I love her."

After that, we sat in silence as we savored the still of the evening—comfortable in each other's company. Except for the sound of a car being started in the distance or a muffled conversation coming from another campsite, we could have been camping by ourselves almost anywhere on the trail. The sky had cleared beautifully, which was a welcome relief after many days of overcast and rain, and an umbrella of stars was twinkling above us on this moonless night. However, the clear sky had also allowed more seasonal air to come back into the region. The temperature was dropping quickly now that the sun had set, and Rex and I pulled on long pants and fleece hoodies to ward off the chill.

The perfect end to this evening would have been to start a campfire in the metal ring at one end of the campsite. Previous campers had left a small stash of wood, including a little bit of kindling. However, we knew that everything was so wet it would take a considerable effort to get a fire going. While a fire would have been nice, neither of us was inclined to try—especially since we were tired and thinking about going to bed. For the time being, we were content to just sit there. I looked down at the fluorescent hands of my watch. It wasn't quite seven o'clock.

Sometimes I've wondered what it would be like to stay up all night and watch the constellations slowly spin their way around the North Star. That's a nice thought, but in reality, after the sun sets, I have a lot of difficulty keeping my eyes open. I was getting very drowsy. I was sure I'd be in the tent, sleeping soundly in the warm sleeping bag on the cushiony air mattress by eight.

As more and more stars appeared, I picked up another point of light out of the corner of my eye. The light appeared for an instant and then disappeared as if someone had switched it on and off. I saw it again a few seconds later. Then it was gone. The light was clearly coming from the woods beyond our campsite, not from another camping spot.

"Did you see that?" I asked Rex after spotting the light a third time.

"No. What?" Rex had been looking the other way.

"Off in the distance. There's a flickering light." We both looked in the direction I was pointing.

"Oh, I see it," Rex confirmed as the light showed up again.

I could now tell that the light was moving, and it was becoming a little brighter each time it appeared.

"I think somebody's comin' up the trail," I offered.

"Yeah, that would make sense."

We watched as the light got closer and closer, moving along quickly and with a distinct bounce. We could now tell that the light was a single narrow halogen beam. The beam became so intense that looking directly into it hurt our eyes. It was almost like looking at a laser. It was a hiker, no doubt about it. Furthermore, the unmistakable and rapid click, click, click of hiking poles told me this was someone with experience. When the light got to within a few yards of our campsite, the clicking abruptly stopped and the light suddenly turned and shone on Rex and me. Even though we were just sitting there, it felt like being caught in a spotlight during a prison break.

"Good evening," said a woman's voice from behind the light. Her voice was a little raspy, as if she hadn't been talking for a while. Although she was only a few feet from us, we couldn't see her.

"Evenin'. How're you doing?" Rex answered.

"Great. Hey, do you mind my asking you where I am?" she asked, a little embarrassed. "I've been hiking on the Appalachian Trail, and I'm not exactly sure where this is." The light abruptly turned off, and for a few seconds all I could see were green spots. The woman was still only a voice in the dark.

"This is Big Meadows Campground in Shenandoah National Park," I replied. I didn't want to sound too patronizing by overstating the obvious—that she was in a national park. However, I also knew that it's possible to be so completely disoriented that you have no idea where you are, especially in the dark.

"Big Meadows. Huh." Then she paused. "Do you have any idea how much farther it is to Rock Spring Shelter?"

"It's about three miles," I answered. I knew this because Rex and I had considered spending the night at that shelter before deciding to press on to Big Meadows so we wouldn't have to hike those extra miles during our second day.

"Three miles, huh?" She pondered this for a second. I knew she was deliberating the same thing that I've considered dozens of times. Do I hike to the next place where I can sleep, or do I stay here?

"Do they charge for these campsites?"

"Yeah, they do. Seventeen bucks," I answered.

"Sweet Jesus!"

"But, you know, you're more than welcome to camp here with us. It's not like we're taking up the entire site," Rex quickly interjected.

"Absolutely," I confirmed.

"You sure? Thanks. That'd be great. I'm too tired to hike another three miles, especially in the dark."

"Where did you start out today?" I asked as she dropped her pack in the darkness and sat down.

"Well, I started at Pinefield Hut, and I was hoping to do about thirty-two miles today. It was a bit of a stretch, and I obviously misjudged things a little."

"You section-hiking the trail?"

"No, I'm thru-hiking."

"What?!" I exclaimed. "You're coming from the south, right?"

"Yeah."

"Isn't this just a tad late to be thru-hiking, Nobo?"

She let out something between a snort and a laugh. "Yeah, you're right. It's a little unconventional. I started at Springer in April, but I banged up my knee in North Carolina. So I got off the trail for a couple of months. Then I got back on in Harpers Ferry so I could still hike with my buddy, and we hiked up to Katahdin. Now I'm finishing up what I skipped."

"Oh, OK. That makes sense."

Without turning on her light, she unzipped her pack and began fishing through its contents. There was enough ambient light from the campground to see that her pack was relatively small and that she was also small of stature.

"Hi, we haven't introduced ourselves yet. I'm Rex."

"I'm BB," she answered.

"BB. Is that your trail name?" he asked.

"Yeah, it is. It stands for Banana Bandana. But after you say that a few times, it's just easier to say BB."

"I'm Two Tents."

Trail introductions had been made.

"Two Tents. That's kind of a funny name."

"It's a long story, but basically I accidentally carried two tents up Chestnut Knob in Virginia."

"How do you accidentally carry two tents?"

"Like I said, it's a long story. How did you get the name BB?"

"Well, you can't see it now, but I wear this bright yellow bandana," BB explained. "At least it was bright yellow when I started. It's pretty faded now, because I've worn it all year, rain or shine."

"That's a good trail name," Rex observed. "I see you use hiking poles. Do they make that much of a difference?"

"They help me keep my balance, I guess. But I don't know how much of a difference they make, because I've never hiked without them," BB said while taking things out of her pack, her thin poles laid far enough to one side so she would not accidentally step on them in the dark.

After she had gotten what she needed, she set the pack aside and began working with the items she had extracted. Our conversation stopped as she concentrated on the task at hand. The setup was done in nearly total darkness although she did flick on her headlamp for a couple of seconds a few times to see what she was doing. BB was preparing her dinner.

"Do you know where I can get some water?" she asked.

"Well, I have a lot in my bag. You're welcome to use that," Rex offered. He handed her a plastic bag that was about half full.

BB flicked her lighter, and for the first time Rex and I got a brief look at her face. Her features were very small—a narrow forehead tapering down to an even narrower, almost pointed, chin. She was very young; right out of college I guessed. Her hair was indeed wrapped in a yellow bandana, and the ends of her hair stuck out straight beneath it. I had already guessed when she approached us that she stood no more than five feet tall, and now I surmised she weighed no more than a hundred pounds.

The flame lit the base of the stove, and except for a few impurities in the fuel that briefly bathed the area with yellow light, the blue glow of the stove barely cut into the darkness. Now that her stove was starting to heat the water for her meal, we resumed the conversation.

"So, I'm assuming you guys are hiking?"

"Yeah," Rex answered. "How did you know that?"

"Well, only hikers would be sitting in total darkness at a campground."

"Good point," Rex laughed. "Actually, we're both section-hiking the entire trail. I'm out for ten days, and Two Tents here is just out for a couple. In total, I've finished about five hundred miles of the trail, and Two Tents just completed two thousand."

"Wow, congratulations, Two Tents," BB exclaimed. "Actually, that's just about how much I've done, too. I think I only have a little over a hundred miles to go."

"Thanks, and congratulations to you, too," I replied. "You said you're finishing up at Harpers Ferry?"

"Yup."

"Then, you're right. It's probably just a little over a hundred, maybe a hundred and ten. I'm planning on finishing up at Harpers Ferry, too, but it won't be until October of next year when I do it."

"How long have you been hiking the trail?"

"Since nineteen-ninety."

"Wow, that's a long time."

I guessed that BB was a toddler in 1990.

"I'm curious," Rex interjected. "Your pack looks pretty small for a thru-hike. How much are you carrying?"

"Thirteen and a half."

"Wow!" both of us exclaimed at the same time.

“That’s got to be without water and food,” Rex continued.

“No, that’s fully loaded with supplies for four days. That’s as much as I usually go out with, although there were a couple of times, like in the Hundred Mile Wilderness in Maine, when I had to pack a little more.”

Rex let out a low whistle that conveyed a mixture of disbelief and awe.

“I’ve seen a lot of ultralights out here,” I commented, “but that’s about the lightest I’ve ever heard of.”

“Well, I knew that I needed to pack really light. I’m not exactly large, if you haven’t noticed. And then I’ve just gotten better and better about knowing what I need and what I don’t. If I don’t need it, it doesn’t come with me. In fact, that’s one reason why I’ve decided to camp here tonight rather than continue on to the shelter.”

“Why’s that?” Rex asked.

“Well, the batteries on my headlamp are good for fifty hours, and I have about forty hours on them right now. I’ve got to be careful that they don’t run down before Harpers Ferry.”

“You don’t have any spare batteries?”

“No, I don’t want to carry the additional weight.”

“What kind of batteries?”

“Oh, they’re just three triple-A’s.”

“So, carrying the spares would add like half an ounce?”

“Oh no, it would be far less than that,” BB answered incredulously, as if half an ounce was the equivalent of a ton.

“It’s funny,” I said. “The first three-person tent that I had weighed eight pounds, and that was one of the lightest ones around at the time. Now they weigh, what, three or four pounds?” I suddenly felt like a hiking dinosaur. I was counting pounds. BB the ultralight hiker was counting ounces.

“Well, that’s one of the things I don’t bring with me,” BB replied.

“What?” I asked.

“A tent.”

“You don’t have a tent?”

“No.”

“Not even a bivy?” A bivy sack is a waterproof covering that is large enough to hold a sleeping bag with a person in it and provide some protection from the wind and rain.

“No, I just planned on hopping from shelter to shelter,” she said.

I didn’t point out what seemed to me to be the obvious flaw in her logic. If she planned to hike from shelter to shelter, she had to make sure she had enough light to do some hiking in the dark, especially at this time of year when daylight lasted only about ten hours. If she wasn't going to bring a bivy, then she should probably pack extra batteries. But I assumed she had probably figured this out on her own and didn't need any coaching from me. It was another example of a hiker deciding for herself what to carry.

I admit it. I'm a hiking packrat. I think through way too many "what-if" situations, and I always carry a lot of "just-in-case" equipment: An extra flashlight and spare batteries. A first-aid kit equipped for every conceivable emergency short of open-heart surgery. Two or three cans of deviled ham that I might consider eating ten minutes before dying of starvation. A friend of mine once told me, "It's better to have it and not need it than to need it and not have it." The only difference was, he did all of his traveling in his car. He never backpacked on the AT. Still, every time I consider leaving something behind, I envision needing it and not having it. So I pack it along even though it adds weight to my load.

Fortunately, I've been blessed with a good back and enough upper body strength so that carrying the heaviest pack around hasn't caused me too many problems. But late in the afternoon, when I'm dog-tired and each foot seems to weigh a ton, hiking with that pack becomes a real chore. Then I kick myself, again, for making it so heavy.

BB was a student of an entirely different school in the hiking world—the ultralights. Those people leave behind everything but the bare essentials and then make sure that everything they do bring weighs as little as possible. Some even cut their toothbrushes in two, pull out half the bristles, and don't pack toothpaste. Fortunately for them, technology has significantly reduced the weight of hiking gear during the past two decades.

The hiking mentality has also changed considerably. When I started hiking in the early nineties, there was a certain machismo, especially among men, about being able to carry a sixty-pound pack day after day after day. Packing everything, including the kitchen sink, seemed to be the cool thing to do.

Now, younger hikers are equally proud to carry only twenty pounds, and they're downright envious when the person next to them is carrying eighteen. I have met ultralight hikers who can tell you the weight of each item in their pack to a hundredth of an ounce. And as soon as they learn that another hiker has some item that weighs less than theirs, they can't wait to buy it for themselves.

Besides being a packrat, I have something else going against me in the weight department: old, heavy equipment. Since I hike only about ten days a year, I do not wear out equipment the way a thru-hiker does. If I were planning to do a thru-hike, I would buy all of the newest gear I could, knowing that I would spend the next six months beating the living hell out of it. But since I hike for shorter periods, my gear tends to last a long time. And with each passing year, the gear that other hikers carry becomes lighter and lighter compared to the antique equipment I carry. Being a very frugal—some would say cheap—Yankee doesn't help matters either. I tend to hold on to things until they wear out, which can take a long time, before I break down and buy something new and light.

By now, the water in BB's dish was boiling, and she dumped in a couple of handfuls of noodles to cook. Rex stood up and began placing some kindling in the fire pit on top of some toilet paper from his pack. "You know, if we're gonna sit here and talk for a while, we might as well have a fire," he observed. "I just hope I can get it started."

"That would be great," I answered. "It'll help take the chill out of the air."

"I could go for that," BB chimed in. "There's been a lot of rain these past few days."

"You're right. It's pretty wet," Rex replied. "We probably won't have to worry about setting the woods on fire like what happened when my brother and I were camping with some Boy Scouts a couple of years ago."

"You started a forest fire?" BB asked, not quite sure whether to believe him or not.

"It wasn't a forest fire, but it could've become one," Rex said. "It only burned some underbrush before we got it out. We were lucky because we were all in our sleeping bags when the fire started. It was kind of hairy for a while."

"How'd that happen?" I asked.

"Tom and I took our Scout troop on a weekend hike near our home in the Harrisburg area. There were ten of us. We hadn't had much rain, and the woods were kinda dry, but the forest fire index wasn't high, so we built a campfire to cook our beans and hot dogs that evening. We were camping right beside a stream. The kids were doing the work, and Tom and I made sure they took all of the necessary safety precautions and didn't build the fire too big.

"Anyway, we ate, and then we talked and roasted some marshmallows, and then everyone turned in for the night. I personally made sure the fire and all the embers were out. Except I guess I missed some. A little breeze came up about the time we all got bedded down in the two lean-tos the Scouts had built. Near as I can tell, a live ember must have gotten blown onto some dry leaves. Someone yelled that they smelled smoke, and sure enough some underbrush was burning just beyond the fire pit.

"We tore out of our sleeping bags. Tom told three or four of the guys to start carrying water in the cooking kettle and anything else they could find, and the rest of us began beating and stomping at the flames with shirts and bedding and whatever else we could grab. We barely had time to get our hiking boots on, so some of the kids had trouble keeping them on to protect their feet. A couple of them used their small shovels to throw dirt on the brush and to beat down the flames. The others hit the fire with water from the stream. They used the kettle and their canteens and dishes.

"We had the fire out within five minutes or so, and then we spent the next half hour soaking the brush thoroughly. Thank God we had flashlights."

"Be prepared. That's what Boy Scouts are supposed to be, aren't they?" asked BB.

"I guess we were," Rex said, shaking his head. "But the rest of the night was interesting. A couple of the kids' sleeping bags were ruined, so they slept in Tom's and my bags, and he and I stayed up to make sure the fire didn't start again.

"We hiked back to town the next morning, and some of the parents were pretty pissed when we told them what had happened and that some of their kids' shirts and jackets and bedding would have to be replaced. Others were pretty good about it. All in all, we were lucky the fire hadn't started any later, when we would have been asleep, and that no one got hurt. The whole woods could have gone up in flames, us included."

"Close call. So I imagine you've been more attentive to campfires since then," I said.

"You bet your ass I've been," Rex retorted. "I'll make sure this one is out cold before we go to bed. Count on it."

BB and I watched as Rex leaned over the fire ring to light the toilet paper and damp kindling with his lighter. We knew it would be iffy, but after a couple of tries, the paper and wood caught, and the little campfire began to crackle and burn and create lots of smoke. Success!

"Now, to change the subject. BB, what do you carry with you so you can keep your pack down to thirteen and a half pounds?" he asked.

If hikers have a recurring topic of conversation, it is about the contents of their packs. What have they brought with them, and what did they leave at home?

"Well, let's see," BB began. "The first thing is the pack itself. It weighs a little over two and a half pounds. If the pack isn't light, then it kind of defeats the purpose. My sleeping bag weighs less than a pound and a half, and my pad is less than a half pound."

"Wow, that's really light for a bag," Rex said. "What's it rated?"

"Thirty-five degrees," BB answered.

Sleeping bags are rated based on how cold the outside temperature can get while you are still comfortable inside. Theoretically, a thirty-five degree bag will keep you snug and warm so long as the temperature stays above thirty-five degrees Fahrenheit. In my experience, the ratings are not all that accurate. I wouldn't want to be in a thirty-five degree bag even if it was forty-five. Yes, the bag might keep me warm at thirty-five degrees if I was tied in tightly and did not move around. But by three in the morning it has loosened enough to let my body heat escape, and I'm damned cold. My bag is rated down to zero, and I've been plenty cold on nights that were a lot warmer than that.

"Doesn't it get a little cold at night, especially this time of year?" I asked.

"It depends," said BB. "If I'm out of the wind and I put on all of my clothing, it's usually not too bad.

"Anyway," she continued. "I go really minimal with clothing, so my cold-weather and raingear are about two and a half pounds. I think that gets me up to a total of seven pounds. Everything that I need for eating—stove, fuel, dish, utensils—weighs just about a pound. Then there's the additional stuff like the first-aid kit, TP, headlamp, pack cover, and stuff sacks. Combined, those all weigh a little over a pound. So now we're at roughly nine pounds. Four days' worth of food weighs about two and a half, and a liter of water weighs about two. Voila! You've got thirteen and a half pounds."

"Well, at least you've included a first-aid kit," I observed. "I've known some ultralights who leave that at home as well. But four days' worth of food doesn't seem like very much for a thru-hike."

"Well, my philosophy has been that by going light I can do a lot of miles, and then every four days I go into town and get resupplied. If I can knock off twenty a day, I can do eighty in four. If I went heavier, then I might only be able to hike ten or twelve miles, and it would take me six or seven days to cover the same distance."

"OK, I see your logic," I answered.

Rex fed the fire with a few small sticks. "So, did you say you banged up your knee?" he asked.

"Yeah," BB answered. "It was in North Carolina."

"Was it really bad?"

"Well, it was a pretty bad sprain. I couldn't walk on it at all for a few days, but it didn't require surgery or anything like that."

"How did you get off the trail if you couldn't walk on it?"

"Well, I actually wasn't on the trail at the time. I was in Hot Springs."

"Oh, I know Hot Springs," I said. "I love that town. I went there several times even after I had hiked way beyond it. Those springs are really awesome!"

"Yeah. That in fact is where I sprained my knee. I was getting out of one of the open-air tubs, and I slipped and landed wrong."

"That's kind of ironic. Here you've been hiking the trail, and then you get injured getting out of a tub."

"Well, I'd had enough to drink so I probably shouldn't have been doing anything at that point," BB answered, noting the irony of the situation.

"WUI?" Rex asked teasingly.

"Huh?" I asked.

"Walking Under the Influence," BB answered. "Yeah, that was me. It also didn't help that I was buck naked at the time."

The campfire was now dancing inside the ring and warming up the three of us. That was a good thing, because this conversation was getting interesting.

## 9

# Rescues and Ribs

"That must have been embarrassing," Rex said, laughing at BB's bizarre tale. I kept my mouth shut because I didn't want to seem like some lecherous old man fixated on the image of a naked young woman taking a bath in public. I needn't have worried.

"Oh, it gets better than that," BB candidly continued. "I'm there with my buddy, Marmot. Both of us are in there naked, because of course you don't pack a bathing suit on the AT, right? He had gone in first, and then I told him to turn his head while I got in. Just like what you do when you're changing your clothes in a shelter. Of course, once the water jets get going in the tub, you can't see anything anyway. It's like skinny-dipping.

"Both of us were pretty toasted to begin with, and we had snuck in the last couple of beers from our six-pack and left them at the bottom of the steps leading down to the tub. So I told Marmot to look the other way again, and I got back out to get the beers. I fell, hit my head, and really twisted my knee. I didn't know if it was broken or what. I wanted to scream because my head was throbbing and my knee really hurt. But I knew if I did, the people in charge would come running, so I was trying to tell Marmot that I needed help without attracting anyone else's attention. I was crying. It was so painful. Anyway, Marmot was a saint. Somehow he got me dressed enough so I was decent, then he put his shorts on and went and got someone to help me. It was probably the most hurt and embarrassed I've ever been, all at the same time."

"Sounds like you got through it with your dignity more or less intact," Rex said.

"Yeah, I guess. But if you don't mind, it's probably best if my boyfriend never finds out."

"Your secret's safe with us," Rex assured her.

"You're lucky it didn't happen on the trail," I offered. "It's not a lot of fun carrying out someone who's been hurt."

"You ever done that?" Rex asked.

"Just once."

The Abol Slide on Mount Katahdin can be intimidating, especially if you're hiking down it. It's nothing but rock and gravel, and it's almost straight down for a mile. Slides are gashes on the sides of mountains, the remains of landslides that occurred many years before. You get the idea that you could fall off the mountain if you trip or even stub your toe. It makes more sense to climb up the Abol Trail than it does to hike down, but we had no choice. This was our way off the mountain on this first Sunday afternoon in September. Besides, there's very little about Katahdin that's easy. Even Aimee didn't object to the steep descent because she had skied a lot as a child, so she was comfortable on the terrain.

Since it was a Labor Day weekend and a gorgeous day, the trail was fairly crowded. All day long our hiking party—Aimee, my sister Elaine, my eleven-year-old niece Erin, and her friend Carl—had encountered small parties of three, four, or five hikers. Sometimes we descended past them, sometimes they went by us, and sometimes we came upon a party that was taking a break. It was typical to exchange pleasantries about the weather or the condition of the trail, and then keep moving.

When we had started our descent, we had come upon three college-aged hikers, a man and two women, who were taking a break. They appeared to be just sitting and taking in the view from above tree line, but as we got closer, we saw that one woman was examining the palm of her hand.

"Hi, there. Beautiful day," Aimee said.

"Yeah, it is," the young man answered.

"Did you hurt your hand?" Aimee continued.

"A little bit," responded the young woman, looking up at my wife. "I skinned it on a rock just up there. It'll be OK."

"Do you want an antiseptic wipe and something to wrap it in?" asked Aimee as she slipped off her pack to get our first-aid kit.

"No, I'll be OK."

"You sure?"

"Yup, I'm sure."

"OK," Aimee shrugged and hoisted her pack back on, a little disappointed that her offer had been rejected because we could have practically amputated the woman's arm with our first-aid kit.

We had bought a good one when we purchased our hiking and camping gear. First-aid kits come in many sizes—very small ones that contain a few Band-Aids and a small tube of antiseptic cream to large ones, like ours, with antiseptic wipes, tape and gauze pads, containers for ibuprofen and antihistamines, an ACE Bandage, Moleskins for blisters, burn ointments, and even a triangular bandage that could also serve as a sling. The woman would never know how much we could have helped her.

We continued down the slide, and the same three hikers caught up with us a few minutes later. They quickly passed us as they hopped from rock to rock in their sneakers. We marveled at the energy and foolhardiness of youth and kept picking our way slowly but steadily down.

We spotted the same hikers about an hour later as we were approaching the bottom of the slide. They had stopped again. When we got down to them, we found only the two women. The one who had scraped her hand was sitting on a boulder. Her left sneaker was off.

"Would you happen to have any ibuprofen?" she asked, wincing in pain. She was either accident-prone by nature or just having a lousy day.

"Of course," Aimee answered, already taking off her pack. "What happened?"

"Well, we were coming down, and I was going a little too fast," she explained. "I bounced off a rock, and I did this somersault. When I landed, I came down hard on this ankle." She pointed to the shoeless left foot. "I'm not sure if it's broken or just badly sprained, but I'm not going to be able to make it down by myself. Anyway, some ibuprofen would help a lot with the swelling and pain."

"You somersaulted? In midair?" I asked, not quite believing what I was hearing. "It's a wonder you didn't kill yourself."

"Yeah, well I didn't have much time to think about it. I just did it," the woman winced again.

By now, Aimee had extracted a couple of pills from the kit, and the girl tossed them down with a sip from her water bottle.

"What can we do to help?" I offered.

"Not much. Our friend has already headed down to get a ranger, so we're just going to wait here."

Something told me I had not seen the last of this woman—that I would be helping to get her off this mountain. I had heard that the park rangers look for able-bodied men like me to help in situations like this and that they don't take "no" for an answer. The ranger would get no argument from me. No responsible hiker could refuse to offer this kind of trail magic.

Aimee, Elaine, and I stepped to one side to discuss this situation.

"Do you think we should stay here until help arrives?" Aimee asked.

"Look, I'm really the only one who's going to have to be here," I answered. "They're going to be looking for folks who can carry her down, and neither of you will be able to do that." As condescending as that may have sounded, it was a statement of fact. Aimee and Elaine are small women, and they weren't going to be able to help carry the injured woman down.

"Besides," I continued, "all of you are getting hungry, and this is probably going to take a while."

"OK, then why don't you stay here, and we'll carry your pack down," Elaine said.

"No, I can carry my pack down until we meet the ranger. Aimee and I will switch packs, and then I'll come back up." As much as I did not relish the idea of hiking back up the mountain, I also knew that Aimee and Elaine were very tired. The less that Aimee had to carry my heavier pack, which held most of the water, the better.

"The four of you can wait for me at the campsite and get some dinner. We've all had a long day."

We hiked another half mile during the next half hour and got to within three-quarters of a mile of the campground. The slide was behind us. That's when we met the ranger and a couple of other guys, including the two women's friend, carrying a stretcher, a first-aid kit, and a couple of blankets up the trail.

"Hi. We need people to help rescue a woman up the trail," the ranger said in a no-nonsense tone. He was looking directly at me, expecting me to volunteer.

"No problem," I replied. "We left her about a half hour ago. We gave her some ibuprofen. She seemed to be doing pretty well, except she can't walk."

"OK, let's go get her," the ranger commanded after pausing just long enough to hear my assessment of the situation. He had obviously done this before. He had perhaps 12 percent fat on his six-foot body, and he wasn't even breathing hard. He was very much in charge.

By this time of day—especially after climbing a mountain like Katahdin—every part of your body hurts. Your feet hurt. Your legs hurt. Your knees hurt. Your shoulders hurt. You hike in a daze, just plodding along. The rest stops that rejuvenated your body earlier in the day no longer help. All you want to do is get this damned thing over with, sit down, eat, and then hibernate.

The last thing on your mind is turning around and hiking back uphill. But that's exactly what I did. Aimee and I exchanged packs. Her daypack seemed refreshingly light compared to mine. Then Aimee, Elaine, Erin, and Carl continued down the trail, and I followed the ranger and the two other men back up the slide.

I was surprised that I had any energy left. It could have been an adrenaline rush, or maybe my legs were so sick of going downhill that they were really happy to be going uphill again. Whatever the reason, I kept up with the ranger's party, even grabbed one of the blankets. We climbed to the two women in less than thirty minutes. The injured one was patiently waiting for someone to take her down.

It was now a little after five—about three hours before sunset. The young woman had fallen about a quarter mile up the steep slide. The trail leveled out considerably at the bottom of the slide for the final mile to the campground.

The ranger first had to make a critical decision. Do we carry the woman a mile and a quarter down to the campground, or do we carry her three-quarters of a mile up to the plateau? From the plateau, a helicopter could fly her to a hospital. However, if we took her up, we rescuers would then have to hike back down. Only the patient could ride in the helicopter. For my money, hiking back down the slide after dark didn't seem like a great idea. But it wasn't my call. The ranger decided that we were close enough to the campground so that bringing her down made more sense than carrying her up.

By now, eleven of us were involved in the rescue—the ranger, the patient, her two friends, and seven other volunteers like me who the ranger had "persuaded" to help. The ranger splinted the injured ankle and had the woman lie down on the stretcher that had been specifically designed for the task at hand—holding a human body that is being carried down a mountain. It resembled a mummy case—narrow at the feet, wider at the shoulders, and then narrow around the head. After the patient was settled in, the ranger covered her with the blankets and strapped her on so she couldn't roll off.

Fortunately, we had about the best patient we could ask for. Her name was Beth. She was very pleasant despite her predicament. Actually, Beth was cute as hell. And while she was in some discomfort, she wasn't in agonizing pain. Nor was she a complainer. However, her greatest attribute was that she weighed only a hundred fifteen pounds.

"I'm so sorry that I got all of us into this situation," Beth said as we clustered around her on the trail.

"Hey, what else were we going to do on a Sunday night?" answered one of the volunteers. We all chuckled.

"OK. I'm Larry, and this is how this works," the ranger instructed us in his forthright manner. "We're going to take this very, very slowly. This is not a race. This is not about anybody proving his manliness. You have to make sure that you're safe as we're bringing her down. So if you don't have a good place to plant your feet, yell it out. I only brought up one stretcher, and it's currently occupied. Got it?"

We all nodded. His message was crystal clear.

"OK, there are eight of you guys who are going to carry her. There are six handholds. Six are carrying, and two are resting. You'll pick her up and carry her fifteen or twenty yards, roughly fifty feet. You'll put her down. Then you'll change positions. Because her body is heaviest toward the head, the two guys at the top of the stretcher are going to move to the middle, the two at the middle will move down to her feet, and the two at her feet will take a break. The two guys who were resting will take over at the shoulders. Each time we switch, everyone moves down. Do you understand?"

"Yes," we all mumbled.

I did the math. If she weighed a hundred fifteen pounds and the stretcher weighed ten to fifteen, then each of us would be carrying only about twenty pounds. We were rugged guys. This was going to be a piece of cake.

What I didn't realize was how difficult it is to safely move a one-hundred-twenty-five-pound object down a very steep slope that is strewn with boulders and rocks. To add insult to injury, the gravel base made the footing extremely difficult. Walking sideways on the narrow trail made it harder. The ranger knew all of this. After only a couple of rotations, I understood why we were switching so frequently. Despite how light we thought our load would be, I quickly realized how heavy a person actually is.

Although she was only about twelve hundred feet up the slide, it took a tremendous amount of time to get her off it. We had to switch places about twenty times on that rocky slope. Although we quickly got into a rhythm of picking her up, walking fifty feet, and setting her down, it was still no picnic. The unfamiliar exertion had us all breathing heavily after a couple of shifts on the stretcher, and all idle chatter ceased so we could hear Larry's curt commands of "Ready. Lift." "Go ahead. Slowly," and "Put 'er down. Gently." Beth did not utter a sound.

Fortunately, after a half hour or so our group of rescue carriers began getting bigger. This trail magic was contagious. We were joined by some hikers who were coming off the mountain, and a couple more came up from the campground. Those guys had finished their hikes and had just taken off their boots. After hearing that a rescue was in progress, however, they had hiked up to meet our party.

With each additional rescuer, it was possible for everyone to rest longer before starting another shift. When we had a dozen rescuers, we formed teams. One team would carry Beth fifty feet, then the other team would take its turn. The team concept also enabled each of us to grab the same part of the stretcher during every rotation. Since I am left-handed and of average upper-body strength, I usually had the middle handhold on the right side.

Finally, we were off the slide. Then the trail got considerably narrower in the dense forest growth below tree line. While the slope on this section was not nearly as steep as it had been on the slide, carrying Beth did not get any easier. The trail is just wide enough for people to walk in single file. But the stretcher detail was considerably wider, so we all had to squeeze through narrow openings between trees and boulders to keep Beth safe and sound.

Thankfully, more and more people arrived to help. At around eight o'clock—three full hours into the rescue—we were still at least half a mile from the campground. While the trail had flattened out and gotten considerably wider, and even though there were now twenty-five to thirty rescuers, it was obvious we could not get her out before dark. But this was not the Baxter Park rangers' first rescue by any means. They had arranged to have someone bring headlamps and flashlights up the trail. I grabbed a headlamp. As darkness fell, the lights lit up the trail well enough so we could see the trees and rocks that we had to avoid so as not to drop our patient. It was the first time I had ever worn a headlamp. I could actually see where I was going without having to hold a light. Cool. I had to get me one of these.

Finally, at around nine o'clock—as the last bit of twilight was fading to black—our rescue party got to the campground. Now at least forty people were helping; enough so that the original rescuers did not have to do any more rotations. Fresh arms and legs carried Beth to a park service truck for the ride to a hospital in Millinocket.

"Thank you all," Beth called out as she was helped into the truck after being released from the stretcher.

"No problem. You'll have to repay the favor sometime," someone replied. We all laughed and dispersed to our campsites—tired and hungry, but satisfied that we had helped a hiker in distress.

However, it has been said that no good deed goes unpunished.

Aimee, Elaine, Erin, and Carl were anxiously waiting for me when I got back to our campsite.

"Guess what?" Aimee asked.

"What?" I wearily replied.

"The keys to our car were in my backpack, and when we switched packs you had them with you. We've been waiting here for four hours, and we haven't had a thing to eat."

"Anyway, you had a good excuse for partying," I said, returning to the subject of BB's injury. "Hot Springs is the first real town you go through, right?"

"Oh, yeah, you're right," BB answered. She seemed distracted. I could tell she hadn't exactly been hanging on my every word about the rescue. I could see from the faint glow of the dying campfire that she was rapidly typing with her thumbs on her cell phone.

"What're you doing?" I asked.

"Sorry. I was just updating my blog," she explained. "It only takes me a few minutes every night."

"You're keeping a blog of your hike?" I asked.

"Well, yeah," she responded in a tone that a teenager wise to the ways of the Internet would use to address a clueless parent. "It's kind of amazing. At first it was how I stayed in touch with my family and friends. But now there's over a thousand people who have logged in to read it. People I don't even know. It's pretty neat. Are you keeping a blog, Two Tents?"

"Well, no," I answered. "When I started doing this, I didn't even know the Internet existed. I think the first time I heard about it was in 'ninety-four or 'ninety-five. And the first time I used email was maybe 'ninety-seven or 'ninety-eight. So the idea of doing a blog would have come pretty late in the game for me. I never really considered starting one."

"Oh, yeah, I guess you're right," BB said, again with the condescending tone of "how did you all survive way back then?"

Suddenly, I didn't feel merely old. I felt ancient.

It occurred to me that BB carried two pieces of gear as an ultralight hiker that I had never included with my heavier load when I had started hiking: a cell phone and hiking poles.

The vast majority of thru-hikers I was meeting on the trail were using slender poles, like the ones cross-country skiers use, to improve their stability. I had gotten so accustomed to making my way on just my feet, and with my hands when I had to do some climbing, that it had never occurred to me to help support myself with hiking poles. And although I did carry a cell phone now, it was only to stay in touch with Donna while I was on the trail. I certainly didn't use it as a means for blogging the world. Fact is, hiking the trail was my way of getting away from the world. I felt no need to send out daily reports about where I was and what I was doing. BB was of the younger generation that had an insatiable desire to stay connected.

"Anyway, Hot Springs wasn't the first place on the trail I had something to drink," BB continued. "Hiking the AT ain't exactly like barhopping, but you'd be amazed at how many chances there are to get off the trail and party. But the most amazing thing was when this couple brought the party to us."

"When was that?" I asked.

"It was right before we got to Max Patch Mountain."

"That's right after you get past the Smokies, isn't it? That's one of the best views on the trail, in my opinion."

"Yeah, well, by the time we got to the top, I'm not sure how much of the view we were seeing. When we got to the road just before the summit, there was an older couple—you know, maybe in their forties or fifties—who had set up their grill and were cooking up a meal. We're talking real Southern barbecue here, and they had ribs going. And they had beer. It was amazing.

"We got to talking to them, and it turns out they'd done this cookout there on the same weekend for several years, and every time, they got a huge turnout because it was during peak thru-hiker season. Except that year it had been raining a couple of days beforehand, so there weren't a lot of hikers coming through that day. They were all bunched up in shelters either a day's hike before or after. So, on that day, it was just Marmot and me and this couple with all this barbecue.

"Now, I thought I'd died and gone to heaven, but Marmot is vegan. So, basically, he could drink the beer, but he couldn't eat the food. This couple was looking at me, figuring that I was just gonna nibble because I'm so 'dainty.' Of course, I hadn't eaten like that since I got on the trail. So I devoured a whole bunch of ribs, but they still had a lot left over. And of course I had to wash the ribs down with a boatload of beer," BB added with a devilish grin.

"Of course. It would only be polite," I agreed with a laugh.

"Yeah, I wouldn't want to offend them. Anyway, it was just an amazing example of trail magic."

"That's a great story. If it weren't for magic, I don't think any of us could complete this trail."

"You're absolutely right," BB replied. "You've been doing this for so long, you must have experienced lots of magic."

"I've seen my share," I said, "but I usually leave the trail magic like water and soda and beer that I come upon to the thru-hikers. If I've got plenty of water and I know that I'm going to be sitting in a restaurant that night drinking a cold Yuengling, it doesn't seem quite right to take something from a cooler. I leave it for the people who'll really appreciate it."

"Ya know, I hadn't thought about it that way, but it makes sense," Rex chimed in.

"More for me," BB laughed.

"Of course, because I do a lot of driving to and from crossings, I've given rides to lots of hikers over the years. There was one guy, Sneakers, who was sitting with his pack next to a crossing in Vermont. He was barely able to stick his thumb out, so I stopped to give him a ride. I figured he was just tired. Turns out he was really sick. Ached all over and was running a fever. He was afraid it was Lyme disease. He'd been able to hike only a few miles a day until he got to that crossing. So I drove him to a hospital. As far as I'm concerned, trail magic works both ways. Sometimes you need the magic, and sometimes you're the magician."

"Why do you suppose the trail is where this magic happens?" Rex asked.

"Well, without waxing too philosophical here, I'm not so sure that it's as much magic as it is an understanding that hikers are pretty vulnerable out here. Even though the trail is well-marked, and pretty well used, once you get away from civilization there are a lot of things that can go wrong. So despite our best efforts to be prepared, we still have to depend on each other to a certain extent. Trail magic is just part of that."

"Nah," BB retorted. "I just think it's because the trail is magical. How do you explain the ribs?"

"Good point," I laughed. "Maybe you're right. I guess we'll never know for sure."

By now, the little campfire that had warded off the evening's chill had burned down to embers. It seemed a little late to get it going again. As it was, it wouldn't take much effort to tamp it down before we went to bed. I could just make out the thin luminescent lines glowing from my wristwatch. It was a little after ten.

"Well, I've got a lot of hiking ahead of me," BB announced. "I think I'm going to turn in."

"Ah, listen," Rex said, not quite sure how to start what he wanted to say next. BB and I both fell silent so he could gather his thoughts. "You said your bag is only rated to thirty-five degrees, right?" he continued, tentatively.

"Yeah?" BB answered.

"Please don't take this wrong, but it's going to get pretty cold out here tonight." He cleared his throat. "Do you want to sleep in the tent?

"In fact," he quickly continued, "if you want us to, we'll sleep outside and let you sleep in the tent by yourself. Our bags are rated to zero degrees. You wouldn't mind, right, Two Tents?"

"No, that'd be fine with me," I immediately answered, not wanting to give BB any inkling that I didn't like this idea. I really wouldn't have minded at all.

BB considered the offer for a few seconds. From a purely practical standpoint, it made sense for her to sleep in the tent. The temperature was hovering around freezing, and there was a very good chance she would have an uncomfortable night in her summer-weight sleeping bag. It would be much warmer in a tent than it would be outside and exposed to the elements. Of course, the ideal solution would be for all three of us to heat that tent with our bodies. But the space inside a three-person tent is smaller than the surface of a double bed, and we would have to cram ourselves into it in our sleeping bags; Rex and I lying with our heads going one way, and BB between us, lying the opposite way. It was hard to imagine any of us getting much sleep.

"Listen, you guys. I really appreciate the offer. But I'm going to sleep outside," BB said. "It's my decision to carry a light sleeping bag and not to pack a shelter. I'm not going to throw you out of the tent you've been packing for your own use. If we were at a shelter, I'd sleep on the floor and no one would give it a second thought. Besides, both of you seem nice enough, but I'm afraid it'd be way too close for comfort with the three of us in that tent. No offense, but I don't know you two very well, and I'm not going to sleep that way.

"There's no wind to speak of. I don't think it's going to rain. And if I sleep in my clothes, which I've done lots of times, I should be toasty warm on my pad and in my bag right here beside the campfire. Who knows? I may sleep better than you do. Don't worry about me. I'll be fine."

There is an unwritten code about the interaction of men and women who meet while hiking the trail. Hands off. Everyone is expected to respect everyone else's privacy and space. It is not a place where people look for chance sexual encounters, although I suppose that does happen now and then. Overall, the ability to hike day after day in sunshine and rain, regardless of gender, is what's important. Rex was not violating that code. His offer to have BB sleep in the tent was about one person making sure that another person would survive. Nothing more and nothing less.

To her credit, BB was every bit a woman of the trail. Self-reliant. Willing to take care of herself. Accustomed to sleeping in the company of men she does not know. Not one bit inclined to play the "helpless girl" card. The trail is a great equalizer. There is no powder-puff version of the AT. Rex and I respected BB's resolve.

"Is that your final answer?" Rex asked with a laugh.

"Yes it is," she answered with conviction.

"Well, if you get really cold in the middle of the night, you're free to change your mind. OK?"

"OK. Thanks again," BB said. "Time for some shut-eye."

With that, Rex used a stick to spread the remaining embers in the fire ring. There was no chance that one of them would set the damp woods ablaze on this night. BB placed her sleeping pad beside the ring and zipped herself into her bag. Rex and I ducked into the tent and crawled into our bags. Sleep came quickly.

**The dreary day did not dampen our enthusiasm when Donna and I hiked to the Mount Katahdin summit, Maine's highest peak.**

**Mount Katahdin: The northern end of the Appalachian Trail.**

**It doesn't look like much here, but I nearly drowned when I first tried to cross the Pierce Pond Dam in western Maine.**

**Hikers, including my niece Erin, have created this unique rock structure on Mount Abraham's summit in western Maine.**

**Mount Washington, as well as the rest of the White Mountains, is not a walk in the park for me or for other AT hikers.**

**The AT is well marked with distinctive white blazes. Most of the state lines are even more prominent.**

**My family and friends turned out in force for my final mile near the Appalachian Trail Conservancy in Harpers Ferry, West Virginia.**

**Erin and I pause near the Blue Ridge Parkway in Virginia.**

Erin and I had a front-row seat to a hailstorm at the Overmountain Shelter in North Carolina.

Springer Mountain: Where most AT thru-hikers begin the journey of a lifetime.

## 10

# Defying Death

The sting of cold air on my nose was my first sensation as I awoke before first light the next morning. The urgent need to urinate was my second. I was as warm in Rex's sleeping bag as I had ever been in my own, but the tent's thin fabric did not prevent the November cold from finding my nose and the rest of my face that was not covered by the hood of my fleece sweatshirt. The clammy dampness of perspiration in my clothes, which I had slept in, added to my discomfort as I came fully awake. And the sleeping pad which had made me comfortable enough to slip into a restful sleep no longer cushioned me from the hard ground.

I knew from past experience that it was useless for me to try to go back to sleep—especially with my bladder demanding immediate relief. It was time to get up and brave the early morning cold, no matter how dark it was. I unzipped the sleeping bag and tent flap and grabbed my boots. Rex was breathing regularly, sleeping deeply, when I exited the tent with as little movement as possible.

The air had gotten considerably colder overnight, and the ground was coated with a white hoar frost. Small icicles hung from every twig and blade of grass. I slipped on and laced up my nearly frozen boots. They would quickly warm up with use. I could make out the dark lump of the sleeping bag that encased BB beside the cold fire ring. I listened to her rhythmic breathing for a few seconds to make sure she was OK.

I made a beeline for the campground bathroom, and then sat at a picnic table beside our campsite to enjoy the stillness of the morning and the surroundings after I returned. This is my favorite time of day when I'm hiking. It's a chance to be alone with my thoughts and to take stock of my circumstances. Like many people, I am accustomed to waking up in a warm house. It's good to sometimes reflect on one's good fortune. Spending a few days in the austere environment of the trail deepens my appreciation for having a nice warm home.

My quiet time ended all too quickly. The lump of fabric on the ground stirred and a head emerged as the sky began to lighten. It was a little after six o'clock.

"Good morning," said BB in a muted voice, still thick with sleep.

"How'd you sleep?" I replied, keeping my voice as low as possible.

"Fine. Once I cocoon inside this bag, it's really warm. I knew I'd be OK as long as it didn't rain."

"Doesn't it get wet, though? You know, from the dew or this frost?"

BB unzipped her bag and crawled out. The rising sun made it possible to get a good look at her. All of her features were small. She was short and thin. Her legs and arms were little more than twigs with skin. Sprigs of straight blond hair stuck out beneath her namesake yellow bandana tied around her head. I wondered if she ever took it off.

"Unless it's really raining, it stays dry inside the bag, and any outside moisture just flies off when I give it a good shake. I love synthetics," said BB, who yawned, rubbed her eyes and began her ritual of preparing her morning meal. The sounds of movement inside the tent a few minutes later told us that Rex was about to join us.

We exchanged the customary morning pleasantries with Rex, and the three of us went about preparing breakfast and breaking camp. As adventurous as hiking the AT may sound to some people, 90 percent of it is doing the same thing—walking, sleeping, and eating—day after day. Hikers develop their own routines which, for the most part, are about as exciting as sitting in church.

Rex focused on preparing our meal, as he had last night, while I packed the tent and rolled up the bags.

"Do you want me to run down to the store and see if I can get some coffee?" I asked Rex as I stuffed the rolled-up tent back into its sack.

"Yeah, that'd be good. It's not too far, is it?" he replied.

"Do you guys need coffee?" BB asked.

"Yeah. I forgot to pack some," Rex answered.

"I think I've got a couple of extra bags," she replied.

"You carry extra coffee bags but no extra batteries?" I interjected.

"Yeah, you know, I've got my priorities."

"You sure you can spare a couple?" I continued.

"Sure can. Here." BB fished inside her pack and handed over two coffee bags.

Rex poured more water into the pot so he and I could enjoy our cups of coffee. BB finished her breakfast and quickly packed her gear. She swung on her thirteen-pound pack with ease and cinched it around her tiny waist.

Had her pack weighed twice as much, she probably wouldn't have had the strength to thru-hike the AT. But because she was packing only the bare essentials, and because everything was so light, she was close to completing a hike that would have been unthinkable for a woman of her size a generation earlier.

"Hope you have a good hike," BB declared as she grabbed her hiking poles and started out of the camp.

"You, too," Rex and I answered.

BB turned north on the trail. Rex and I finished our coffee, strapped on our considerably heavier packs, and headed south.

"I understand why a hiker like BB has to go ultralight," Rex said. "I mean, a good gust of wind could send her sailing. But being out here for six months without so much as a bivy and without a spare set of batteries; that's just a little too ultralight for me."

"I agree that the battery thing is a little over the top," I answered. "But I've known a lot of thru-hikers who don't pack a tent or bivy. They just depend on the availability of the shelters and then take their chances. There are definitely two schools of thought on that one."

"So said the guy who likes tents so much he brings two of them with him."

I just laughed. "Of course, there's also a downside to bringing too much with you."

"Yeah, I know. Things like aching shoulders and back strain."

"Well, there's that. But I've almost died on this trail a few times, and carrying a heavy pack certainly didn't help."

"They say that Kinsman always takes a blood sacrifice."

Bones' words from the night before echoed in my head as I examined my scraped hands and the lines of dried blood from the cuts on my legs. Overall, it wasn't so bad. The scrapes stung but did not hurt badly enough to indicate serious harm. A little antiseptic and a little time would heal them just fine. And, best of all, Kinsman was behind me.

I had met Bones the previous evening as I was sitting on the bank of Lonesome Lake in the White Mountains of New Hampshire.

"You thru-hiking?" he asked.

"No, I'm just out for a few days," I said.

"I could tell by the size of your pack that you're not just hut-hopping."

"Yeah, I'm pretty well packed."

"How much does that pack weigh?" he asked.

"I don't know. Something like fifty pounds."

"That's about what I carry, too," he said.

Bones was a thru-hiker in his fifties. He had given himself his trail name because he was an orthopedic surgeon. We ended up talking most of the evening about—what else?—hiking. I told him I was hiking between eight and twelve miles most days. He looked me over and concluded that, considering my age and fitness, I should be able to knock out fifteen or twenty miles a day.

While I had been hiking the AT for well over a year, this was the first time I was planning to be out for more than three days. My wife, Aimee, had moved out of our house ten days before, and I had decided that a five-day hike was a good way to escape my misery for a while.

Bones' admonition had persuaded me to push myself. Originally, I had planned to hike twelve miles today. Now I was planning to do twenty. That meant I had to climb over the two Kinsman peaks in the morning, hike about seven miles over a couple of smaller mountains after that, go over Mount Moosilauke late that afternoon, and finish at the Jeffers Brook Shelter that evening. Three four-thousand footers in one day. Piece of cake. Especially if I was doing it without Aimee.

Bones had also warned me about one section of South Kinsman that many hikers consider to be the worst part of the trail.

A large granite outcropping sits in the middle of the trail about halfway down the mountain. Rock outcroppings can present some of the greatest challenges to hikers. The only way to climb up or down one is to take advantage of the cracks and crevices in the rock face. These can be used as hand- and footholds. While most outcroppings on the AT are fairly well broken up, the one on South Kinsman is almost as smooth as a sheet of ice. It's about sixty feet long with only a few cracks and bumps. The heavy brush on both sides precludes any possibility of going around the rock. I had to go straight down it, hopefully without killing myself.

I reached the outcropping in the late morning, about when I expected to, and spent a few minutes looking down it, hoping to find some footholds on its face. There weren't many. I knew I should figure out the best route down before I started, because I probably wouldn't be able to change course once I was on the rock. There were some fissures at the top, but I couldn't see any cracks farther down. I hoped that once I got down there, I could figure out how to get the rest of the way down. So much for my planning.

Fortunately, I could lie flat on the granite slab. As I inched my way down, using a very narrow seam as my foothold, I pressed my body and backpack as close to that rock as I could so I could stay on it.

The crack ended about halfway down. There was nothing else to hold on to. I looked again. Nothing. That rock looked as smooth as a baby's behind, although by no means as soft. I spent the next couple of minutes wondering what I should do now. There was a wide ledge at the bottom of the outcropping—about thirty or forty feet down. If I kept myself pressed against the rock, I could slide down the outcropping and, hopefully, land without too much force on the bottom. Basically, I would slide down on my stomach. I hoped my body would create enough friction to slow my slide, but the weight of my pack would certainly work against me. I wished I had packed some rope to lower the pack down first. Oh, well. Next time.

I stretched my arms above me, spread my hands as widely as I could and, except for my head, pressed myself as closely as possible to the rock face. I took a deep breath and flexed my toes just enough to dislodge them from the foothold. I started sliding down the rock. My arms and legs were much like the runners of a sled, bumping over the rock. I accelerated as gravity pulled me and my heavy pack down. It was a scary and painful ride. After a few seconds, however, I was at the bottom of the outcropping. My feet landed squarely on the ledge and I flexed my knees to absorb the impact.

Some of the cuts and scrapes on my legs and hands were bleeding, but not badly. South Kinsman had claimed its blood sacrifice from me, as I'm sure it has from many others. Luckily, I had made it down in one piece without serious injury.

I readjusted my pack and kept picking my way down the steep, rocky trail. I got to Eliza Brook Shelter at the bottom of the mountain and examined my cuts and scrapes. They had stopped bleeding, but I cleaned off the abrasions with antiseptic wipes to prevent infections.

It was now a little after one in the afternoon. It had taken me about five hours to hike a little more than five miles. The next shelter was seven miles away, and I deduced it would take me about seven hours to get there. Seven plus one equals eight. Eight o'clock was a lot later than I wanted to be hiking. There was no way I was going to make it to Beaver Brook today. Instead of hiking twenty miles, I would complete five.

It had taken a little more than five hours and a slide down South Kinsman to undo an evening of pep talks from Bones. It's one thing to think that you're going to hike twenty miles in a day because you're in the prime of your life. It's quite another thing to actually do it.

I'd learned my first lesson about listening to thru-hikers. Don't. A thru-hiker who has made it from Georgia to the Whites has become a hiking machine. Thru-hikers have developed their muscles, lost any excess weight, and learned how to efficiently maneuver over the trail. They've discarded any unnecessary items from their packs, and they've acquired the discipline and stamina that enables them to hike for hours at a time without breaks, day after day after day.

While I consider myself a strong and competent hiker, I don't come close to matching the abilities of thru-hikers who have done more than three-quarters of the AT.

I hiked the seven miles from Eliza Brook to Beaver Brook on my third day out. While the trail didn't go over any major mountains, it had a series of short ups and downs over a rough terrain. I could never get into a steady pace. By the time I was going down a long set of stone steps into Kinsman Notch near the next shelter, I realized that I didn't have enough gas left to make it up and over Moosilauke. I had hiked about fifteen miles in three days.

I started hiking up Moosilauke the following morning. Initially, the trail followed Beaver Brook, which certainly wasn't a "brook" in the true sense of the word. Beaver Brook flowed over huge, unbroken slabs of granite that have been smoothed by the water over many millennia. The brook cascaded down the mountain over the granite slabs, the water separating into fingers and then flowing back together into a single stream.

The AT followed the brook closely, and in many places the trail was on the granite streambed itself. Since the granite had very few fissures, iron rungs for hand and footholds had been set in places where the rock face was particularly steep. The rungs were U-shaped with both ends cemented into the rock and the straight part of the "U" wide enough for two boots. The rungs were about the thickness of a broom handle. Sometimes only one or two rungs were needed, and other times several were required to climb up or down a particularly difficult section.

One of these steep sections was especially high, and a long series of iron rungs had been set into the rock face to serve as a ladder. Stand on one rung, hold onto another, take the long step up to the next rung, grab onto the next rung as you're lifting yourself up. It was a chore.

I had repeated this laborious task several times, my fifty-pound pack feeling a little heavier with each step. It felt like I was training to be an Olympic weightlifter. I was getting sick and tired of lifting myself and my pack by the time I was approaching the top of this iron ladder. I could see that I had only a few rungs to go. I took a brief break to catch my breath. I stood there, standing on one rung and holding another at shoulder level. A rung in between those two was even with my hip. I took several deep breaths, replenishing my strength for the final few steps to the top.

My pack was feeling particularly heavy and uncomfortable as I prepared to take my next step. I let go of the rung to rotate my arms up and back to relieve the discomfort in my shoulders. That was not a wise thing to do. The weight of my pack shifted my center of gravity. The pack began to pull me backwards. Since the rung I was standing on was positioned just in front of my boot heels, under the arches of my feet, I now made a perfect fulcrum. My feet started to pivot on the iron bar and my body began to swing away from the mountain. I must have looked like one of those glass birds sold at novelty stores—the ones that pivot down and drink up a red liquid until their center of gravity brings them upright again. But the feet of those glass birds are attached to a perch. My boots were not attached to anything. I was about to fall off this steep cliff. I was seconds from being dead.

Thank God for quick reflexes. Almost before realizing what was happening, I thrust both arms forward and down, extending them as far as I could. My right hand slapped down hard on the iron bar, and I curled my fingers around it. I held on for dear life as my left hand also grabbed the bar just as my pack began twisting me to the right. I pulled myself close to the bar and brought my center of gravity back to where it belonged—next to the cliff. I clung to that bar like a drowning man to a life ring. I was safe.

The entire incident took less than two seconds. It was over almost as soon as it began. Yet, those two seconds marked the difference between living and dying. Had I not grabbed that rung, had I been just a fraction of a second slower getting my hand down, I probably would have been carried off that mountain in a body bag.

I stood there panting for a couple of minutes, happy to be alive, angry with myself for doing something so stupid, weak-kneed that I had almost killed myself. I regained my composure, kept a very tight grip on the iron rungs, and climbed to the top. I still had miles to hike before I could sleep.

Rex and I turned a corner and saw a sliver of asphalt through an opening in the trees just ahead of us. We had reached Milam Gap and were about to cross Skyline Drive. As close and omnipresent as the highway would be throughout this hike, this would be the only time we would actually cross it. A couple of cars were parked in the large lot. This was a good place to take a short break.

"I guess I'm prepared to deal with anything the trail can throw at me," Rex began. "Things like iron rungs and outcroppings are all part of the game."

"You could look at it that way," I replied.

"The thing that would concern me most is being caught in the middle of a thunderstorm. I'm sure it has to do with some deep-seated, irrational fear I have from childhood, but those things scare the bejesus out of me."

"Well, I've hiked during several thunderstorms, and mainly they're just a pain in the ass—especially if you're not near a shelter. The least that's going to happen is you'll get soaking wet. The worst thing would be getting hit by lightning. And the thunder and the possibility of getting hit can scare the crap out of you. Sometimes there isn't much you can do except get out of harm's way as quickly as you can. If you can't, you realize that if you're hearing the thunder then you haven't been hit by lightning. And if you do get hit, you probably won't know it. You'll be dead in a heartbeat."

We pulled on our packs and crossed Skyline Drive.

"That's kind of fatalistic," Rex observed as we continued down the trail.

"You're right. But after you've been in the middle of a thunderstorm above tree line in the Whites, you look at them a little differently than you did before. If it's your day to die, there are probably worse ways to go."

Aimee's new apartment was available August first, and she decided to move her things out of our house the following weekend. As luck would have it, we had already made a reservation for the Mizpah Springs Hut for that Friday night, and we had an even more sought-after reservation at the Appalachian Mountain Club's Lakes of the Clouds Hut for that Saturday. Those reservations made it possible for me to get out of the house for a few days so Aimee could pack her stuff.

Lakes of the Clouds is the AMC hut closest to Mount Washington's summit. It is the largest of all the AMC huts, and it is also the busiest—which explains its nickname, "Lakes of the Crowds." On a clear day, the view to the west from atop the Presidential Range is simply unsurpassed. That's why so many people want to stay at Lakes of the Clouds.

I drove to Pinkham Notch on Friday and grabbed an AMC shuttle to the AT crossing at Crawford Notch. Driving up there by myself reminded me that I was about to be alone a lot more than I was used to. As tumultuous as my eight years with Aimee had been, there had been someone with whom I could share my life. That connection would be gone when I returned from this trip. I was thirty-one, and my life was about to start over.

The hike was steep but uneventful. By early afternoon, I had climbed to the summit of Mount Jackson at the northern end of the Presidential Range. The wide-open summit was a great place to lie down and enjoy the view on this warm and very clear day. I spent a little time there and then proceeded along an almost level footpath to the hut at Mizpah Springs.

I enjoyed a hearty breakfast the following morning and resumed my hike. I reached tree line about a half mile out of Mizpah. I spent that entire August day hiking above tree cover, something that I couldn't have done if I had traveled a thousand miles in any direction. The sky was cloudless and the visibility was incredible—well over a hundred miles.

I completely forgot about what was happening at home. I reached Lakes of the Clouds by midafternoon. I checked in, dropped most of my gear in my room, and easily hiked the mile and a half to the Mount Washington summit. I spent a few minutes in the Summit House, where I bought a candy bar and used a real flush toilet. I made my way back down to the hut. I ate dinner with my fellow hikers and settled down for the evening. I was sound asleep by nine o'clock.

I awoke in the middle of the night to the distinct sound of wind-driven rain pelting the windows and roof. Except this rain sounded like hail—raindrops making little pings as they hit the hut. I hoped it was a passing shower and fell back to sleep.

It was early morning when I awoke again. I could see through the window that we were socked in a cloud and that it was raining torrents. These raindrops had tiny ice crystals in them—not quite hail and certainly not snow. Hiking conditions today were going to be considerably worse than the balmy temperatures and unlimited visibility of yesterday.

Since the weather was so foul, I considered bagging my hike for that day and hunkering down right where I was. Hikers are strongly encouraged to seek shelter and stay there if conditions are bad in the Whites. I was in a shelter. I was warm. I was dry. There was food. It only made sense for me to stay put. I settled in for another hour of sleep.

Then it hit me. Aimee needed my car. Shit!

I had promised to return the Mazda so that Aimee and two of her friends could move furniture to her apartment on the roof rack. I had agreed to this arrangement because I was trying to be mature about splitting up.

My mood instantly turned as foul as the weather. My mind and my body were out of sync. "I have to be out of my mind to go out into this shit," I argued with myself as I forced myself out of the bunk bed, dressed, hit the bathroom, ate breakfast, and grabbed my pack. "I can't control the goddamned weather," I muttered as I put on my boots. "She'll have to find some other way to move the furniture. I'm not leaving here today," I kept telling myself as I pulled on my raingear and lifted on my pack.

The weather's fury struck me full force as I stepped outside. The sleet was hitting me horizontally, and I was walking directly into it. Within seconds the tiny icy crystals encrusted my glasses. I put them in my pocket. Now the sleet was pelting my unprotected eyes. All I could do was squint and blink. I am somewhat nearsighted. It was almost impossible to make out distant objects. On top of that, I quickly got cold as the wind cut through the fleece pullover under my raingear. Then I got wet because the sleet soaked through the raingear. I might as well have been standing out there butt naked.

Having hiked in heavy cloud cover before, I was fairly adept at staying on a trail in adverse conditions. I looked for the cairns. Cairns are manmade piles of rocks, generally between two and three feet high, that mark the trail. In places like the Whites, cairns may be only a few feet apart. Hikers barely notice them when the visibility is good because the footpath is so well defined. We search for them as a parched man gropes for a canteen when the trail is obscured by low-hanging clouds or heavy rain. They can mean the difference between living and dying.

Following cairns is pretty simple. Stand by a cairn, pick out the next cairn in the gloom, walk to it, repeat the process. If what you see is not a cairn, turn around, go back to the one you just left, and try again.

The progress was agonizingly slow. Finally, after following the cairns for a thousand feet on the AT, I turned onto the Tuckerman Cut-off Trail which would lead me about three-quarters of a mile to the Tuckerman Ravine Trail. That trail would lead me back to Pinkham Notch and my car.

But getting there would not be easy. I had trouble seeing because ice kept building up on my eyebrows. I had to keep clearing my eyes. The cloud cover was so dense it was nearly impossible to make out the next cairn. Sometimes I could only guess where the trail was by following rocks that looked like they had been walked on by a few million feet. That was hard to do in the sleet and the gloom of that morning. So I continued peering ahead for the cairns. I knew it could be disastrous if I got off the trail. I could wind up wandering around the plain, hopelessly lost and without adequate shelter. No one would know to come looking for me. Hypothermia could kill me.

The fact that I didn't actually have to be out in this stuff made the situation even more aggravating. It would not have been the end of the world had I not gotten home with the Mazda today. So what if Aimee had to wait an extra day to move her furniture? But I had made a promise, and I was going to keep it, come hell or high water.

One of my favorite movies is the Mel Brooks flick *Young Frankenstein*, and one of my favorite scenes is when Gene Wilder's character, Dr. Frankenstein—pronounced with a long "e"—and Marty Feldman's character, Igor—pronounced with a long "i"—are digging up a grave. Wilder comments about what a horrible situation they're in, and Feldman says, "Could be worse." Wilder asks, incredulously, "How could it possibly be worse?" Feldman retorts, "Could be raining."

Well, it was already raining. And it was about to get worse.

I heard a low rumble in the distance—more of a vibration than a sound. Another minute, another rumble, this time a little louder. *Holy shit! Thunder!*

Of course, it wasn't the thunder that alarmed me. It was the lightning that comes with it. And it was coming my way. Although I had hiked during thunderstorms before, I had always been *under* the storms. Here, in the clouds, I would be *in* the storm.

What I knew about thunderstorms was that lightning is discharged in several ways—from cloud to cloud, from within the same cloud, and from cloud to ground. I didn't like the idea of being caught in the middle of any of those scenarios.

To make matters worse, the rocks in the immediate area were only about hip high. I knew that lightning is attracted to the highest object in its vicinity. At that moment, that was me. Not good!

Until now, I had been going very slowly, making sure that I could pick out the next cairn on the trail. Now I wanted to get off that ridge as quickly as I could. My first thought was to walk hunched over to lower my height and hopefully fool the lightning. But that made it a lot harder to follow the trail. I switched tactics and walked kind of like Groucho Marx—keeping my back and head straight but my legs and hips as low to the ground as I could.

Fortunately, I reached the junction with the Tuckerman Ravine Trail in a couple of minutes. This is the primary trail used by hikers who climb Mount Washington from Pinkham Notch. It was fairly easy to follow because it had been so heavily traveled. I raced along that trail in the downpour, the thunder getting louder and louder every minute, and reached the headwall where the trail leaves the ridge and begins descending to the valley below. I plunged down that trail as if my pack were a rocket engine. The thunder and lightning reached the area a minute later with a loud BOOM-BOOM. Now, at least, I was off the ridge and no longer the tallest target for the lightning. I was merely another fixture on the landscape.

I stopped to catch my breath—bent over, hands on knees, gasping for air. Now what? If I stayed put, I would be in the clouds during the thunderstorm. I decided that the safest place was below the clouds. So I continued hiking down the trail as quickly as I could, my boots getting more waterlogged with every step.

The thunder crashed around me. The lightning flashes repeatedly turned the cloud cover into hues of bright white. I was in the middle of my very own Fourth of July fireworks, and it was not fun. I reminded myself several hundred times that if I was hearing the thunder and seeing the flashes then I had not been hit.

I dipped below the clouds about halfway down the headwall. Now, at least, I was no longer in the thunderstorm. I was merely under it. Thankfully, the storm began to subside a few minutes later.

By now, the sleet had turned to rain. From the moment I had left the hut, my flimsy raingear had been no match for the wind-whipped sleet. But while I had been concentrating on picking my way across the ridge and then racing down this trail to beat the thunderstorm, I hadn't given much thought to the fact that I was thoroughly soaked. Now that I could see where I was going, now that I no longer feared for my life, I realized that I probably looked like a drowned rat. I certainly felt like one.

From the bottom of the headwall, I still had to hike another two and a half miles to my car at Pinkham Notch. I had not seen a soul since leaving Lakes of the Clouds. But as I was hiking down the trail, I met a family hiking toward me: two parents in their late twenties or early thirties and three children, all under the age of ten. The parents were wearing a semblance of raingear, but the kids were clad in garbage bags with armholes cut in the sides.

"Hey, did you just come off the mountain?" the father asked me.

"Yes, I did," I replied.

"What were the conditions like?"

"Well, it was the worst weather I've ever hiked through. High winds. Driving rain. It was sleeting up on the ridge itself. And for a while I was in the middle of a thunderstorm. Other than that, it was just fine."

"Oh, OK," the man said, and the family continued up the path toward the mountain.

Having read the sign in the Mount Washington Summit House that tells who has died in the Presidentials, in what years, and under what circumstances, what struck me at that moment wasn't that a lot of people die in these mountains but that it's a miracle that more people don't die out here.

A little more than three hours after leaving the hut, I got into my car and cranked up the heat. The steam rolling off my body fogged the windows as I headed south on Route 16. I kept the windows cracked open and the defroster on full blast as I began drying out during the drive back to Amesbury.

I returned late that afternoon to what had been "our" house but was about to become "my" house. Aimee had packed her things and taken all of her light stuff during the weekend. Now her friends had arrived to help move out the big boxes and furniture.

The events of the day and all of the petty resentments that had built up during our relationship poured out of me.

"I'm soaked. I'm tired. And I'm pissed off!" I barked as I entered the house, not caring whose feelings I hurt. "All I want to do is take a goddamned shower!" I stormed upstairs to the bathroom.

"We need your keys to the Mazda," Aimee called up to me. I pulled my key ring from my damp shorts and threw it down the stairs. The keys crashed to the floor just a couple of feet from her friend.

I stepped into the shower and let the hot water soothe my aching body for a long time. Both cars were gone when I finished. I got dressed and went downstairs.

Alone.

# 11

# Memorable Men

Rex and I had been climbing steadily since leaving Milam Gap, and now we were on top of Hazeltop Mountain. The trees on the summit had shed their leaves by this time in November. That opened up spectacular views that we could not have enjoyed during the summer. Radio towers stood out prominently on another range to the east, and the Shenandoah Valley was visible to the west. It felt good to take a breather as we stopped for a few moments on an outcropping.

"Sounds like you were pretty lucky to make it out alive up in Maine and New Hampshire," Rex said after we had slipped off our packs and pulled out candy bars. "Maybe I should just stick with hiking down here."

"Well, I wouldn't advise that," I responded. "Sure, the Whites and Maine are difficult, but the tradeoff is some of the greatest views you'll ever see. The good offsets the bad, but the good comes with conditions. You have to work for it. Anyway, I think that a lot of my problems during the early years were caused by my inexperience. It might have been better if I'd waited a few years and had a better understanding of what this hiking thing is all about before I tackled the toughest sections of the trail. On the other hand, I took my lumps and learned my lessons. And it was good to have the hard parts behind me fairly early on. I sure wouldn't want to have the Whites ahead of me at this point."

"Yup. Sometimes the only way to learn is to just do it," Rex acknowledged.

"Have you met any really interesting people on the trail?" he asked, changing the topic.

"Well, a few. I did meet one guy who was running for president."

"Was it that Mark Sanford guy?"

"No, it wasn't him. I've never seen him out here." We both laughed. "No, this guy was really running for president."

"Seriously?"

"Yeah. At least he thought he was."

"Hey, how're you doing?" I asked. I had just rounded the corner of the lean-to at Joe's Hole, a few miles east of the southern end of Moxie Pond in Maine. The spot was about halfway between the New Hampshire line and Mount Katahdin. Or, put another way, in the middle of nowhere. The lean-to faced away from the trail, and the man inside hadn't heard me coming. He had jumped up in surprise at the sound of my voice.

"Oh, sorry I startled you," I apologized.

"No problem. I just didn't hear you coming," he replied, regaining his composure.

It was a Sunday morning, and I was on the final day of a three-day hike. I was in no particular hurry because I only had to hike two and a half miles to the road crossing where my brother Bob would pick me up and drive me to my truck. The lean-to was just a little over a mile from where I had camped. Normally, I wouldn't have stopped this early into my hike. But the brook flowing past the lean-to was inviting, and I had some time to enjoy it.

The man and I made the usual AT small talk about the weather, where we had hiked from, and where we were planning to go that day.

"Did you know that I'm running for president?" he asked rather nonchalantly.

Now, when I had initially seen him, presidential candidate was not the first thing that came to mind. My first impression was that he was a thru-hiker because of his scraggly beard and the really dirty clothes that hung limply from his thin, wiry body. He obviously hadn't taken a shower in many days. His appearance was perfectly acceptable for the Appalachian Trail, but it certainly wouldn't do for the campaign trail.

I had to make a decision. Was this guy a total nut job, so I should make my exit as quickly as possible? Or was this guy a total nut job, but harmless enough to talk with for a while?

*What the hell,* I decided. *I've got a couple of hours to kill. Let's see where this one goes.*

"No, I have to say I wasn't aware that you're running for president," I said to the guy. "President of the United States, right?"

"Yes. President of the United States. I've actually run several times. Of course, I haven't won yet."

I knew that. I stay up on current events pretty well, so I've got a good idea of who has and has not been elected president. I think I would have remembered if this guy had served between, say, Jimmy Carter and Ronald Reagan.

"Here, I'll show you an article," he continued. He dug into his backpack and pulled out a clear plastic re-sealable bag. Several newspaper articles were inside. He pulled one out and passed it to me.

I began to read. The piece had been cut out of a local weekly paper from a town in northern Maine. A black-and-white picture of the man standing in front of me—scraggly beard and all—was printed with the story about how he had declared his candidacy for the 1996 Republican nomination for president. The article explained who he was, what he did, and why he was running. I was sure that Bill Clinton was shaking in his boots, seeing his re-election chances go up in smoke.

"Wow, that's interesting," I said as I handed back the newspaper clipping. "You really are running for president."

"Did you know that I was also the keynote speaker at the Republican Convention when I was twelve?"

"No, I didn't know that," I answered.

He took another clipping from the plastic bag, this one considerably more yellowed than the previous one. It included a picture of a rather handsome young man wearing a sports coat and tie. The article gave his name and hometown and noted that he had spoken to the national convention as a junior member of the Republican Party.

At this point I'd have believed this guy if he'd told me he'd walked across the Grand Canyon on a tightrope. I was certain he could have produced a newspaper clipping from his plastic bag to show me he had done just that.

So here I was, sitting in a shelter on the AT with someone who was running for president. Yes, he seemed a little peculiar, but no more so than some of the politicians I already knew. And, since I don't get the chance to talk to a presidential candidate every day, I started talking politics with him.

As a registered Democrat in 1995, I could finally take pride that a Democrat was in the White House after two Republican administrations. Bill Clinton had been in office for a little over two and a half years. Despite a disastrous midterm election in 1994, when the Republicans had won control of both the House and Senate, I thought Clinton had found his niche. My new Republican candidate acquaintance, however, wasn't nearly as enamored with Clinton's performance.

Yet, despite our political differences, he and I did agree on some issues. We were both concerned that America's role in Bosnia could escalate into a greater involvement and that the entire region was a potential powder keg. Anyplace that had been the catalyst for the First World War and that had been controlled by the former Soviet Union had to be handled with kid gloves.

One of our primary concerns was the bombing of the Oklahoma City federal building the previous April, and the threat that right-wing extremists like Timothy McVeigh posed for the U.S. I was very concerned that this was only the beginning of those people's efforts to topple our government. Even if they did not succeed, a lot of people might die during the attempt. My new acquaintance considered the extremists to be a manifestation of the discontent that many people felt toward the government. Although he thought changes were necessary, he agreed that people should not get hurt.

We also agreed on one other matter. Given the evidence the jury was hearing during that year's O.J. Simpson trial, there was no doubt that Simpson had murdered his ex-wife, Nicole Brown Simpson, and her friend, Ronald Goldman, and that the only logical verdict was "guilty."

I was curious about his campaign—how he was actually going to run. I had read that it is relatively easy to get your name on the ballot for the New Hampshire presidential primary. The cost was something like a hundred dollars. No signatures had to be collected. You just pay the money. Typically, therefore, dozens of candidates from both parties appear on the New Hampshire primary ballot. Most are unknown fringe candidates who get only a few votes and the satisfaction of having run for president.

"So," I asked, "are you going to enter the New Hampshire primary?"

The question obviously took him aback.

"Oh, no. You need millions of dollars to do that. I don't have that kind of money," he replied.

"Oh, I thought all you needed was something like a hundred dollars to get your name on the ballot. I might be wrong, but I thought I read that somewhere."

The tenor of the discussion changed abruptly. Whereas a minute earlier we had been having a pleasant conversation about world and national affairs, now my question about his campaign seemed to make him very uncomfortable.

"Well, I guess I'm going to have to look into that," he said with a harrumph as he began putting things back in his pack.

I realized I had crossed a line and that it was time to leave. I quickly put my water bottle back into my pack and strapped it on.

"Hey, good luck with the campaign," I said as I shook his hand, and resumed hiking toward Moxie Pond Road.

"Do you think this guy was really crazy?" Rex asked.

"No, I really don't think so. In fact, as I've thought about it more, I think I was the crazy one."

"How so?"

"Well, in his mind, declaring for the presidency was something that you told your local newspaper. It would make him a local celebrity. Maybe some of the folks in town would call him 'Mr. President' when they saw him at the store. But I don't believe for a minute that he really considered himself a legitimate presidential candidate.

"My vision of running for president is very different. If you really want to do that, you declare your candidacy, raise some money, get into the primaries, shake some hands, kiss some babies, and hope for the best. He didn't see it that way. All he wanted to do was declare. When I crossed that line and began asking how he'd run for president, I found out that he knew he didn't have a chance in hell.

"So, no, he wasn't crazy," I concluded. "Eccentric, yes. Quirky, yes. But in the long run, declaring that he was a candidate for president was just his thing. He wasn't hurting anyone, and it gave him lots of satisfaction. Kind of like what hiking the AT does for me."

We had lingered longer at the top of Hazeltop than we had intended. We pulled on our backpacks and continued southward.

"While 'Mr. President' was probably the most eccentric person I've met on the trail," I continued, "I'd have to say that the most memorable person I've met out here was a guy who was in danger of killing himself, and most of his family, too. And don't think that you can only get into trouble in remote places like Maine and New Hampshire. He was on one of the most traveled sections in Pennsylvania."

"How did he do that?"

While I normally park my truck at my destination and then ride my bike to my starting point, I had decided to do the opposite on this October morning in 2003. Flat tires on my bicycle had seriously delayed the start of my last two hikes, and I desperately wanted to get in a good one without any problems. So I decided I'd hike first and bike later. That meant hiding my bike in the woods where I planned to finish, and driving to where I wanted to start. Then I'd ride my bike back to my truck.

I hid my bike in the woods where the AT crosses Route 61 near Hamburg, Pennsylvania, and then drove to the parking lot at Hawk Mountain Sanctuary. The road distance was seventeen miles—about an hour-and-a-half-long bike ride back to my truck. If I got a flat along the way, I'd just have to deal with it.

It was a little before ten o'clock when I pulled into the Hawk Mountain parking lot. I had a fourteen-mile hike ahead of me. I had to be off the trail and on my bike by five o'clock to ride back to my truck by dark. That gave me seven hours to hike this stretch of trail. I had certainly maintained a two-mile-per-hour pace before. So as long as the trail conditions were as good as I expected them to be, I could pull this off.

The trail guide told me that a place called The Pinnacle offered an excellent viewpoint a little over five miles away. I figured I could get there around noon. It looked like a good place to eat lunch.

I was not disappointed. The Pinnacle is a massive outcropping that juts out from Blue Mountain. It provides an expansive view of the small city of Hamburg and neat Pennsylvania farms that extend across the valley for as far as you can see.

I've looked over many valleys from the tops of mountains, but the view from The Pinnacle is unique. Blue Mountain is not a mountain in the traditional sense. It is, rather, a ridge that runs nearly continuously for one hundred fifty miles. It sits at a uniform height above a valley of flat farmland. The Pinnacle juts out from the ridge and curves back almost like a talon on an eagle. The outcropping sits at the very tip of that talon. From this vantage point, you can see the entire length of Blue Mountain and the valley below it.

This mountain is so long that it disappears from view because of the curvature of the earth. It was a phenomenon I had never seen so clearly before. It could only work with a mountain that is as long and as uniformly high as Blue Mountain.

I lingered at The Pinnacle until one o'clock—longer than I should have. I still had nine miles to go. I had fallen off my two-mile-per-hour pace, and I had to make up for lost time. I resumed hiking with a newfound determination, walking as fast as I could without spraining an ankle or tripping on an exposed root and banging up a knee. I kept my breaks to a minimum. I paid no attention to the view or to anything else except the trail in front of me. There were no two ways about it. If I wanted to get to my truck by sunset, I had to be off this trail by five.

I pulled out my trail maps during my first break after lunch and calculated when I should reach some specific points on the trail to keep to my schedule. I should get to Windsor Furnace Shelter by two fifty. Then I'd get to Pocahontas Spring an hour after that, and I'd reach another overlook at four thirty. From there, I could get to Route 61, and my bike, around four forty-five. I figured I could take some short breaks if I reached those milestones with a little time to spare. But if I was running behind, I'd have to pick up my pace even more to get off the trail on time.

I arrived at the shelter with a couple of minutes to spare, but decided to keep on hiking without resting. I got to the spring at three forty-five, and stopped just long enough for a drink and a candy bar. I arrived at the viewpoint at four twenty-five, five minutes ahead of schedule. I had only six-tenths of a mile to hike. As long as I didn't have a problem with my bike, I would be back to my truck before dark.

I began descending from the viewpoint, beginning to believe that my plan would work out after all. It turned out that the god of hiking had other ideas.

I spotted two youngsters walking toward me on the trail a couple of minutes later. The boy looked to be around ten, and the girl was about eight. We passed without saying a word. I supposed they were coming up to look at the view. The number of people on the trail increases substantially if it is close to a road crossing. For anyone hiking the entire trail, the sight of day hikers is akin to a sailor spotting a shore bird out to sea. It's an indication that you're getting close to a road or highway—civilization.

I rounded a corner a few minutes later. Now a man and two young boys were coming up the trail. I guessed the boys were six and four. The man appeared to be in his mid-to-late thirties and of average build—somewhere between thru-hiker-hard and office-soft. So that was it. He and his children were making a late afternoon hike up to the viewpoint.

I didn't really give the family much more thought because I was focused on getting to my bike and riding to my truck. Time was not on my side, and I wasn't interested in any chitchat.

"Hi, how ya doin'?" I asked as we drew within speaking distance. But I really didn't care if they answered, and I didn't slow my pace a bit.

The three of them stepped aside to let me pass. Then, after I had gone by them, the man asked, "Did you happen to see a couple of kids on the trail?"

I stopped and faced him. "Yeah. A boy and a girl, right?"

"That's right. My son and daughter."

"I met them about five minutes ago." I turned to resume my hike.

"Can I ask you another question?" he asked.

I reluctantly stopped again. *Jeesh. This guy wants to talk,* I whined to myself.

"Yeah, sure," I replied a bit impatiently.

"Do you know how far it is to Hawk Mountain?"

"By road or by trail?" I asked back.

"By trail."

It took me a couple of moments to remember how far I had hiked today. I had been focused all afternoon on how much trail I had left to go, not on how many miles I had come. "It's something like fourteen miles," I replied.

"Fourteen miles?!" the man exclaimed, much more emphatically than I had expected. "You can't be right. It can't be fourteen miles!"

"Yes, it is. I've got the maps to prove it." I took off my pack and pulled them out. *This jerk is costing me too much time,* I muttered to myself.

I unfolded the maps, got my bearings, and showed the father this section of the trail. "Look, the road crossing that you just came up from is here. We're probably about here, and the trail winds all the way along here until you get to Hawk Mountain. That's about fourteen miles."

All the while, I was asking myself why this guy wanted to know how far it was to Hawk Mountain. Maybe he was thinking about hiking this section sometime in the future, but I was in no mood to spend my precious time helping him now. He should get his own damned maps and figure it out for himself.

"Do you think we'll be able to get there before dark?" he asked me, somewhat plaintively.

It hit me like a bucket of cold water. This guy wasn't asking out of curiosity. He was actually planning to hike this section today. He was planning to hike a fourteen-mile section of the AT with four kids under the age of twelve with about two hours of daylight left. Unbelievable.

Whereas a few moments ago I had been completely lost in my thoughts about my upcoming bike ride, I now realized that these five people were in a very dangerous situation. And they didn't even know it. They needed some help.

I took a deep breath. "There's absolutely no way you're going to be able to hike this section before dark," I said very firmly. While temperatures had reached the mid-fifties that afternoon, I had scraped a little frost off my windshield that morning, and it would probably drop below freezing again that night. The father and his children were wearing long pants and sweaters, and they were all carrying some water. They were only marginally prepared to be out here on a pleasant fall afternoon. They certainly weren't equipped to spend a very cold night.

"Well, we don't have any other choice," the father said. "My wife's waiting for us at Hawk Mountain." With that, he and his young sons continued walking up the trail—away from me.

"Hey. Listen," I said as adamantly as I could without yelling at the man. "There's no way you can make it that far on your own before dark. And you're certainly not going to make it with four kids." I had to convince this guy to turn around. If he and his children kept hiking, they were in for a hell of a night.

"Well, I don't know what else to do," he replied.

"Look, I'm sure we can figure out something," I offered. My mind was racing, searching for a solution. "Do you have a cell phone so you can call your wife?"

"No, I don't," he answered, as if to say, "We don't believe in them."

*Great! He's out here with four kids, and he has absolutely no way to contact his wife. This has to be the biggest idiot on the planet!* I thought.

"I'm feeling so stupid for being out here," he said as if he was reading my mind.

OK. He may not be the sharpest pencil in the box, but he was beginning to see that he needed some help. I backed off a bit. If I came on too strongly, he might blow me off and start hiking toward Hawk Mountain again. That was the last thing I wanted. I had to boost his ego a bit.

"It's all right. This could happen to anyone," I said. "I'm section-hiking the entire trail. That's why I have these maps. But a lot of people are out here without them. These trail distances are very deceiving."

Then I personalized the relationship. "I'm Jim."

"I'm Bill, and this is Joshua and Jacob," he answered as we shook hands. "That was Adam and Rachel who you met earlier."

Joshua was six, and Jacob was four, their father told me. Adam was ten, and Rachel was eight. I was right about their ages, for whatever that was worth. I knew they were all too young to hike fourteen miles of the AT under the best of circumstances, and they were certainly too young to spend the night out here under these conditions.

"Look," I continued, "I've got a bike down at the road crossing, and I'm riding back to Hawk Mountain where my truck is parked. You guys can wait at the crossing. I'll find your wife at Hawk Mountain, and then she'll come back to pick you up." It sounded easy enough. There were only about a thousand things that could go wrong, but I couldn't think of anything else to do.

"OK, that sounds like a good plan," Bill agreed. "We're not imposing on you, are we?"

"No, of course not," I replied. "I'm going that way anyway."

*What a moron,* I thought sarcastically. *I always ride my bike and look for women I don't know who are parked in their cars after dark. Happens all the time.*

Then something else occurred to me. Bill's two other children were still out on the trail. As we were talking, the sun was getting closer to the horizon, and Adam and Rachel were getting farther and farther away. Bill couldn't catch up with them if the two younger boys were tagging along with him. I somehow had to persuade Bill to leave his sons with me so he could race ahead and bring the two older children back.

But, being a father myself, I knew that idea would go against every paternal instinct he had. How could any father leave his children with a complete stranger? But that's what I had to convince him to do—quickly.

I pulled my wallet from my daypack and took out my driver's license. "Bill," I began in a firm voice that I hoped showed resolve without sounding overbearing. "Adam and Rachel are up ahead. We don't have a lot of daylight left, and I have a long bike ride ahead of me. You have to go get them, and you're not going to catch them if Joshua and Jacob are with you. Here's my driver's license. Take this, and leave your boys with me." I handed him my license.

He considered this idea for a few seconds as he examined my license.

"Look, I know this goes against anything you'd normally do," I continued. "I have a six-year-old myself. His name is Jason, and I can't imagine letting anyone do something like this. But we're in a heck of a predicament here, and you and I have to figure out how we're all going to get out of it."

Bill agreed that this was the only solution. "I don't need your license. I trust you," he replied. He tried to hand the license back to me, but I raised both of my hands. I wouldn't take it.

"No, you take the license so you know you can trust me."

Bill put his arms around both little boys and told them he had to go get Adam and Rachel. He said that I was going to take care of them, and that they were to obey me just like they would obey him. The boys looked a little apprehensive, but they didn't argue with their father. Bill started jogging up the trail a few seconds later.

I sat with the boys for the next twenty minutes. I asked them about their friends, the games they liked to play, school, anything to keep their attention so they wouldn't worry about being left by their father and perhaps start crying. It was lucky that Joshua was the same age as Jason. That gave me some common ground. Both boys probably liked the same things. Like Jason, Joshua had just started first grade. I asked him about his teacher and the kids in his class. Jacob was quick to chime in on the conversation so he could get some of my attention. I looked at Jacob, the youngest, and thought about how he would be most at risk had they spent the night on the trail.

It was after five thirty when Bill returned with Adam and Rachel. He had caught up with them fairly quickly because they had stopped at the viewpoint to wait for their father and brothers. It took us about ten minutes to hike out to the road. Thankfully, my bike was where I had hidden it. Bill told me his wife's name was Marcia as he handed me my license.

She would be waiting in a turquoise minivan. I wrote down the license plate number on my map. I strapped on my helmet and began pedaling. It was about five forty-five, three-quarters of an hour later than I had wanted to start riding. The sun wasn't going to wait. I had to move.

Even though I pedaled as fast as I could, I could not beat the dark. The sun set while I was still on the road. I continued pedaling uphill to Hawk Mountain. I was exhausted after a full day of hiking. My light daypack didn't slow me down, but my feet were sore, and my ankles were killing me. They were stiffly bound inside my hiking boots, which were higher and heavier than my sneakers and were not designed for pedaling bicycles. I would ordinarily have walked my bike the last mile or two to my truck. But I knew I would need whatever light was left to locate Bill's minivan and his wife. So I gritted my teeth and pushed on.

I finally pulled into the sanctuary, tired but relieved to be off the relentless hill. The parking area was really a number of small, unlit openings scattered among the trees. There was just enough daylight remaining to read the license plates. I rode my bike through several openings, looking for the vehicle, until I finally saw a woman sitting in a minivan. The license plate number matched the one Bill had given me. I pulled my bike around to the driver's side, and the woman rolled down her window.

"Hi, is your name Marcia, by any chance?" I asked her breathlessly.

"Yes, it is," she replied. I could now see that a toddler was sitting in the backseat and that Marcia was very pregnant with child number six. "Could this be about my husband and kids?" she asked quite cheerfully.

"Yes, it is. I met them on the trail and convinced your husband that they wouldn't be able to make it here tonight. They're back at the crossing where you dropped them off."

"Oh, OK," she replied, rather nonchalantly. "I wasn't sure if they'd be able to make it or not. I'll go pick them up." She did not appear to be the least bit concerned that her husband and four of their children might have been stranded on the trail all night while she and her baby waited in the van. It was almost as if she knew that someone would come to their rescue if things didn't work out as planned.

"Thank you for your help, and God bless you," said Marcia as she started the engine. A bumper sticker on the back of the van caught my attention as she drove away: "Honk If You Love Jesus!"

# 12

# Son and Sunrise

Rex and I had reached a junction with a side trail that led to the top of Bearfence Mountain. Because it had been raining hard when I had hiked this section before, I hadn't gone up there. Now I wanted to see if there was any kind of view from the top. We were not disappointed after making the short climb. A large outcropping provided us with a view all around. We dropped our packs and took a break.

"Wow, I can't believe somebody like that father could be out here and be that irresponsible," Rex remarked between bites of a candy bar. "I mean, it's one thing to be out here by yourself after dark. But it's quite another thing to have four kids with you."

"Well, maybe something else was going on," I said after taking some satisfying gulps from my water bottle. "Of all the things that have happened to me in my life, it was the encounter with that family that got me to wondering about my ideas about God."

"How so?" Rex asked.

"Ever since my late teens I've been pretty much convinced that God doesn't exist. I went to a very conservative, fundamentalist church with my family when I was a kid. But by the time I'd finished high school and was getting ready for college, I just wasn't buying what that church was selling—probably because of my contrary nature. The idea that there's this one omnipotent God that controls everything we do just didn't make sense to me. Then, whenever I doubted that idea, I'd tell myself that if there is a God, it would only be involved in the big-picture things. You know, like creating the world and keeping the moon and the stars in order. The day-to-day stuff would still be left to chance.

"But I began to wonder about that soon after I met that family. That father and his kids were in trouble. Bill assumed they only had to hike three or four miles to get to Hawk Mountain. That's about the distance as the crow flies."

"Yeah, but crows didn't lay out the AT," Rex chuckled.

"You can say that again. It was a *fourteen-mile* hike because of the trail's long sideways sweep to pick up The Pinnacle. So they were in for a very long night on the trail unless someone like me came along to help them. The chances of that happening were almost infinitesimal. I hadn't seen another soul on the trail since I'd left The Pinnacle. It was mid-October, so the thru-hikers had already come through. Most people wouldn't attempt to hike that stretch then because the days were pretty short to do that kind of distance. If they met anyone, it would most likely be someone who was just going up to the lookout in the late afternoon, as I had assumed they were doing.

"What they needed was a guardian angel, someone who was hiking the trail and could show Bill the error of his ways and help his family. And lo and behold they got one—me. Marcia's reaction, when I finally met up with her, told me she just assumed that God would take care of them.

"So, was my encounter with them entirely by chance, or was it part of some grand plan that I had unknowingly become a part of? While I'm inclined to believe it was the former, I'm sure they're thoroughly convinced it was the latter—that God had put me there to help them. And, who knows, maybe they're right."

"That's some food for thought," said Rex as we again lifted on our packs. We still had more miles to cover today.

"Did you ever think about calling it quits?" Rex asked after we had come off Bearfence and settled into a comfortable pace along this stretch of the trail.

"What do you mean?"

"You know. Giving up this section-hiking business."

"You mean after I've twisted an ankle or spent an entire day and night soaking wet?" I laughed. "Sure. I imagine everyone has thought about quitting. But I got over it after a day or so."

"No. I mean, did you really seriously think about chucking the whole thing because it took too much of your time, or because it was costing you too much money, or because you were just losing interest?"

"Actually, I did. Just once. Eleven years ago. It was right after we had adopted Jason. I was in lousy shape, and I thought I was spending too much time away from home. So I told Donna I was hanging it up. She's the one who convinced me to stick with it. In fact, she practically insisted on it."

I was thirty-seven before I discovered that there's nothing quite like having a baby fall asleep in your arms.

I looked down and saw that the nipple on the bottle had slipped out of Jason's pouting lips. They were open just enough so I could see the tips of his two lower teeth—the only ones that he had so far. His eyelids were shut, and his lashes perfectly matched his mass of curly, jet-black hair. But what was truly amazing was the look of absolute contentment on his face and his state of complete relaxation. He trusted me enough to fall soundly asleep, somehow knowing that I would take care of him. I wouldn't jar him. I wouldn't poke him. I certainly wouldn't drop him. After all, I was his dad. That he had known me for only half an hour didn't matter.

Part of me was trying to concentrate on the discussion that Donna and I were having with Carlotta, the adoption agency's attorney. Carlotta was telling us everything we would need to know during the next two days, such as when we would go to the United States Consulate and what would happen there. The other part of me was focused on the little boy who was sleeping so peacefully with his head in the crook of my arm and his feet dangling just beyond my fingertips. I'd look up to listen to Carlotta as she talked to us from behind her cluttered desk. Then I'd look down at the peacefully sleeping Jason. The rest of the world didn't exist.

After Donna and I had returned from our Vermont weekend in late September 1997, the adoption process, which had been interminably slow during the previous eight months, quickly gained momentum. We began receiving telephone calls from our agency nearly every day, and paperwork was express-mailed between the agency's office in New Mexico and our home in Massachusetts.

Finally, we got a call late one evening in early November from the agency's director, telling us that the adoption had been approved. We were advised to fly to Guatemala City as soon as possible. We arrived on November twelfth, still not totally believing that the dream of getting our son was about to come true.

A very short, middle-aged Guatemalan man and a young woman, holding a sign with HASKELL printed on it, were waiting for us outside the customs area. We immediately began to feel better.

"Hola, mi nombre es Jim Haskell," I said in broken Spanish as we approached them.

"Very nice to meet you, Mr. Haskell," the man replied in easily understandable English. "My name is Carlos, and this is my daughter, Nancy. I'm going to be your driver while you're here. Nancy will be able to take care of your child. Here, let me take your bags. Come with me." With that, Carlos grabbed two of our bags, and Nancy grabbed the other one.

Although we were only supposed to be in Guatemala for two days, we had packed enough for a week. We had no idea what Jason would need, so we had packed everything for him we could think of. We had also brought a laundry list of items including diaper wipes, baby oil, baby powder, pacifiers, and bottles to replenish whatever Jason had used during his stay in foster care.

Carlos and Nancy led us to their car, a 1964 Dodge Dart, and put our things in the trunk. Donna and I got into the backseat, and Carlos began weaving through the streets of Guatemala City. Carlos put us at ease by telling us about himself as he deftly maneuvered his car through the crowded streets. He had left school after the sixth grade. He had twelve children, including Nancy. He had spent his adult life doing what he was doing now—driving people around and attending to the needs of tourists. In the process, he had learned Spanish, German, French, Italian, and English. A Mayan dialect was his first language. He considered English to be his weakest language, but Donna and I told him he was quite well-spoken. He nodded, apparently appreciating the compliment.

We stopped at our hotel just long enough to check in, then we were off to the lawyer's office to meet Jason.

The long wait and the aggravations over the adoption process evaporated when we were escorted into Carlotta's office. Standing on wobbly legs, and steadying himself with one hand as he leaned against the wall near the door, was the most beautiful nine-month-old baby boy in the world. Our baby. In that second, everything in my life changed. I became Jason's dad.

Seated on the couch and in two other chairs were his foster parents, Roxana and Julio, and their daughters: Gaby, who was eight, and Erica, who was seven.

I knelt down in front of Jason, holding my glasses in my hand. I reached out so he could toddle over to me. Donna was leaning against the doorframe, tears streaming down her face.

"He isn't walking yet, but he's obviously cruising," Carlotta said, breaking the silence. Instead of grabbing my outstretched hand, Jason reached for my glasses. He clutched them and tried to take them away from me.

"No, no, no. You probably shouldn't have these," I said, gently pulling my glasses from his grasp. Jason lost his balance and sat down with a *thud* on the thin carpet. By now, Donna was kneeling on the floor beside me. For the next couple of minutes we marveled at this child we had just met.

It was then that we looked up and saw his foster family taking in the scene. This was a bittersweet moment for them. They were happy to see that we were so thrilled with Jason. They were sad knowing that when they left the room, this little boy who they had loved and nurtured for nine months would not be going with them. I realized at that moment that as wonderful as an adoption is for the couple that is getting the child, it is also a tremendous loss for those who have already been part of that child's life. That process had started when his birth mother had realized that she couldn't care for this child that was growing inside her. Now it was culminating in the loss that the foster family was feeling because the baby was leaving them.

They all took turns hugging Jason and smothering him with kisses. He squealed with delight as each person held him. Finally, the foster family departed, and the only ones left in the office were Carlotta, Donna, Jason, and me. Carlotta's secretary prepared a bottle, and Jason drank the warm milk and fell asleep in my arms.

The next forty hours were a whirlwind of visits to the U.S. Consulate, to make sure Jason's immigration papers were in order, and to the upscale home of Jason's foster family, on the outskirts of Guatemala City, to see where he had lived. On Friday morning we flew to Miami and then into

Boston during a mid-November blizzard. Welcome home, Jason Haskell.

Jason was a lively and healthy boy. He was inquisitive, but not to the point of being reckless. He thrilled in activity and attention. It was obvious that he had been very well socialized by his foster family. He loved being with people and being the center of attention. He took his first step on Christmas Day. He then apparently decided he wasn't ready to walk quite yet, and didn't take another step for two months. However, when he did begin to walk, he hardly ever fell down.

Donna and I watched in amazement as he grew by leaps and bounds, physically and emotionally. I stayed away from work as often as I could during the first month that Jason was with us. I went back to work in mid-December, but Donna remained on leave from her job until mid-February. She returned to work soon after Jason's first birthday, and we placed Jason in a daycare center nine miles from our home when both of us were working. We began juggling the demands of our jobs and his needs just as many parents do. We were busier than we could possibly have imagined as we tried to be good parents and professionals.

In the grand scheme of things, Jason was an extremely easy child to care for. Both of us gained a tremendous appreciation for single parents, for parents who have more than one child, and for parents who have a child with special needs. We were exhausted from caring for an "easy" child.

Ever since college, I had run three or four times a week. However, soon after Jason arrived, I stopped running altogether. After a while, I couldn't run for more than a mile or two when I did manage to get out. My breathing was labored, and I had lost a lot of muscle tone.

Nonetheless, in mid-May I decided to hike a nine-mile section of the AT in western Massachusetts near Interstate 90. It was fairly close to home, and it would be an easy day hike, provided the weather cooperated. I planned to hike from Pittsfield Road, where Donna and I had finished one of our hikes in 1996, to U.S. Route 20 just outside of Lee.

I parked my truck on Route 20, rode my bike back to Pittsfield Road, and hit the trail. A high cloud cover made for ideal hiking—warm with little chance of rain. However, the trail was still very muddy from the winter's snow. I had hiked three miles when I discovered I didn't have my keys with me. Now what? I hoped I had dropped them when I put on my pack at Pittsfield Road. I knew I had to find them. I couldn't drive home without them, and having Donna drive all the way out here with Jason was not such a good idea either.

I hiked another mile until I reached a road where I could get off the trail. I doubled back to Pittsfield Road. The keys were right next to the bike that I had chained to a tree. So much for security. I then rode my bike back to my truck on Route 20. I was disappointed that I had hiked only four miles and that there wasn't enough daylight left to get back on the trail. While it certainly felt good to be on the AT again, hiking all nine miles would have felt even better.

When Aimee and I had done our original planning for hiking the AT, we had included two "half-years" in our itinerary. The period from 1990 to 2010 is twenty-one years. We had decided to hike a little over a hundred miles for nineteen of those years. We planned to do only fifty miles for the other two. Those would be our half-years. Aimee and I had planned to have two children, and thought we would save those half-years for when our children were born. That plan had obviously not worked out.

Later, when Donna and I were planning to start a family, I kept those two half-years in mind. Now that Jason was with us, I had decided that 1998 would be my first half-year. I only had to hike a little more than fifty miles to stay on schedule. But I had not planned for one of those hikes to be shortened for some reason such as dropping my keys. Now I still had to hike forty-six miles to meet my goal for this year.

In June, I decided to really push myself and get in a hike that would cover some ground. I chose a sixteen-mile section in Connecticut that began at West Cornwall Road and ended at Route 341 near Kent. Although that was a long stretch for one day, five of those miles followed an absolutely flat woods road beside the Housatonic River. Nor did the other eleven miles appear to require a great deal of climbing. It was just what the doctor ordered.

I left home very early and pulled into Kent by nine o'clock. I began riding my bike along Route 7 toward West Cornwall Road. I reached that trailhead two hours later. It was eleven o'clock. I still had to hike sixteen miles, but I was feeling strong, and there would be plenty of daylight to do the distance.

I hid my bike in the woods, put on my boots, made sure my keys were in my backpack, and started hiking. I had determined from the trail map that this hike would be broken up into three distinct sections. There were four hills during the first seven miles, but none of them was more than five hundred feet high. Then the trail flattened out for five miles along the woods road. It was probably one of the longest sections of absolutely flat terrain on the entire AT. At mile twelve, the trail climbed uphill for about a mile. The last three miles were a gradual descent into Kent.

I wasn't exactly flying, but I was making pretty good time. I had covered the initial seven-mile hilly section and was nearing the end of the five-mile flat section by late afternoon. I was tired but still confident that I could hike the final four miles before dark.

The trail turned toward the west away from the river, and began climbing up to an outlook called St. John's Ledges. Caleb's Peak was just beyond that. It was steeper than I had anticipated. I began to sweat profusely. I could barely lift my feet. I stopped to gather my strength and readjust my pace. One of the problems about going from an easy stretch of the trail to a difficult one is that you want to keep hiking at the easy-trail pace. But you have to adjust. I told myself to slow down and shorten my stride. I took ten deep breaths and resumed hiking.

That usually works for me. I hike slower, and therefore convert speed into power. But that's if I have any power left in my body. Today, the gas tank had unexpectedly run dry. I hiked for another fifty feet and was exhausted again. I stopped, rested for a minute, and started again. I had to stop after another fifty feet. This was not going well.

Since I'd always been a strong hiker, I had never had to wonder whether I could get over the next section. Now, hiking up a short but steep hill, something I had done a thousand times before, I was questioning my ability. I was beat. I did not know if I could get up that hill.

It suddenly hit me. I was completely out of shape. I was working altogether too hard to climb this little five-hundred-foot hill.

I plodded on. I'd walk a few feet, stop, catch my breath, and repeat the process. It was torture. My legs were burning from fatigue. My pack seemed to weigh a ton. I was sweating as if I was in a sauna. Finally, I reached the ledges and the overlook, and stopped for several minutes to try to gather my strength. Then I began the final climb to Caleb's Peak. It was only three hundred feet to the top, but it seemed like three hundred miles. When I finally got to the summit, I dropped my pack, sat down, massaged my legs, and told myself what a wonderful job I had just done by climbing all the way to the top of this insignificant hill. It was a classic example of how something that should be incredibly easy could become incredibly hard. I was pissed off because I had let myself get so badly out of shape that this climb had exhausted me. I was suddenly overwhelmed with the desire to get off this trail, get to my car, and get home to my wife and son.

I made two seemingly contradictory decisions as I drove home that evening. I would get back in shape. I would stop section-hiking the Appalachian Trail—perhaps for good.

I realized I had been spending all of my time since November either taking care of Jason or doing my job. My own health had taken a backseat. Spending time maintaining my health wasn't being selfish. It was absolutely necessary if I expected to be part of Jason's life as he grew up.

My father had died at fifty-five, and his father at fifty-seven. Neither of my father's brothers had lived to retirement. Having adopted Jason at thirty-seven, I didn't want him to lose me before he was out of high school. That meant I had to exercise regularly. My father had been a blue-collar worker. He had also been a farmer and had worked in the woods. He got his exercise from his labors. Yet, he still died of a heart attack when I was twenty-one. I didn't get that kind of exercise sitting in meetings or answering phone calls all day. If I didn't change my ways, I was heading for a heart attack before I was fifty. Jason would barely be a teenager.

The fact that I was so happy that Jason was a part of our lives and that I really loved being his dad led me to the second decision. It would be better for everyone if I gave up these section hikes.

Donna was a great mom, but taking care of Jason by herself and doing her job while I spent a week or ten days every year walking through the woods didn't seem fair. Hey, I told myself, this had seemed like a really good thing to do when Aimee and I had agreed to spend twenty-one years hiking the AT, or when it was just Donna and me. But Jason had changed our lives, and it was time for me to change as well—to grow up and be a father. Besides, I could still go hiking when the spirit moved me. There were plenty of places to hike in New England, and the three of us could go to the White Mountains whenever we wanted to. I could still hike to my heart's content. I just wouldn't hike the entire AT. So what? I'd already hiked more than eight hundred miles of it. How many people could say that?

I pulled into my driveway a little after eleven, satisfied that I had made the right decisions.

Donna disagreed. Adamantly.

"You're WHAT?" she asked the following evening after I had told her of my decisions, and the reasons, while we were washing the dinner dishes. "You're going to stop hiking the trail? Oh, no. Not because of Jason and me. The hell you say." If looks could kill, I was dead meat. She was that serious.

"I just think ..." I began, fully prepared to explain my decisions in greater detail.

"Yeah, yeah, yeah. You've just told me what you think," Donna interjected, handing me another plate for the dishwasher. "And I don't want to hear it. You've started this thing. It's practically all you've talked about, other than adopting Jason, since I've known you. You have to finish it. You won't be able to live with yourself...I won't be able to live with you if you don't."

"But what about...?"

"What about what?"

"You know, taking off to go hiking a couple of times a year? I'm going to have to start hiking southern sections of the trail pretty soon. Trips to Virginia, Tennessee, and North Carolina. That'll keep me away for quite a while."

"So?"

"So how will you manage taking care of Jason and working and being here alone?"

"What do I look like? Twelve? Jim, I'm a grown woman. Jason is already in daycare. My family lives all around us. It's not as if you're leaving us alone in a log cabin in the middle of the woods—while you go looking for gold. We'll be fine. Honest. Go hike your trail. And, oh yeah, get back into shape so you don't kill yourself out there. Then I'd be really upset."

"Are you sure?" I finally managed to get in a complete comment. "Because if you are, I'll do my damnedest to see this thing through."

"Jim. Do it," Donna said, her tone more gentle and encouraging now. "You're always telling me how your father told you guys to finish whatever you start. To never quit. Well, do what he said. You Haskells are a driven bunch. Once you set your minds to do something, you can't live with yourselves until you do it. Look at Elaine. She was divorced and raising two daughters, and she still went to seminary when she was in her thirties and became a minister.

"All I know is this. If you quit hiking the AT, twenty years from now, when Jason's in college and we're a middle-aged couple, you'll be kicking yourself for not following your dream. However, if you do quit, don't you dare blame Jason or me because we are behind you *one hundred percent.*

"Look, Jim. We've both agreed that we can't hike the trail together and leave Jason with someone else for days at a time. But that doesn't mean you shouldn't finish the trail. The only thing I ask is this. You take care of Jason for a week or so every year so I can do what I want to do. If you can agree to that, I'll be happy and you'll be happy."

I suddenly saw my wife in a new light. This woman was practically demanding that I continue with my hiking rather than agreeing with my decision to stay home with her. It was a special moment in our marriage. I pulled her close to me and gave her a big hug to let her know how much I appreciated her. And, yes, I assured her, I would be happy to care for Jason so she could have a week to herself every single year.

I ran three miles the next morning. I ran five more two mornings after that. My legs ached, my breathing was labored, and my chest hurt, but I refused to stop until I had put in those miles. I hobbled around the house the day after each run as if I had just done a marathon. But I was determined to rebuild my strength and my stamina. By the end of the summer, my body was strong, it no longer screamed in pain after a good run, and I felt ready to try an overnight hike.

I put myself to the test the first weekend in October. A seventeen-mile stretch of the AT, between Jug End Road in Egremont, Massachusetts, and Connecticut Route 41 in Salisbury, Connecticut, seemed ideal. I'd hike eight miles the first day and nine miles the second. It would require climbing three moderate peaks—Mount Everett, Race Mountain, and Bear Mountain in the Taconic Mountain Range. The highest of those, Everett, topped out at a little more than twenty-five hundred feet.

The only drawback, I believed, would be a lack of scenic vistas that I had so thoroughly enjoyed while hiking the White Mountains in New Hampshire and the Green Mountains in Vermont. Having hiked other sections in this vicinity before, I resigned myself to spending two days hiking under tree cover, what hikers call "the green tunnel." Oh well, the trail had to be walked, and the weather forecast of clear skies, low humidity, and daytime temperatures in the fifties and sixties could not be beat. Most importantly, I'd be back on the trail without any reservations about neglecting Jason or leaving Donna to fend for herself.

It was a splendid weekend for a number of reasons. One of them was that I had picked up a new hiking partner. Robert was several years younger than me, but, like me, he was directing a small non-profit in Salem. That gave us plenty to talk about.

After driving to the road crossing in Salisbury, we chained our bikes to the signboard and drove back into Massachusetts. We parked near the Jug End Road crossing and headed south on the trail. We were immediately confronted with a steep, thousand-foot climb up to the Jug End summit. I leaned into the trail, my pack set comfortably on my back, and I made the climb almost without breaking a sweat. This was very encouraging.

We stopped to savor the view from the summit and then began hiking along a ridge. The elevation was less than two thousand feet, and I assumed we would soon enter the green tunnel. But I was wrong. The ridgeline is quite narrow, the slopes on both sides are very steep, and there are numerous rock outcroppings along the way. There were long stretches of the trail that offered spectacular views of the valleys below. While the mountains aren't very high by New Hampshire standards, they are the highest points in that area. Robert and I could see for miles in both directions.

Furthermore, the fall foliage was near its peak at this elevation, and the yellow and red leaves were framed by a deep blue October sky. We hiked for nearly four miles along the ridge, and I was so taken with the scenery that I had to keep reminding myself to pay attention to the trail so I wouldn't twist an ankle on a rock. I had never seen anything quite like it.

While the views from atop Katahdin and above the tree line in the Whites are certainly impressive, those mountains are so high that much of the detail is lost because of the distance. From the much lower Taconics, however, we could make out individual trees and other features in the valley. We could clearly see barns and animals. It was like looking at a tabletop display of farms and forests.

We were hungry, and ready for lunch, when we reached the fire tower at the Mount Everett summit in the early afternoon. But I was feeling little or no fatigue after hiking four miles. So far, so good. The view of autumn's splendor made our lunch break even more satisfying before we descended the mountain and hiked the final four miles to Bear Rock Falls, where we would camp for the night.

It was obvious when we got there, at close to five o'clock, that we were not the only ones who had taken advantage of this wonderful weekend to do some hiking. Dozens of little hiker tents, a rainbow of fabrics, were scattered through the woods of brown and yellow leaves in this rather expansive camping ground. Still, we found an area fairly quickly, and set up my tent to make it our home for the night. Dinner was done as darkness settled in. We spent a few minutes talking with some other hikers, but fatigue quickly overcame my desire for conversation. The nature of my fatigue was encouraging. I was tired because I had just hiked eight miles over some fairly difficult terrain. I was not exhausted because I was out of shape. My sleeping bag beckoned, and I answered the call, quickly falling into a deep, satisfying slumber.

I awoke a bit before six. The full moon that had bathed the ground in light the night before had set. The camp was dark and still. I realized I could do something that I rarely got to do. I could watch the sun rise.

Strange as it may seem, I rarely had the chance to do that. Most of my AT hikes were one-day excursions, and most of the shelters where I had camped overnight were located in valleys and gaps where there were too many trees to actually see the sun rise above a distant horizon.

The conditions were ideal this morning. A nearby outcropping faced to the east, and I was up early enough to get there before the sun came up. I slipped out of the tent without disturbing Robert, strapped on my headlamp, and made my way to the outcropping before daybreak.

A sunrise is not rare. It occurs every day in much of the world. Maybe that's why so few people take the time to appreciate it. I was in the right place at the right time to enjoy this one. At first, the sky was entirely black. Then I could make out a small bubble of blue, barely discernible from the black surrounding it. The bubble continued to expand, sort of like a blue balloon that is being inflated on a helium tank at an amusement park—only much more slowly. The blueness gradually encompassed more and more of the cloudless sky as the blue on the horizon became lighter and brighter. I tried to determine exactly where the sun would show itself, but the sky wasn't quite bright enough to give that away. Finally, the sky was entirely blue except for one spot on the horizon that by now was almost white. That was where the sun would rise.

What would be the exact moment that the top of the sun would peek over the horizon? I'd think the sun was about to do that, but it would remain hidden for another few minutes. Finally, I could see the very top of the bright yellow orb rise above the trees on the horizon. Then, in a matter of minutes, the entire sun was sitting on the horizon. Our sun had risen for yet another day, just as it had for a few billion years. The light was so intense that I could look at it directly for only a few seconds before I had to turn away. Immediately, I could feel the warmth on my face. It was a spectacular sight and sensation. I understood why so many cultures have worshipped and marveled at our planet's primary source of life.

Returning to the tent, boiling water for coffee and hot oatmeal, and packing for another day of hiking seemed anticlimactic, so ordinary, after savoring the sunrise. But it was another day, and it was time for Robert and me to get back to reality. We hiked into Sages Ravine about an hour later, and then climbed over Bear Mountain. Our bicycles were where we had left them at the Route 41 crossing, and we rode to my pickup near the Jug End Road crossing without incident. We had come full circle in two days without a hitch. It was the end of a perfect hike.

Donna was right. I needed to do this. Now I knew I could.

I had been entirely focused on Jason and work for two years. This weekend had been the first "me" time I had allowed myself in many months. I truly loved being Jason's dad, but I still really wanted to hike all of the Appalachian Trail.

# 13

# Carnivores and Canoes

The trail had led us to a crossing with a forest road. Rex and I were hungry. It was a little after noon, and we had hiked more than eight miles. The signpost told us that Bearfence Mountain Hut was two hundred yards down the road to the left. We could eat lunch there. Or, if we went a little farther along the AT, we could have lunch at Lewis Mountain Campground, which had picnic tables. We liked that idea, so we stayed on the trail.

Now all we had to do was find the side trail to the picnic area. We walked in silence for a couple of minutes, thinking only about our noon meal because our stomachs were growling.

We came upon a rather large hardwood tree that had fallen across the trail. Trail maintainers had chopped a two-foot-wide notch about halfway into the trunk so hikers could stay on the trail by climbing over the tree rather than detouring around it. However, the footing was tricky, and we had to be careful. It was a speed bump on this otherwise unobstructed path. Rex climbed over first. Then it was my turn. After I had climbed over, I saw that Rex had stopped dead in his tracks. His right arm was bent at the elbow and his hand was pointing straight up. He was signaling me to stop. I immediately saw why.

There was a black mass ahead of us and slightly off the trail. We were less than a hundred feet from a female black bear, as big as a very large dog. She was probably just a few years old—old enough to be on her own, but probably not old enough to have cubs. That was a relief on both counts. We wouldn't have to contend with this bear's mother or with her own maternal instincts for protecting her cubs.

She seemed to have sensed our presence at about the same time that we saw her. We engaged in something of a standoff for the next couple of minutes. The bear wasn't entirely comfortable with humans around, but she wasn't scared enough to run away. Nor did she seem inclined to attack. However, we had to wait for her to move farther off the trail before proceeding because we did not want to do anything to provoke this bear. Besides, she was only a few feet from the side trail we were looking for.

Rex and I stood there and waited until the bear sauntered into the woods—putting a comfortable distance between herself and us. We continued on to the picnic area. We grabbed a table and prepared our lunch.

"Wow, that's the first bear I've seen on the trail," Rex remarked as we munched on tuna salad and crackers. "Is that pretty typical? What we just experienced?"

"Let me see." I had to think a minute. "I think that's the sixth bear I've seen on the trail. Three of them were similar to this one. The bears were off the trail and didn't seem particularly concerned that I was there. I just waited for them to get far enough away so I could continue. One other time, I scared a bear somehow, and about the only thing I saw was bear butt as it disappeared into the woods. But the first bear that I ever saw, that was a different story."

"Shuckstack is a killer!"

"Shuckstack just keeps going on and on, and you don't think it's ever going to end."

"Oh, my God, Shuckstack! That was the worst climb I had on the AT."

Nearly every thru-hiker I had spoken to south of the White Mountains had warned me about this climb. Shuckstack is the first mountain that a northbound AT hiker climbs in the Great Smoky Mountains National Park, which runs along the North Carolina–Tennessee border. The trail rises about two thousand feet over four miles. Most of that elevation comes during the first three miles.

Just before climbing Shuckstack, northbound thru-hikers come to the town of Fontana—the first community of any significant size they've seen on the trail. Many thru-hikers take at least one "zero"—a full rest day—at Fontana. Quite a few take several zeros. The hike up Shuckstack is the wakeup call that you're back on the trail, or so the thru-hikers claim.

Making matters worse, everyone coming out of Fontana has a fully loaded pack. There are very few places in the Smokies where hikers can readily get supplies, so most are carrying a minimum of six days' provisions. Some are carrying enough for ten days.

I had heard so much about Shuckstack that I had envisioned something like the Bataan Death March up the Matterhorn: a steep, relentless uphill hike; the unforgiving weight of a heavy pack; crawling at a snail's pace, hand over foot over hand; reaching the top thoroughly exhausted, parched, and famished, an inch away from death.

What I experienced was a fairly routine uphill trek that I completed much sooner than I had expected. Shuckstack was a piece of cake. If the Whites are the major leagues of the Appalachian Trail, Shuckstack is in the minors.

After I had passed the side trail leading to Shuckstack's summit, the AT leveled out quite nicely. The sky was overcast, threatening rain, on this May afternoon in 1996. But for the time being, the clouds were keeping the temperature fairly comfortable. I hiked along easily and at a good pace.

I passed a couple of women hikers who were taking a break after returning from the summit.

I began to daydream. I have found that exceedingly easy to do when I'm hiking over a relatively flat section deep in the forest. My mind will drift to other places, and I will have little or no memory of actually hiking that part of the trail.

I had a lot to think about. I was the executive director of a small nonprofit in Salem, Massachusetts. It was my dream job that I had landed two years earlier, in 1994. The agency worked in Salem's poorest neighborhood, known as The Point, which was home to a Dominican immigrant community. While the agency's primary work was developing and managing housing, we also offered English classes and helped organize the community so it would have a greater say about its own destiny. We tried to do all of this with a staff of four. The job was exciting, but it also was tremendously demanding; sometimes all-consuming.

I came upon another hiker who was taking a break. We chatted for a couple of minutes, and I continued on, again quickly consumed by my thoughts. The agency's board of directors had approved a strategic plan a month earlier. The plan called for a major expansion of our work and an increase in staff to accomplish that. Now all I had to do was figure out how we were going to pay for all of that and sustain ourselves into the future. A lot of things had to happen before…

ROOOOOOOAAAAAAARRRRRR!!!!!!!!

I jerked my head up quickly as the sound ripped through the still mountain air. A fully-grown male black bear was clinging to the trunk of a huge spruce tree about twenty-five feet ahead of me. The tree was right next to the trail. The bear's butt was hanging just a few feet above the ground, and his front claws were about five feet below the first main branches. This bear was very big. He was also very unhappy.

He roared at me again—not quite so loudly as the first time, but with enough gusto to make it perfectly clear that he was not pleased that I was so close to him. The day-dreamy state I had been in a couple of seconds earlier had totally evaporated. I was now intently focused on the fact that I was standing very close to a very large, pissed-off bear.

I instantly knew I was in a great deal of danger. What I did during the next couple of minutes could very well determine whether I lived or died. A million things rushed through my head.

Fortunately, Donna and I had spent four days at McNeil River—a bear sanctuary on the Alaska Peninsula—during our honeymoon two years earlier. A group of us spent several hours each day watching the bears catch and eat salmon at the river. Those were brown bears, considerably larger than the black bear that confronted me today. But bears are like hurricanes. They're all dangerous if you're close to them—no matter the size or category. And this bear was certainly big enough to be dangerous.

I tried to remember everything I had learned about bears at McNeil.

I knew that one thing was working in my favor. Bears generally don't hunt humans. There is a theory that most predators don't like to eat people because we're not very appetizing. Luckily, we don't taste like chicken. But that doesn't mean we can't trigger a bear's predator instinct. So I might get mauled to death, but at least there would be something of a corpse left if I totally screwed this up. That was comforting.

What I remembered from McNeil was that there are four things that typically trigger a bear's killer instinct. The first two are interfering with a food source, such as trying to wrestle a fish away from a bear, and posing a threat to a female's cubs. Fortunately, I was not violating rules one and two right now.

The third thing is entering into a bear's "personal space." You don't want bears to think you're close enough to pose a threat to them. Their personal space can vary considerably depending on the terrain, species, and territoriality of any given bear. But twenty-five feet is way too close under any circumstances. This bear's roars had let me know that he thought I was too close for his comfort.

The fourth thing is running away. I knew that bears are incredibly fast for their size. You can't outrun them. If I were to start running back down the trail, the bear would consider me prey. His instinct would be to barrel after me, bring me down, and clamp his jaws around my neck.

Unfortunately, there's an inherent contradiction between rules three and four. If a bear is pissed off because you're in his personal space, your first inclination is to put some distance between you and the bear as quickly as possible. But if you move away too quickly, such as at a dead run, the bear may chase you down anyway. It doesn't make much sense, but bears aren't required to pass Logic 101.

I also remembered from my McNeil experience that bears don't have great eyesight. They have trouble seeing things at a distance that aren't moving. So the first thing I did was freeze in my tracks and try not to move a muscle. I tried not to breathe. I even managed to keep my knees from shaking. I hoped to make the bear forget I was there by standing completely still.

I did not move for several minutes, which seemed like a week, until the bear seemed to lose interest in me and resumed climbing the tree. Then, when I thought he wasn't looking, I very slowly moved my right foot behind me. I shifted my weight ever so slightly so that my entire body moved back a couple of inches. But that was enough to get the bear's attention, and he quickly focused on me again. He let out a low growl. I became a statue for another couple of minutes.

By now I was concerned about a lot of things. I was afraid that if I made any sudden movement, such as tripping over my big feet and falling, the bear would be all over me. I was also concerned that if I didn't get out of there pretty soon, the other hikers that I had recently passed would come along and provoke an attack. I tried not to imagine how threatened and infuriated the bear would be if another person ventured into his space.

Fortunately, none of the above happened, and the bear seemed to lose interest a second time. I placed my left foot behind me and slowly backed away again. The bear didn't get agitated. I stopped for a couple of seconds and then moved my right foot. The bear sniffed loudly and looked in my direction. I froze in mid-step. I waited for a couple of minutes until he turned his head away.

My actions were entirely counterintuitive. When the bear was agitated, I wanted to get the hell out of there as quickly as possible. Instead, in those moments I had to freeze. On the other hand, when the bear wasn't paying attention to me, I wanted to stay and watch him for a while. But those were the times when I could safely back away.

The trail bent around a sharp corner about fifty feet behind me. If I could get back there, I'd be out of the bear's line of sight. It took me fifteen or twenty minutes to make my way back around that corner. The man I had recently passed caught up with me a couple of minutes later.

"There's a big black bear in a tree right next to the trail," I told him in a hushed tone. "I was only about twenty-five feet from him when I startled him, and he let me know it. I just got back around this corner, so I'm pretty sure he's still there."

"Oh my God! What do you think we should do?" he asked.

"Well, let's look around the corner to see if he's still there. If he is, then I guess we'll just have to wait until he gets out of the tree. I especially don't want the women that we went by to surprise him."

"OK," he replied.

We both looked around the corner, cautiously, keeping low to the ground. We must have looked like two of the Three Stooges. The bear was still in the tree. However, he had climbed another five feet or so. He was resting on the first main branch, but he still could easily have climbed down and come after us. At least that's what we thought.

"OK," I said, "let's wait here until the two women come along and then see where he is."

We retreated back around the corner, and I gave him more details about my encounter. The women came along several minutes later.

I explained what had happened, and the four of us looked around the corner to see where the bear was. We looked the tree up and down, but he was nowhere to be seen.

"OK. Looks like the coast is clear. I guess it's OK to keep going," I whispered to the group. "Let's all stick together. If he's still around, maybe he'll be less likely to chase the four of us than he would just one of us."

We made our way to the tree and looked up. The bear was resting on one of the higher branches, at least thirty feet above us.

The branches were much smaller at that height than they were lower down, and I had a fleeting thought that one of us could still be killed by this bear. Not from having him attack us, but from having him fall out of the tree and land on us.

We passed underneath without incident. The bear either chose to ignore us or didn't know we were there. We continued down the trail.

Rex and I packed our things and hoisted on our packs. A quick check of the trail guide told us that we only had to hike a couple more miles to reach Rex's destination for the night and my Civic hybrid. This would be the final section we would hike together. We made our way back down to the AT.

"Weren't you afraid you'd be attacked by a bear after that?" Rex asked.

"Well, I was certainly much more cautious after that, especially for the rest of that trip in the Smokies. If I was hiking through an area where there was a blind corner or thick vegetation, I'd make some noise so that any bear would be well aware that I was in the neighborhood. But I also knew what I had done wrong to get myself into that predicament in the first place. So I figured that as long as I was more careful I'd be OK."

"What's that?"

"Well, if I'd been paying attention rather than daydreaming, I probably would have seen the bear when I came around that bend in the trail, well before he roared at me. I'm sure the bear had seen me as soon as I came into view, and that's when he started to climb that tree. He had said to himself, 'OK, maybe this idiot will see me now and stop.' When I kept walking toward him, he did the only thing he could short of eating me for lunch. He roared. It was his way of saying, 'You stupid jerk, don't you realize that I'm a bear and you shouldn't be getting this close to me. Stop walking—NOW!'"

"I see your point," Rex laughed.

"The other thing I realized later on was that I should have said something to the bear rather than being absolutely quiet. Bears have bad eyesight, so they identify things as much by sound and smell as they do by sight. If I'd talked quietly to the bear, he might have recognized me as being human and not prey and not been so agitated. Fortunately, that little mistake didn't kill me. It just goes to show that most of the dangerous situations I've found myself in out here have been my fault. It's not so much that the AT is dangerous, but it can certainly be unforgiving."

"Aren't you being a little hard on yourself?" Rex countered. "Yeah, I guess you could say you should have been paying more attention, but that doesn't mean you would have seen that bear any sooner. From what I can tell, you've got a lot of experience under your belt."

"Well, I've put in a lot of miles. But I'm still amazed at how I can be totally oblivious to some of the situations I've found myself in. There was one time that the signs of trouble were all around me for hours, and I didn't realize anything was wrong until I was a couple of seconds away from killing myself."

"Again?" Rex retorted in disbelief.

"Yeah, again."

If anyone deserves sainthood, it's Steve Longley.

The Appalachian Trail is a continuous footpath that stretches from Maine to Georgia with one major exception—a two-hundred-foot section where the trail crosses the Kennebec River in Maine.

In every state but Maine, AT hikers cross major rivers and streams on bridges—highway bridges or pedestrian bridges specifically built for the trail.

Such is not the case in Maine. Most major rivers and streams are crossed on foot by a process called fording. Simply put, you have to walk through the water, not over it. The fords are located where the rivers and streams have become wider and where the water is relatively shallow and calm. Most fords have gravel bases that provide pretty good footing. They are generally from calf to waist deep. Yet, fords can be treacherous even under the best of conditions. Even a relatively slow current exerts constant, strenuous forces on your body, and a backpack quickly becomes an anchor if you fall during a crossing.

As treacherous as Maine fords can be, the place where the trail crosses the Kennebec River stands alone. The Kennebec is one of Maine's major rivers. It is about two hundred feet wide at the trail crossing, and the water is about waist deep under ideal conditions. However, melting snow or heavy rains or discharges from a hydroelectric dam upriver can make the waterway run very fast and deep. The river is too deep for fording at certain times.

In the past, hikers were advised to use extreme caution while fording the Kennebec. If the water was too deep or the current too strong, hikers had to make a thirty-mile detour to get to the other side. There were only two problems with this. First, it is nearly impossible to determine how deep a river is or how swiftly the water is flowing when you're standing on the bank. The river always looks shallower and slower than it really is. Second, telling a hiker to either risk a crossing or take a thirty-mile detour is kind of like saying, "You can go directly to your grocery store on this road, or you can take a detour through Chicago. Which do you prefer?" The idea of hiking an additional thirty miles—at least two extra days—after you've been on the trail for several months does not appeal to many thru-hikers who, by now, just want to finish this thing.

So the hikers risked the crossing. Finally, in 1985, the inevitable happened. A hiker drowned while trying to ford the Kennebec.

Enter Steve Longley.

He was an outdoors-adventure outfitter in Caratunk, the town where the trail crosses the Kennebec in western Maine. In 1986, the Maine Appalachian Trail Club and the Appalachian Trail Conference hired Steve to ferry hikers across the Kennebec. For several hours each day, Steve paddled his Old Town canoe back and forth across the river, taking hikers and their gear across that two-hundred-foot stretch. A white blaze was painted on the side of his canoe, thus making it an official part of the AT. You hadn't officially hiked the trail unless you had been in Steve Longley's canoe.

My work schedule was unusually frenetic during the summer of 1996, and by August I knew I couldn't take a full week off to go hiking as I had done in the past. However, I could easily hike the seventeen miles from Caratunk to Long Falls Dam Road in Maine in two days. I would drive to Maine and stay with my mother on Friday night, hike on Saturday and Sunday, and be back at work on Monday. No sweat.

Everything went according to plan. I drove to Caratunk that Saturday and got down to where the AT crosses the Kennebec early in the afternoon. I was amazed that anyone could ever ford that river. The water was flowing very fast, creating rapids over underlying rocks that drove the water high into the air. I assumed that water was being released from the dam. There was no way I could wade across. I would need the services of Steve and his canoe to get to the other side. Besides, I really wanted to experience that unique aspect of the trail. Luckily, Steve was still there.

After a few words of greeting, I stowed my pack in the middle of Steve's canoe, put on my life jacket, got into the bow, and grabbed a paddle. Rather than paddle directly across the rapids, Steve pointed the bow upstream. We paddled hard against the current for the next several minutes. Steve kept us in the slower water next to the bank, but we still had to work hard to make any progress.

When we reached a certain point, Steve turned the canoe downstream. We then paddled diagonally across the churning river and landed at the AT trailhead on the western side of the Kennebec. While we were only two hundred feet from where we had started, we had paddled several hundred yards to get there. Steve had obviously done this many times before, and he knew exactly how far up the river he had to go to get across safely and close to the trail. There was clearly a lot more to this canoe ferrying business than meets the eye.

"Wow, that was amazing," I remarked as I disembarked. "You should have gone down to Atlanta on the U.S. Olympic canoe team. I bet you could have come home with a medal."

"Nah, those guys are really good. I'm just fair to middlin'," Steve replied in the self-deprecating manner that's common among Mainers. "Besides, if I did the Olympics, who'd be here to take you guys across?"

I laughed and thanked Steve heartily for his service. With that, he turned his canoe upstream to return to the other side.

Now that I was on the western side of the Kennebec, I figured the hard part of the trip was over. All I had to do was hike seventeen miles of mostly uneventful trail.

I knew from my trail guides that the AT follows Pierce Pond Stream upstream until it reaches its namesake pond and a shelter that sits on its bank. While I don't particularly like fording streams, I really do like waterfalls. So for the next few miles I looked at some of the most spectacular waterfalls I had ever seen on the trail. By mid-August, even the largest falls have normally slowed to a trickle. While a fall might be a hundred feet high, the water just drizzles over the edge and dissolves into spray as it hits the rocks below.

This was not the case with Pierce Pond Stream. The water was cascading down the stream with springtime ferocity. As the water raced along the rocky stream bottom, it occasionally jumped high in the air and then came splashing down to continue its journey. And where there was a legitimate waterfall, even one of only a few feet, the water was shooting out from the top and arching down to the base with a tremendous roar.

Since I had to hike only four miles to get to the shelter, and I had the entire afternoon to do it, I took my time making my way up the trail. I stopped numerous times to watch the water racing downstream.

I finally got up to Pierce Pond, a medium-size body of water by Maine standards, late that afternoon. The trail made an abrupt turn to the left, and I could see that it led across Pierce Pond Stream right where the stream flowed out of the pond. The stream was fairly wide here, and it was not flowing nearly as swiftly as it had been farther down. However, there was still a definite flow to the water. I took off my boots and socks and stepped into the cold water. It was up to my thighs after a few steps, and I could see that the water was going to get deeper and deeper. The bottom of my pack was about to be immersed, which was the last thing I wanted to happen.

*OK, I guess this isn't going to work,* I thought to myself. I turned around and waded back to the bank. My wool socks and boots quickly warmed my feet. I pulled out my AT guide and read it again. "Cross wooden dam at outlet of Pierce Pond," was all it said.

*OK, so there's supposed to be a wooden dam under there, but the guide didn't tell me the water would be so deep. So what do I do now? How am I supposed to cross here?*

The pond was to my right. To my left, several trees were lying across the stream at the place where it was pouring over what must be the dam. On one side of the trees was a relatively calm body of water. On the other side was a roaring waterfall. *I guess I'm supposed to go along the trees,* I reasoned.

I climbed up onto the first tree, a solid looking spruce, and began picking my way along the trunk while grasping the branches. The tree started to thin out after about thirty feet. I was getting closer and closer to its top. At the same time, I could see the water rushing beneath me. The water from the calm pond was cascading over the dam in a spectacular and dangerous waterfall. The roar from the waterfall became more intense as I got closer to the middle of the stream and as the tree continued to thin out. The top was bending low enough to dip my boots into the water. This tree could not hold my weight. I took another couple of steps. The tree bent down and then back up each time. It felt like I was riding a bucking bronco—holding the reins for dear life.

Then I heard a voice. It took me a couple of seconds to realize that the voice was coming from inside my head. It was as if one side of my brain was having a friendly conversation with the other.

"Hey, Haskell," I said to myself. "So how's this working out for you?"

"Right now, not so well," I replied.

"You know, you might want to seriously consider turning around and going back," I calmly continued, "because if you walk any farther out on this tree, you're going to die."

Here I was, nearly halfway across the stream, two or three feet above a pounding waterfall, and I was precariously perched on something that could not support my two hundred fifty pounds. A few more feet, and the tree would give out. The rushing water would carry me over the dam, probably to my death.

"Yeah, you're right," I agreed. "I think I'll turn back now."

With that, I began slowly working my way back along the fallen tree. Finally, I was back on the shore where I had started. I was still in the same predicament, but at least I wasn't dead.

I took out my guidebook again to look for another way to cross the dam. Was I missing something? I could clearly see the white blazes leading across the dam, so I knew I was still on the trail. It's just that the trail was going someplace that I couldn't.

I found the solution. The guide revealed that two-tenths of a mile behind me the AT intersected with a side trail that led to Harrison's Camps. I had barely noticed the trail junction on my way up. A closer look at the map revealed that the side trail crossed the stream and led to the camps on the other side. Another trail led from the camps back to the AT on the other side of the dam. If I could cross the stream on the side trail, I could get back to the AT.

The only other option was to go back to the Kennebec, sleep overnight on the bank, and wait for Steve to canoe me back across the river the following morning. I didn't like that idea because I really wanted to finish this hike. Besides, this was supposed to be an easy section.

I backtracked to the side trail and followed it to a footbridge that crossed over the roaring stream and then on to the camp buildings.

Harrison's Camps appeared to be a fairly substantial operation, with a main house and several small sleeping cabins. In short order I followed the trail from Harrison's back to the AT. The Pierce Pond Lean-to was beside the trail, with a great view of the pond, just a few feet from the trail junction.

Two hikers—young bearded guys, obviously thru-hikers judging from their lean bodies—were sitting in the shelter.

"Hey, how's it going?" I asked.

"Good. How about you?" the sandy-haired hiker asked back.

"Good, but I really had a scare trying to cross that stream. I was trying to come across on some trees and then realized that wasn't going to work. So I had to backtrack down to the camps, and then make my way up this side."

"Oh, yeah. The pond's overflowing the dam. The only way across is to go down to the camps and then cut across the stream that way," he answered rather nonchalantly. "We had a huge thunderstorm come through a couple of days ago. Dumped something like five inches of rain in a few hours. Flooded everything out."

"You didn't know they'd had that kind of rain?" Rex asked.

"Nope, I had no idea," I replied. "Of course, once the hiker told me, then all of the pieces of the puzzle fit together. The swollen Kennebec, the spectacular waterfalls, and the impassable wooden dam. All of that rain had created the spring-like conditions on the stream and the rapids on the Kennebec. All of the clues were there, but I was totally clueless.

"I also realized I had fallen victim to White Blaze Syndrome."

"What's that?" Rex asked.

"Well, if the white blazes told me the trail went this way, then there must be a way to get there. Otherwise, they wouldn't have put the white blazes there in the first place, right? I had become so used to following the blazes, I just assumed the trail was always going to be passable no matter what."

"Sounds like you learned some valuable lessons on that trip."

"Yeah, two in particular. First, even though there are white blazes showing you where the trail is, you still have to use your head because the trail can be impassable in places. But what I learned even more was that you can't take any part of the trail for granted. This was supposed to be an easy section and a short hike, and I very nearly died because I didn't take it seriously."

# 14

# Boomers and Battles

Rex and I came out onto a fire road. The sign told us Pocosin Cabin was a tenth of a mile down the road to the left, and Skyline Drive was a tenth of a mile up the road to the right. We had come to the end of our trail.

"I'm feeling a little guilty about the thunderstorm story I told you a while back," I began. "I know you're concerned about getting caught in one, and you might never get back on the trail after what I told you about my experience in the Whites. But like so much else on this trail, something that may be a really negative experience one time can be one of your best experiences another time."

"You got caught in another thunderstorm?"

"In a manner of speaking. Do you have a couple of minutes?"

"Sure, I don't have anywhere else to go." It was only midafternoon, and Rex knew he wouldn't have much to do at the cabin after I left.

Roan High Knob is nearly as high as Mount Washington, but after spending four days climbing it, I found the summit very disappointing. Most of the mountain was forested with various types of evergreens. The trail guide stated that this was highly unusual; a hiker wouldn't see trees like this until reaching New England.

Big whoopty-doo. I grew up in New England. I know what a fir and a spruce look like. Give me a view. There was a limited view from a picnic area near the Roan summit, but there was nothing close to the three-hundred-sixty-degree panorama that I had hoped for. Having done most of my hiking in the Northeast, I had come to expect that climbing a tall mountain would result in a great view. The South could be disappointing that way. The most prominent feature on Roan was a bathroom with flush toilets and a sink. Erin and I took advantage of those marvels of modern plumbing.

This trip in 2002 was my college graduation present to Erin. It was also the first long hike she and I were doing together. Any misgivings I had about spending a week with my niece were soon put to rest. I had wondered if we would find enough to talk about, considering she's about twenty years younger than me. To the contrary, we found lots to discuss—including our family and world events—during the drive to Tennessee and while we were on the trail.

We talked about how we had experienced the events of 9/11 the previous fall. Both of us were fortunate. No one in our family nor any of our friends had been killed by the terrorists. Erin had been at a Westchester County hospital in New York where she was performing a clinical internship during her senior year in college. The hospital had spent that day preparing for a crush of victims from the World Trade Center, but they never came. Erin bore witness to one of the remarkable things about the 9/11 attacks on lower Manhattan: people either walked away unharmed or they died. Relatively few went to hospitals.

My connection was a little less direct. Jason and I had been riding the train from Washington to Boston on September fifth after spending the previous week in the DC area with my friend Seth and his family. It was a picture-perfect Wednesday. Jason, who was about to start preschool, looked out the window and asked: "Daddy, what are those buildings?"

"Those are the twin towers of the World Trade Center," I answered. "At one time they were the tallest buildings in the world, but, believe it or not, now there are some others that are even taller."

"Oh," he replied and went back to his coloring book.

Six days later, those buildings were rubble.

Erin and I had started our hike near Erwin, Tennessee, a large town near North Carolina's western border. We had steadily gained elevation for four days. The high point was going to be Roan. Now that we had reached the summit, our disappointment about the limited view put a damper on what had been a really great time.

After eating lunch at the picnic area, we began hiking down the mountain toward Carver's Gap. I hadn't read too much about the trail on the other side of Roan, but I could tell by the trail profile that we would make a series of descents, interspersed by short climbs, that over the next two days would lead us fifteen miles to the road crossing with U.S. Route 19E where my truck was parked.

We reached the road crossing at Carver's Gap after hiking a little over two miles. We had obviously entered an area that many others knew about. A large parking area was filled with cars. The reason was immediately apparent. The exposed slope ahead of us was dotted with day hikers who were climbing or descending the open field that sloped up from the road. Maybe we would get our view after all.

The wide stretch of trail up the slope was packed gravel. It was like walking on a freeway. This section had obviously been designed to accommodate a lot of hikers. A great many had driven out to wander up this mountain on this Memorial Day weekend. For the past four days, Erin and I had been exclusively in the company of other long-distance hikers, complete with their full packs and body odor. Now we were the anomaly, carrying our packs among others who were pushing baby strollers. Several people asked us how we could climb this slope with those huge packs strapped to our backs. We pretty much ignored them. We were, after all, the seasoned hikers.

Erin and I climbed for half a mile until we reached the top of the slope. This was the spectacular view we had hoped to find on top of Roan. But where the heck were we? I dug out my trail maps to figure that out, and perhaps determine why I hadn't known this was coming up. I discovered that we were at the top of something called Round Bald. I also discovered that there was another open summit, Jane Bald, about half a mile farther. Having spent the past four days in the green tunnel, we were now in an area where there was one exposed peak after another.

We pressed on to Jane Bald and stopped to enjoy that view. The openness of that area reminded me of the exposed peaks in the White Mountains. Furthermore, when we left Round Bald, we left behind the throngs of casual hikers. We were back into the relative seclusion of the trail, but with open vistas all around.

We stopped frequently that afternoon, wherever we could savor a view of the valley below. We reached Yellow Mountain Gap around five o'clock, and turned down a short side trail toward our shelter for the night.

Shelters on the AT are generally utilitarian structures. The typical design doesn't change much from place to place. From the side, a shelter looks like a small house; except that someone forgot to build the other half.

Overmountain Shelter, our destination for the evening, didn't fit that mold. The shelter was an old barn that, somebody told us, dated back to antebellum days. It stood at the top of a large open field that sloped down into the valley. A series of wooden posts under the main floor supported one long side of the barn, which extended out over the slope. Sitting under the barn afforded an excellent view of the valley and the mountains that formed a parallel ridge beyond that. Several sleeping platforms had been built under the barn, and one of them had not been claimed. That's where Erin and I placed our packs. It was our home for the night.

We fell into the routine that we had developed during the previous three evenings. It was almost automatic. Erin went to fetch and treat water, and I started cooking dinner. All the while, storm clouds filled the sky. We watched as they got heavier and darker. Soon we could hear the distant rumble of thunder. Lightning exploded up and down the valley. A huge white mass of pouring rain began moving across the field directly at us. Our vantage point beneath the barn was the perfect place to witness the origin and fury of the storm without being caught in it. It was spellbinding.

We could tell when the rain would begin hammering the barn a few seconds before it arrived. A strong, gusting wind came with it. But the barn sheltered us from the storm. We laughed at its inability to get to us even though it was pouring and blowing just a few feet away. Lightning flashed all around us, and thunder clapped almost immediately. We were right in the heart of the storm. We could barely hear ourselves think. Then the sound of the rain changed. It was as if someone was running their fingers through a pail of pebbles off in the distance. That sound grew louder and louder, and the raindrops suddenly began bouncing as they hit the ground. We were now in the middle of a hailstorm.

The hail came down in buckets, bouncing around like miniature Ping-Pong balls before settling on the ground. The first few quickly dissolved. But the hailstones began to cover the landscape with a layer of white, like a new coat of paint.

The hail stopped after a couple of minutes—as quickly as it had started. The rain and wind let up a few minutes later. Before long, rays of late afternoon sunshine were cutting through the clouds. The storm, and the show, were over. Dinner and then bed under the barn were the next orders of business.

The final day of our hike was equally as spectacular as the previous afternoon had been. The trail took us over Little Hump and then Hump Mountain, both of which had views rivaling the ones we had enjoyed the day before. We ate our lunch on the summit of Hump Mountain, but we had to cut it short because approaching clouds warned of another thunderstorm rolling into the area. It was time to make tracks for my truck on 19E. We didn't get there quite quickly enough. The clouds opened up for the second straight afternoon, forcing us to put on our raingear for the first time during this trip.

"Twice I've been right in the heart of a thunderstorm, but each experience was completely different," I told Rex. "In the Whites, I was scared to death because I was totally exposed. But when I was protected by a shelter, being in a thunderstorm was one of the most thrilling experiences I've had on the trail.

"Say, I just had an idea," I continued. "If you're interested, we could drive down to Elkton and grab some dinner."

Rex thought for a couple of seconds. "Sure, that sounds great!"

"Of course, I wouldn't want to get in the way of your scrumptious freeze-dried meal."

"No, that's a sacrifice I'm willing to make," Rex laughed.

We hopped into the car and headed south along Skyline Drive toward its intersection with Route 33.

"Karen tells me you guys work at a software company," I began as we meandered down the parkway.

"Yeah, everybody needs a day job," Rex replied. "It seems funny to be asking you this now, seeing we've been hiking the last couple of days, but what do you do for work?"

"I know. It's almost as if jobs are a taboo topic on the trail, and then the second you get off it you're allowed to talk about them again. Anyway,

I do consulting work. I help nonprofits that are developing housing. I've been doing that for a little over three years now."

"How'd you get into that?"

"Well, I was director of an agency in Salem, Mass., for twelve years, which did that kind of work, and then I decided I should spend more time with my son, so I started consulting. I work out of my home."

"That must have been quite a transition."

"It was. But I had to do it. I fell victim to a double-play ball."

"A what?"

"You know, a double play in baseball. My son was eight years old, and he was playing Double A Little League ball where we live. At that level, they put all the kids on the team out in the field when they're on defense. So there were something like twenty kids on the field, and Jason was playing between first and second—kind of like a shortstop.

"There was a runner on first, and the kid at the plate hit a pop fly. Jason camped out underneath the ball and caught it as if he'd done that a thousand times. Of course the runner on first went as soon as the ball was hit because he didn't know he should stay put. Jason saw that the runner had gone, so he tossed the ball over to the first baseman. Double play."

"That's amazing. You must have been really proud," Rex remarked.

"Problem is, I wasn't there to see it. I was stuck at a neighborhood meeting because of my job, and that was just one of many times when I couldn't be there for him. That double play was the straw that broke the camel's back. That's when I realized I had to choose between being a dad and focusing on my career. I chose the former. I left the agency the following February, and I've been doing consulting ever since."

My gas gauge was reading uncomfortably close to Empty. "I need gas," I informed Rex as I pulled into a convenience store.

"Actually, that'll be great. I want to get some coffee before I get back on the trail. I'm sure the store will at least have some instant."

Rex came out of the store with a jar in hand just as I was twisting the cap back on the full tank. "You all set?" I asked.

"Sure am. They didn't have any bags, but this will do. I also asked the clerk if there was a good place to eat. He suggested a barbecue place called the Log Cabin a couple of miles up on 33."

"Sounds good to me. Anyway, we should have some barbecue in honor of BB."

"This certainly beats freeze-dried," Rex exclaimed thirty minutes later as he bit into his dinner of North Carolina pulled pork. "Kind of a vinegary taste to the sauce they use. It's really different, but I like it."

"Yeah, Southerners take their barbecue very seriously," I replied before biting into my order of ribs. "There's nothing like a good meal after a day of hiking."

"You're absolutely right. You know, when my brother and I are out, we tend to stay on the trail for the entire time. Maybe we should change our routine and get out to eat once in a while."

"Well, you're learning something that took me about thirteen years to figure out. My philosophy used to be that once I got on the trail, I'd stay on the trail for as long as I was hiking. Then, one year I hadn't fully recovered from pneumonia. I was hiking in Tennessee, and I was absolutely miserable. I had one of those long sit-down talks with myself, and I decided I really don't like to backpack."

"You don't like backpacking?" Rex replied, somewhat surprised.

"No, I don't. If I can, I much prefer to slack-pack. I love hiking the trail, but I don't have to carry a heavy backpack to do it. I much prefer eating a good meal and sleeping in a comfortable bed at night than I do eating freeze-dried and sleeping in a shelter. So I started looking at the trail in an entirely different way. Was it possible for me to go from one crossing to another in a day? If so, I could ride my bike or get a shuttle and do a day hike. Since then, the only backpacking I've done is over really long sections where I couldn't get to the next crossing in a day."

"And you think that's better?"

"Yes, for me, it's much better," I answered. "I'm learning a lot more about the areas I'm hiking through than I did before. It's changed the entire experience."

"Like finding good barbecue restaurants to eat at?"

"That and a whole lot more."

I really wasn't expecting much when I entered the Museum of the Middle Appalachians in Saltville, Virginia, on a rainy afternoon in early July 2005. Saltville isn't exactly near anything. It's situated in the western tip of the state, an eight-mile drive from Interstate 81, and there isn't a major city anywhere near the place. But the three-dollar admission charge was considerably less than what it costs to get into Boston's museums, and I had some time to kill because of the weather and a flat tire on my bicycle that was being repaired. So what the hell.

I was pleasantly surprised. I had always taken salt with, well, a grain of salt. I got an unexpected education about that region's history in relation to the mineral sodium chloride and, even more interesting, about its importance to the Confederate cause during the Civil War.

Saltville is still known as the "Salt Capital of the Confederacy," and the museum's exhibits do an incredibly good job of explaining how salt shaped the town. A large-scale model of the town occupies the center of the museum floor. Exhibits surround the model. One explains how a combination of geological forces created the vast salt deposits. Another exhibit, complete with a dinosaur skeleton, explains how the salt had attracted a vast number of prehistoric creatures to the region. Other exhibits focus on the history of Native Americans—who used salt to preserve their food—and how those people were ultimately displaced by white settlers looking for the same thing. Yet another exhibit addresses the subject of Saltville as a company town and what it was like to live there.

The depiction of the Civil War battles that occurred in October and December of 1864 particularly interested me. By happenstance, most of the soldiers fighting for the North and South during the October battle were from Kentucky. Furthermore, many of the regiments were from the same Kentucky counties and towns. The Civil War is often referred to as a conflict of brother against brother. That was very much the case during the first Battle of Saltville. Cousins could be shooting at cousins. Men may have killed their neighbors. These depictions helped me better understand the personal tragedies that the Civil War wreaked upon countless families and communities throughout the country. I also found out about the Saltville Massacre—how victorious Southern soldiers murdered black Union troops following the first battle.

"I've never heard of Saltville," Rex said between bites.

"Neither had I. I found a pamphlet in the hotel lobby that morning. The museum sounded interesting, so I decided to go."

I am particularly interested in history, and the regions that the AT goes through are steeped in the past. Much of the Revolutionary War was fought in the vicinity of the trail's corridor in New York, New Jersey, and Pennsylvania. But even in Maine the trail crosses the route that Benedict Arnold followed during his ill-fated invasion of Quebec. For Civil War enthusiasts, the trail runs close to the Antietam battlefield in Maryland and Gettysburg in Pennsylvania. The Shenandoah Valley in Virginia was also important Civil War ground.

These regions also offer a lot more history than battlefields. The entire trail corridor was once inhabited by a variety of Native American tribes. Some tribal names are familiar: Cherokee, Shawnee, Delaware, and Mohican. Others, such as Catawba, Tutelo, Saponi, Susquehannock, Lenape, Munsee, Quiripi, Abenaki, and Penobscot, are not so well known. All of those tribes, however, have interesting histories.

The history of European exploration and settlement along the East Coast is another tale of the trail. The diverse cultures included frontier woodsmen and trappers in northern New England, the Puritans of Massachusetts and Connecticut, the Dutch in New York and New Jersey, Quakers and Germans of Pennsylvania, Catholics in Maryland, and Scotch-Irish who settled the Shenandoah and the New River Valley of western Virginia and the uplands of Tennessee, North Carolina, and Georgia. Their descendants give different sections of the AT some distinct characteristics.

The history of the Appalachian region is really the history of how white settlers expanded westward from the Atlantic coast and how that expansion inevitably conflicted with and decimated the native peoples.

The geological history of the Appalachian Mountains is also fascinating. At one time, the range was as high as the Himalayas are today. The Appalachians were created when the African and American subterranean plates collided some three hundred million years ago to form Pangaea, the single landmass in which all of the continents used to be connected.

Mount Mitchell in North Carolina is possibly the highest mountain ever to have existed on this planet. The Rockies and the Sierra Nevadas out West are puny by comparison. It was only when the African and American plates separated that the Appalachians began to erode. They are now less than 20 percent of their original height.

The northern Appalachians have been further shaped by a much more recent climatic effect—the succession of ice ages that have altered and scoured the region. Much of the topography of Maine through Pennsylvania has been shaped by the advance and retreat of glaciers.

"Tell me about the battle and the massacre in Saltville," Rex encouraged me.

"Well, there were actually two battles. The Union lost the first one, in October 1864, but they were still determined to shut down the Confederate salt works, which they did after winning the second battle that December. The massacre occurred after the Southerners beat the Yankees in the first battle."

"Why was Saltville so important?" Rex asked.

"It was the only place still producing salt for the Confederacy that late in the war, as I recall, and the Confederacy needed the salt to preserve meat for the troops and its other citizens. It was such a valuable resource that most of the states had their own salt works there to provide for their own people. The rate of production increased about tenfold during the war. Four million bushels were produced there in one year.

"The Southern troops were badly outnumbered during the October battle, but the Union commander was not exactly Patton, so the Rebels won the day. The Union force included African-American troops in the Fifth U.S. Colored Cavalry. Apparently they fought extremely well, but some of them were wounded and got left behind when the Union force retreated.

"A number of those wounded soldiers suffered a terrible fate because the Southern soldiers hated the idea that people they considered slaves were fighting against them. The irony is that some of the black soldiers may still have been slaves even though they were in the Union army. They were from Kentucky, and Kentucky was still a slave state even though it had stayed in the Union."

"Wait a second. Didn't the Emancipation Proclamation free the slaves?" Rex interjected.

"No, that's a big misconception. The Emancipation Proclamation freed slaves in the states that were still in rebellion, but it didn't do anything for the slaves in Union states like Kentucky and Maryland where slavery was legal. We needed the Thirteenth Amendment to accomplish that, and that didn't get passed until after the war was over."

"I never knew that. History was not one of my strong suits," Rex admitted between mouthfuls.

"Anyway," I continued, "at Saltville the wounded soldiers were outright executed instead of being taken as prisoners of war. Historians don't agree on how many were killed. Some say less than ten. Others claim as many as a hundred fifty. We'll probably never know the actual number. What we do know is that some black soldiers were shot in cold blood. That was the Saltville Massacre.

"But there was a degree of revenge or justice or whatever you want to call it. The Union army returned to Saltville that December under another general named George Stoneham. He commanded the same troops who had been defeated in October. He was apparently a good leader. His men captured key towns in the region and took the salt works at Saltville. Stoneham gave his soldiers plenty of incentive. He told them to remember the Saltville Massacre.

"Now consider this. Lee surrendered to Grant at Appomattox four months later. Lee's army was starving. There are those who claim that cutting off the Confederacy's supply of salt hastened the end of the war."

Rex and I decided to finish our meals with slices of pecan pie topped with mountainberry ice cream—a combination of raspberries and blackberries. Our waitress returned a couple of minutes later carrying generous portions.

"So I spent the better part of an afternoon at the Museum of the Middle Appalachians," I concluded. "As I was driving back to my motel, I realized I had already squandered many opportunities to learn about the regions where I had been hiking. Before that, an AT hike meant getting to the crossing, putting on my boots, and hiking until I was finished. Then I would hop into my truck and drive home. And, yes, even though the AT was the reason I was there, it didn't mean that the AT was the only thing I could do while I was in the area. So, since then, I've tried to do at least one thing off the trail whenever I've done a hike. It's really made the experience much more fulfilling."

"I'd never really considered doing stuff off the trail," Rex acknowledged.

"Well, it's really easy to get into the mindset that you're cut off from humanity when you're on the trail. You forget that there's usually stuff to do all around you."

With dessert finished, all that was left to do was pay the check and get going. My Honda was soon carrying us back along Route 33 toward the national park.

I resumed the conversation. “Some of my off-trail experiences have fundamentally changed how I see people and view different regions.”

“How so?”

“Do you remember me telling you about the hike when I was recovering from pneumonia?”

“Yeah?” Rex replied.

“Well, I was two days into a four-day hike. I was coughing and feeling really horrible. There was a side trail that I could follow back to Hampton, Tennessee, which was where my truck was parked. So I figured, ‘You know what? I’m not having any fun. Screw this!’ I hiked into the town and got my truck. I took the next day off, and I still hadn’t decided if I would try to hike some more or just bag the rest of the trip and go home.

“Michael Moore’s film, *Fahrenheit 911*, had been released the previous week. I really wanted to see it, so I checked the movie listings in the area. The film was playing in Johnson City, just a few miles away. I was a little apprehensive about going to such a highly partisan flick in what I presumed was a really conservative part of the country. I felt a little like Dorothy in *The Wizard of Oz*. I knew I wasn’t in Massachusetts anymore.

“I got to the theater early. At first I thought I’d be the only one there. But others began trickling in, and then the trickle became a steady stream. By the time the previews were rolling, the theater was packed. The crowd really got into the movie. It was the best audience participation I’ve seen since my college days when I went to midnight showings of *The Rocky Horror Picture Show*.

“It really changed my whole perception of this region,” I continued. “You know, there are liberals in Tennessee, and there are conservatives in Massachusetts. We’re so quick to stereotype a region or a profession or a race. It’s so easy for us to be prejudiced in our own way, and it’s good for me to have my own prejudices challenged from time to time.”

I drove into the parking lot near Pocosin Cabin. It was dusk, but Rex had to walk only a short way down the fire road. Both of us got out, and Rex pulled his pack from the backseat.

“I’ll ship your brother’s pack back to him after I get home,” I said. “What’s his address?”

“Here, let me write it down for you,” Rex replied.

“Well, looks like this is it,” Rex said with a bit of regret as he handed me the address. It seemed to me that he had enjoyed hiking with me, and he was now facing eight days of hiking alone—something he had never done before.

Having hiked most of the trail by myself, I could tell Rex that hiking solo can be a thoroughly enjoyable experience. It gives me the chance to reflect on anything I want, something I rarely do off the trail.

But Rex would have to find out if the same held true for him. My experience would mean nothing to him.

"I've really enjoyed this hike. I hope I didn't bore you with all my war stories," I said.

"No, not at all."

"Well, I hope you have a great hike."

"Thanks," Rex replied. "And good luck finishing yours."

"Thanks. You'll only be a few years behind me."

We shook hands, and Rex pulled on his pack for the last time that day. He headed for the cabin, and I began the long drive back to Massachusetts.

A long ride home gives you a lot of time to think. It was somewhere in Pennsylvania, perhaps only a few miles from where Rex and Karen lived, that it finally hit me. My encounters with hikers like Rex and BB were the same as the friendships I had formed as a boy while camping with my parents. Instead of meeting another boy my age and playing basketball and swimming for a weekend, I was meeting other hikers on the trail. Sometimes I would hike part of the trail with them as I had with Rex. More often, I would meet hikers at a shelter and get to know them around a campfire, as Rex and I had done with BB.

We would do things we'd never dream of doing off the trail. We'd share our stories and discuss parts of our lives that we'd rarely divulge to our loved ones. We'd even sleep in close proximity to total strangers, women as well as men. But the next morning, after having shared so much just a few hours before, we'd go our separate ways and never see one another again. Contrary to the tagline for the popular TV sitcom *Cheers*, nobody would even know our names.

# 15

# The Rookie Returns

People have been telling me how smart I am for as long as I can remember. I've given them good reason to do so. I was a whiz at the card game cribbage when I was ten. I graduated at the top of my high school class. I was elected to Phi Beta Kappa at Boston University and graduated summa cum laude in history. My older brother, a master of self-deprecation, claims that when it comes to our college transcripts, mine was mostly A's and his looked like Scrabble.

There have been times, however, when I have been too smart for my own good. Or, as my mother would admonish, when I wasn't nearly as smart as I thought I was. I have done my share of stupid things on the Appalachian Trail, and fortunately, lived to tell about them. Good old common sense and paying attention to details—qualities valued highly by my father—are just as important as intellect on the trail, because just when you think you know it all, the trail slaps you upside the head and reminds you that you don't. That is especially galling after you've been hiking the AT for twenty straight years; when you're convinced that your stupid mistakes are behind you.

By any measure, the Appalachian Trail is long. If you placed one end in Manhattan, it would stretch all the way to Salt Lake City.

At the beginning of 2010, I only had 138 miles of the AT left to hike. That was less than 7 percent of the entire trail. However, that's still a long way. It's the distance from my home in Ipswich, Massachusetts, to

Hartford, Connecticut. It would be like hiking from Baltimore to Richmond, Virginia; from Cleveland to Columbus; from Los Angeles to San Diego.

Furthermore, the 138 miles were not in one continuous section that I could hike end to end in a couple of weeks. They were in four different places—stretches of the trail I had orphaned during previous years; the loose ends I had to tie up so I could truthfully claim that I had hiked every foot of the five-million-step trail.

There was a fifty-four-and-a-half-mile section between U.S. Route 522, near Front Royal, Virginia, and Harpers Ferry, West Virginia. I intended to do that section in October. My last footstep would be in the center of Harpers Ferry.

A twelve-and-a-half-mile section was in the middle of Shenandoah National Park. A fifty-one-mile stretch extended from Tye River near Montebello, Virginia, to the southern section of Shenandoah Park.

But the section I dreaded the most, and the one farthest to the south, was the twenty miles between Pearisburg, Virginia, and a remote road crossing in a place called Stony Creek Valley. To put it bluntly, the logistics for that section sucked. Ideally, I would carry my backpack and do this hike over two days—except that the distance between the road crossings and the location of the shelters didn't work for me.

Rice Field Shelter is less than seven miles from Pearisburg. So if I hiked from Pearisburg to Stony Creek Valley—south to north—I'd be doing seven miles the first day and thirteen miles the second. That wouldn't be so bad.

But another consideration reared its ugly head. Vandalism. Stony Creek Valley is in a pretty remote area, and the trail guide cautioned that cars parked there had been broken into. I surmised that leaving a foreign-made hybrid with Massachusetts plates at that crossing overnight would be like putting up a neon sign stating "Help Yourself." Since I couldn't park my car in Stony Creek, I couldn't do the hike south to north. That meant I had to get a shuttle from Pearisburg to Stony Creek so I could hike back to Pearisburg—north to south.

If I were to do that hike over two days, I would have to backpack thirteen miles up the ridge to Rice Field Shelter. Then I'd have to hike only seven miles to Pearisburg the second day. But backpacking for two days was the hard way to do it. I preferred carrying a considerably lighter daypack. So I decided to suck it up and do the entire twenty miles in one day.

I knew the terrain would be somewhat challenging, but I had done that kind of distance before. I would just have to be careful and keep humping. I was sure I could do it.

I drove ten hours to Luray, Virginia, on Friday, June fourth. My overall itinerary for this trip was ambitious—hiking eighty-three miles in six days. I was still in good shape, but I knew my fifty-year-old body would not stand up to the rigors of hiking that many miles over six straight days, especially if I was going to do twenty miles during one of them. So I decided to hike three days, take a couple of days off, and then hike the final three days before heading home. Fortunately, my sister Elaine lived not too far away in northern Ohio, and it happened that the Red Sox would be playing the Indians in Cleveland during one of my off days. So I'd get a couple of days rest, go to a ballgame, and visit my sister at the same time.

I hiked two sections in the national park during the first two days, and drove to Pearisburg for my third day of hiking—for what I expected to be my toughest hike of the trip. I had arranged to meet my shuttler, a guy named Ronnie, in Pearisburg at seven o'clock Monday morning. I checked into a motel in nearby Christiansburg on Sunday evening, and spent a fitful night thinking about and then dreaming about disasters that might befall me the next day. It was as if I had never done anything like this before. All told, I may have slept for two hours.

I checked out of my motel at a little after six, gulped some orange juice, black coffee, and a tasteless breakfast sandwich at a nearby convenience store, and drove into Pearisburg a little before seven. Timing was everything. I had to be on the trail early so I'd have enough time to hike all twenty miles in one day. In fact, I had planned this hike for June so I'd have as much daylight as possible. So far, so good. I was getting my shuttle at seven, which meant I should be on the trail by eight. Sundown was sometime after eight thirty. I'd have over twelve hours to do the twenty miles. The weather forecast was for clear skies and temperatures in the upper seventies. Perfect.

Ronnie was waiting for me at a parking lot where I would leave my car for the day. He was finishing a cigarette and sipping coffee from a plastic travel mug. He was about six feet tall, thin, and he had a scraggly beard that suggested he had simply stopped shaving some time ago. I guessed he was about my age, but he was one of those guys who could have been anywhere between thirty and sixty. His pronounced drawl told me he'd probably spent most of his life right there in Pearisburg.

"Throw your pack in the back, and we'll get goin'," Ronnie instructed, gesturing with his coffee mug toward a battered green pickup truck. "I gotta go to work after I drop ya off." Black smoke billowed from the back of the pickup as we headed for Stony Creek Valley a minute or two later.

Ronnie wasn't much of a talker, which was just fine with me. I was still groggy after my restless night, and I was trying to focus on the day's hike. After a couple of minutes, Ronnie looked at me and asked, "You plannin' to do the nineteen-mile hike today or the twenty-two?"

What with the roar of the motor, the rush of air coming through the open windows, and Ronnie's drawl, I had trouble understanding him. I had him repeat himself a couple of times before I understood what he was asking. Finally I responded, "Nineteen."

Big mistake. I should have asked him what he meant. I didn't, because I believed I knew the answer. While I had read that the hike would be twenty miles, I had also read that a trail relocation was being considered for this section. Maybe the relocation had taken place since my guide had been published, and the trail had been shortened by an entire mile. Cool. Less hiking for me. I had no idea about the twenty-two mile hike Ronnie was referring to. Maybe there was another trail of that length that some other hikers used. No worries. I had read my guide. I knew what I was doing.

Ronnie turned his pickup onto Virginia Route 635 toward Stony Creek Valley. Some of the scenery looked familiar because I had been down this road a couple of years before when another shuttler had dropped me off at Stony Creek so I could hike north. It was about quarter to eight when Ronnie turned his truck into a little parking area beside Route 635. The area didn't look familiar. But I didn't ask Ronnie where we were. Another big mistake.

Again, I believed I knew the answer. A new hiking bridge had recently been built across Stony Creek, and I assumed this parking area had been built as part of that project. There was a kiosk with a big map of the area, and I assumed the map would explain everything. I paid Ronnie for the shuttle and grabbed my pack. Ronnie headed back to Pearisburg.

I checked the map. Uh-oh. This wasn't the crossing where I had been two years before. This was the trailhead for a short spur that led to the AT. The place where the trail actually crossed the road was a considerable distance beyond where Ronnie had dropped me off.

"Oh, shit!" I exclaimed out loud. "What the hell? He couldn't take me all the way to the crossing? This is bullshit!"

I was furious. Ronnie had left me in the middle of nowhere, and now I had to walk a long way just to get to the crossing where I wanted to start. I had two choices. I could walk up the short spur trail to the AT, walk north until I got to the road crossing, turn around, and walk back. Or I could walk along the road until I got to the crossing and then get on the AT and head south from there. The second option would be easier, but I would risk missing the crossing. Having been to the crossing once before, I decided to take my chances. I started walking along the road.

I walked for at least two miles and finally came to an area that looked familiar. Fortunately, I hadn't missed the crossing, but I was still very upset with Ronnie. I should have started on this hike forty-five minutes ago. Instead, I had needlessly added two miles to my hike. I was now starting my twenty—check that—nineteen-mile hike at eight thirty. But I still had twelve hours of daylight to hike nineteen miles. I could make it.

The first two miles on the trail were proof that the AT doesn't need a mountain to be difficult. While the trail ostensibly followed Stony Creek, in several places it led straight up the steep bank and then descended as steeply back down to the stream. This process was repeated over and over again.

It took me over an hour to get to Pine Swamp Branch Shelter. By then I was thoroughly exhausted. What added insult to injury was that the shelter was only about a quarter mile from where the spur trail intersected with the AT. I had walked two miles on the road and then two miles back along the trail, and basically I was back to where Ronnie had dropped me off.

Even though it was a little before ten, four thru-hikers, all guys, were still at the shelter. They didn't seem too concerned that they weren't on the trail yet. I reached into my pack for a snack and my trail guide. We got into a long discussion about trail conditions and whether Obama or anyone else could straighten out the mess created by the Bush administration. So I didn't pay too much attention to my guide. The mistakes just kept on coming. It was well after ten when I glanced at my watch. I still had seventeen miles of trail to cover. I threw my stuff into my pack, said "So long," and hit the trail.

The topographical description of this section was pretty simple. Start at a low elevation, walk two miles of flat trail, climb fifteen hundred feet, walk along a relatively flat ridge, descend about fifteen hundred feet, and walk two miles to my car. The next section had the only major climb I would have to make this day. Fortunately, the section had been pretty well engineered, with a number of switchbacks that kept the pitch of the trail consistent as I climbed the ridge. I reached the crest at eleven thirty and sat down for a much-needed rest.

Now that I was by myself, I examined the trail guide that I had ignored at the shelter because of my conversation with the thru-hikers. The first thing that jumped out at me was that the shelter was only three-tenths of a mile from the beginning of the section. That just couldn't be. I had walked for at least an hour to get to the shelter. "Maybe the shelter was relocated," I reasoned. However, the guide also stated that I would reach the crest of the ridge after I had hiked another two miles. That timing was right. Now I was completely confused.

I read the description for the section north of this one; the section I had hiked in 2008. That description held a bombshell. I had to hike two more miles than I had planned. The road crossing that I thought marked the beginning of the section was actually two miles farther down the trail. Ronnie had dropped me off at the intersection with the spur trial, not where the AT crossed the road.

I still had seventeen miles to go—not the fifteen I thought I had left. It was now eleven thirty, and I had to hike those miles in about nine hours of daylight. I would have to hike two miles an hour, including breaks, to get back to Pearisburg by dark.

I concluded that Ronnie had not screwed me after all. He had asked me if I was doing the nineteen-mile hike or the twenty-one. When I had said I was doing the nineteen, he had dropped me off at the place where he knew that hike began. If I had asked a follow-up question, if I had actually asked him what the difference was, he would have set me straight, and I would not be in this mess. But oh, no. I was just so smart I didn't have to listen to him. After all, I had my trail guides.

"Haskell, you're a goddamned idiot!" I cursed myself. This was something that a rookie would do. No, on second thought, it wasn't. A rookie would have read the goddamned trail guide in the first place.

Now that I'd gotten myself into this predicament, I had to get myself out of it. I had two options. Try to make it to Pearisburg or turn around and go back to Stony Creek Valley. If I chose the latter, I'd wind up back in a remote area where it might take hours to hitch a ride. Also, if I retreated I would have to return to do this section later this year, and I didn't see how I could find the time to do that. If I chose the first option, I had a very long walk ahead of me without a lot of daylight remaining. However, I had hiked at a two-mile-per-hour pace before, although not for seventeen miles. So, yes, it would be a long, difficult day. But at least I could cross off this section if I just kept moving forward. I pulled my pack back on and started hiking toward Pearisburg.

I knew that the trick to hiking a long distance in a relatively short time was to minimize my breaks rather than walk faster. If I tried to go faster, I risked injury—especially to my inherently weak ankles. I could ill afford a sprained ankle today. Minimizing my breaks was the only alternative. Normally, I like to hike for an hour and rest for ten or fifteen minutes. That leisurely pace would not be possible today.

I had read in my trail guide that a campsite was located about five miles up the trail and that Rice Field Shelter was five miles beyond that. Then it was seven miles to Pearisburg. Those would be my only stops: campsite, shelter, final destination.

The ridge I was on is part of the Virginia–West Virginia border. If I was hiking on the right side of the ridge, I was in West Virginia. If I was on the left side, I was in Virginia. The ridge was quite wide, as I'd come to expect in this part of the country, but the trail was considerably more difficult than what I'd experienced in the Shenandoahs. This section wasn't used by many people other than thru-hikers and section hikers like me. Grass had overgrown the trail in many places, and I had to be careful I didn't twist an ankle on a hidden rock. I wanted to be quick but safe. I had already screwed up enough for one day, thank you.

I got to the campsite a little before two that afternoon. I had finished the first segment without incident. I sat down and ate my lunch quickly, rechecked the trail guide, and resumed hiking a few minutes later. The condition of the trail improved considerably over the next five miles. This section was more heavily used, probably because it is closer to Pearisburg. However, after hiking a couple of more miles, the bottoms of my feet began to hurt. I could feel a tingling, burning sensation with every step. It wasn't the pain from a blister, which I had experienced before. No, this was a dull ache that told me my feet were just plain tired.

I reached the vicinity of the shelter at about four thirty. I had seven miles to go in four hours of daylight. At this pace, I could finish with maybe half an hour to spare. However, my feet were hurting badly enough that I was concerned they would swell up if I sat down. So I took a break standing up.

The shelter was on the far edge of a small field where I had stopped, and I could see and hear three people talking from where I was standing. They could see me. Trail decorum dictated that I go over and make myself known, but I wasn't the least bit concerned about being polite. I ate a candy bar, gulped some water, and watched them from afar—not caring if they were concerned or merely curious about who I was.

I checked my trail guide for what I assumed would be the last time today. I didn't plan to take any more breaks because my feet were aching and the daylight was dwindling. Stopping would not rejuvenate me in any way. The only thing to do was to keep plodding along.

I made a mental note about the rest of this hike: two more miles along the ridge, three miles downhill, and then two miles of relatively flat hiking into Pearisburg. I would cross several roads when I got close to the town. At one of those crossings, the AT would follow the road until it intersected with U.S. Route 460. The Route 460 bridge over the New River would bring me into Pearisburg and my car at the motel. Finally, the end of this grueling day was in sight.

I continued plodding along. I had absolutely no appreciation for anything around me. A woods fire was about the only thing that would have gotten my attention. I was focused only on getting this hike behind me so I could get off my feet and head for my sister's home. I had to keep moving.

In about an hour, the trail began descending from the ridge. Five miles to go. I had hoped the descent would be similar to the ascent: a series of switchbacks that gave the trail a gradual pitch. Not so. This section was more like Vermont than Virginia. The trail was rocky and uneven. Even though I was thoroughly exhausted, I had to pick my way slowly and carefully, because the last thing I wanted to do was sprain an ankle or slip and bang up a knee. Anything like that would probably force me to stop, and I was pretty sure that no hikers would come along this late in the day to help me. I was on my own.

Finally, after three arduous miles, the trail flattened out. I was now on the homestretch to Pearisburg. It was a little after seven. Despite all of the obstacles, I was still covering about two miles an hour. Better yet, I had only two miles to hike and an hour and a half to do it. Amazing.

I remembered that I was about to cross some roads. The trail would follow along one of them to Route 460 and, finally, to my car. A new sense of hope surged through me but did not renew the strength I had used while hiking down from the ridge. I was now simply a walking machine, putting one foot in front of the other because that's what feet do. I focused entirely on getting to that road.

I crossed a dirt road, hiked some more, and came to another road. This one was paved, and I could see that the road intersected with a main road—Route 460—quite a ways off to my right. The AT didn't appear to cross the road to the other side, so I decided this must be where the trail followed the road down to 460 and then crossed the river. Finally, I was almost there!

If walking on dirt and rocks had been painful, walking on asphalt was even worse. The asphalt was hard and hot, and my feet were already burning up. I trudged along, barely picking up my feet. I could see the intersection in the distance, and that was all that mattered. Once I got to the intersection, the bridge would be right there. And on the other side would be my car.

The only thing that bothered me now, besides my aching feet and tired body, was the absence of white blazes along the road. I was perturbed that whoever maintained this part of the trail had not marked it very well.

I have frequently found it ironic that the most difficult places to follow the AT are when it follows stretches of road. It's as if some trail maintainers don't think it's necessary to mark the roads as carefully as they mark the trail in the woods. The opposite is closer to the truth. It's pretty easy to distinguish a trail in the woods, although the white blazes certainly eliminate any doubt that a hiker is on the AT. On a road, however, the white blazes are the only things that indicate it is part of the trail. But white blazes can be hidden among all of the other things—including mailboxes and signs—that are found on most roads. So as I plodded toward Route 460, I just assumed I was so tired that I was missing the white blazes along the way. Another big mistake.

Then, to make this bad day even worse, when I finally reached the intersection, there was no bridge to be seen. I wasn't anywhere near a bridge. I was sure, based on my trail guide, that I would come onto 460 very close to the bridge. Something wasn't right. So, very reluctantly, I stopped, took off my pack, and dug out my trail guide. What the hell was going on?

I reread the description for this section and realized that the place where the trail connected with 460 was, indeed, very near a bridge. That meant I was off the trail. That would explain why I hadn't seen any blazes. This wasn't the AT! Shit!

"Screw it!" I said to myself. I'd had enough. I knew that 460 would eventually lead me across the bridge and to my car. I declared a mutiny. This was the end of my hike for today.

I began walking along the side of 460 toward Pearisburg. A major industrial complex was to my right. I began walking past a field to my left. Then I spotted a single stake at the far edge of the field, maybe a hundred yards away. A blotch of white paint appeared to be on the stake. From the distance of a football field, a blotch of white on a stake could be anything. It could be an irregularity in the stake that appears to be white in the evening light. Someone could have painted the top of the stake white as a boundary marker. Or it could be a white blaze marking the AT. Hmmm.

I stopped and studied that stake for a couple of minutes. If I continued following this road, I would get to my car, and I would end this torture. But then I'd have to come back to complete this section later this year—before October tenth. Then again, if I walked across this field to check out the stake and it had nothing to do with the AT, I would add another couple of hundred yards to this already sucky, sucky hike. However, if that stake really did mark the AT, I just might figure out where the hell I was and actually complete this part of the trail today.

What is it they say? When the going gets tough, the tough get going? "Only one way to find out," I sighed. I started walking toward the stake.

As I got closer, I could make out a definitive white blaze on the stake. Son of a bitch. I had rediscovered the AT. Now, if I was going to complete these twenty miles, I had to hike southbound until I came to the road that I had mistakenly turned down.

I backtracked along the trail and eventually came to the road. I figured out where I had made my mistake. Instead of turning right to go down the road, the AT had taken a left up the road for less than a hundred feet and then followed a steep gully down the other side. Had I walked a few feet more when I had been here before, I would have seen where the trail descended. But because I had just assumed that the trail went down the road, I had added more than a mile to this hellish hike. And I still had nearly two miles to go and not a lot of daylight to do it. The sun was hovering just above the horizon. It was almost eight o'clock. I dutifully walked down the road to the point where I had originally made my most recent mistake of the day and did an about-face.

Every part of my body hurt. I had been up for fifteen hours. I had been hiking for twelve hours, after two hours of sleep, since Ronnie had dropped me off at Stony Creek Valley. My legs felt like gigantic cramps waiting to happen. My head was throbbing, my throat was parched, and my feet were screaming at me nonstop. I was so lightheaded and wobbly that I'm sure I would have been arrested for public intoxication had a cop come by.

I even contemplated something I'd never thought about before. At what point would I not be able to do this anymore? There will come a day when this body will tell me that it's had enough. It will refuse to go another step. In twenty years of hiking I have pushed it to the limit many times, but it has always come through. That won't always be the case. Could that day be today? I sure hoped not.

The trail followed a series of short up-hills and down-hills as it led to the bridge. Normally, I love this kind of trail. It's almost like riding a roller coaster. Today it was not fun. I was convinced that every one of these undulations had been placed there by the evil geniuses at the ATC and their minions at the Outdoor Club at Virginia Tech. These were the people responsible for maintaining this section and for torturing my body and soul. Why in God's name would anyone put a trail here when there was a perfectly good road just a short distance away?

Then I saw the bridge. Thank God! When I reached the northern end, I knew I was only seven-tenths of a mile from my car. The light was fading, but I had made it. With each step, the concrete bridge seared through the soles of my feet, up my legs, and straight to my pounding head. When I got to the southern end of the bridge, the trail turned up a steep bank from the road. The last three-tenths of a mile would be through the woods. I willed myself up the bank, stopping a couple of times to catch my breath. Normally, I would have flown up something like this without a second thought. Not tonight.

Finally, I reached my car. I let my pack drop to the pavement, and I opened the driver's-side door and sat down. I had hiked for thirteen miles without sitting down. I was as bone tired as I had ever been.

After changing into my sneakers and resting for a few minutes, I drove to a Dairy Queen and shuffled in for a cheeseburger. As hungry as I was, I couldn't eat very much. The food made me nauseous.

Sitting there, I thought about all of the things I had done wrong that day. It was a pretty long list. My first mistake was in the preparation. I had looked at the trail guide before the hike, but I hadn't really studied it. Because I had debated doing this in one day or two, I had focused on where the shelters were located. I hadn't made sure I knew where the section began and ended. That mistake had added two miles to the hike. Had I known that, I probably would have spent two days backpacking that section. I certainly wouldn't have tried to hike it in a day.

I had compounded my first mistake by not listening to Ronnie. He had asked me a question that didn't seem to make any sense, and I had simply dismissed him. It's a terrible thing to think that you're smarter than somebody else, because it usually shows just how stupid you are.

But I did not smarten up after realizing I had made those mistakes. I compounded my misery at the end of the hike. Had I simply taken the time to turn left up that road for a few feet and see if the trail crossed to the other side, I would have saved myself that extra mile or so at the end of the day. And once I was on the road, it never dawned on me that the absence of the white blazes meant I was off the trail.

But the biggest mistake I had made all day long was to take the trail for granted. After twenty years of hiking the AT, I had become cocky. On that day, the trail had shown me it could still whack you around if you're not careful and if you don't plan ahead. Even though I was a veteran hiker, it had made me feel like a rookie.

Two good things did happen that day. I did knock out those twenty miles so I'd never have to face that stretch again. And, one more time, in spite of myself, I did not die.

At the beginning of 2010, I thought I had 138 miles of the Appalachian Trail left to hike. In fact, I had 140. Those two miles may not seem like much, but they made a very big difference.

# 16

# The Last Leg

During twenty-one years of hiking the Appalachian Trail, I had experienced many emotions: anger, fear, joy, contempt, bliss, amusement, empathy, concern, boredom. As wide-ranging as those emotions are, none had brought me to the point of tears. That is, not until I had only forty-one miles to go.

In October 2006, I was on the verge of accomplishing a major milestone. I was about to complete the northern "half" of the AT. In the early nineties, when I had just started this journey, I had read that Harpers Ferry, West Virginia, was traditionally considered the halfway point of the trail. The actual halfway mark is some distance north in Pennsylvania. However, since trail relocations change the length of the trail from year to year, it makes sense that there be a permanent place that is always considered halfway. What better place than Harpers Ferry for that milestone?

After all, the Appalachian Trail Conservancy is located there. It is also famous for the event that did much to bring on the Civil War. The center of town is a national historical park and depicts Harpers Ferry as it was in 1859 when John Brown led his ill-fated attempt to capture the federal arsenal and start a slave rebellion. Many Americans have heard of Harpers Ferry.

I had decided very early on to complete the AT in Harpers Ferry. Most people hike the trail from one end to the other. But I had chosen to hike it from both ends toward the middle. In the fall of 2006, I was about to finish all of the AT north of Harpers Ferry—everything from Maryland to Maine. As I walked the last couple of miles along the Chesapeake & Ohio Canal, I began to think about the next time I'd be walking into Harpers Ferry. That would be sometime in 2010.

Every family has its traditions. My family celebrates each member's fiftieth birthday with a big party. The tradition started with my brother Bob, and then Elaine and Patti had their celebrations as well. They weren't huge affairs. We didn't rent a football stadium. But everyone in the family—including siblings, nieces, and nephews—tried to attend.

The first three of these parties came in relatively rapid succession because my three siblings were born within a five-year period. But there was a seven-year lag between Patti's fiftieth birthday and mine. That had given me some time to think.

As I neared the bridge that would take me over the Potomac River from Maryland into Harpers Ferry, I realized what I wanted for my fiftieth birthday. I wanted my family and friends with me as I completed the Appalachian Trail.

I knew that would be a big sacrifice for a lot of people. The majority would have to come to Harpers Ferry from Maine or Massachusetts, which isn't exactly a short drive. I knew that would probably limit the number of people who could make it, but I could live with that possibility. After all, some people might not come to the party if it were held in Massachusetts. I knew Donna and Jason would be able to make it, and that my siblings would probably come as well. I knew my mother was doubtful because traveling any great distance had become a problem for her.

Erin would probably be able to come down from Connecticut without too much trouble. My best friend from college, Seth, lived in the DC area, so Harpers Ferry would be convenient for him and his family. Anyone else who could come would be icing on the cake.

Donna and my siblings liked the idea and promised to try to be there. However, it was kind of hard for them to get excited about a trip that was four years in the future. But now that I had something to plan, I would occasionally dig out the Maryland-to-Northern Virginia trail guide and do some Internet research about places where people could stay and things they could do while they were there. A party in Harpers Ferry became my vision.

Most hikers finish the AT on their own or with one or two others who have also hiked the entire trail. They don't invite their friends to witness their achievement. Thru-hikers typically finish at the peak of Katahdin, and it's not easy to predict when they will do that. Besides, Katahdin isn't usually a hospitable place in late autumn. Snow falls early on the summit. Few people want to climb the mountain at that time of year for any reason—if they can even get into Baxter State Park. Even the thru-hikers who finish at Springer can't predict exactly when they'll do that, and Springer isn't especially easy to get to either.

Having hiked the trail as I had, I had the luxury of picking a place and a date that would be convenient for a large group of people. Harpers Ferry had the added advantage of being accessible by air and road, and even by rail if people wanted to travel that way.

By the fall of 2009, I was heavily involved in planning for my Harpers Ferry celebration. I decided it would be on the Sunday of Columbus Day weekend the following year. That would enable people to get there on Friday or Saturday, hike the final mile with me Sunday morning, go to the party in the afternoon, and return to their homes on Monday. Having spent a number of Columbus Days in Virginia during previous years, I knew the weather would probably cooperate—not too hot and not too cold. The Sunday before Columbus Day 2010 was October 10th. Perfect. October 10th, 2010, or 10-10-10. It was easy to remember and went well with my trail name. Two Tents would complete the trail on ten-ten.

I put the word out to my family and friends during the late fall and winter of 2009-10. I told a lot of people, but I did not pressure anyone. If they wanted to come, I would be thrilled to see them. But I would certainly understand if they chose not to join me. It was a long way to travel just to take a walk.

The response was overwhelming. As I had expected, Donna, Jason, and my siblings promised to be there. So did Seth and his family. Erin said she would come, and so did my two other nieces.

What really surprised me was the response from other people. College friends Ann and Diana would travel from Connecticut and Massachusetts. Two families on Donna's side, my in-laws, would drive from New Hampshire and Massachusetts.

Two people I had worked with said they would come. One was

Molly, who said she'd bring her husband Jake and their two sons from Oak Ridge, Tennessee. Molly and Jake had hiked with me in Maine and Tennessee. The other was Marcos, who couldn't understand why anyone of sound mind would walk a great distance when you could drive. He would fly down from Boston.

A family that Donna, Jason, and I had met during a trip to Guatemala three years before, and that lived in the Harpers Ferry area, would join us. And through the miracle of social media, I had made contact with Kim, an old high-school friend. She had asked me to be her date for her high-school senior prom thirty-three years before. She now lived in the DC area, and would be there with her husband.

In all, thirty-eight people were planning to be with me in Harpers Ferry on October 10th as I completed the trail. Even more amazing, this group included all but six of the people who had hiked parts of the trail with me during my twenty-one-year odyssey.

Of course, one person who would not be in Harpers Ferry was Aimee. She and I had hiked eighty-three miles of the trail together, but, more important, we had originally shared the idea of section-hiking the entire trail as a married couple. Now I was about to achieve that goal without her. I knew that Aimee had remarried and started a family of her own. So far as I knew, she was much happier than she had been with me, and I was happy with my new life. We had gone our separate ways, and it didn't seem appropriate to invite her.

As I drove toward West Virginia on the morning of October 2$^{nd}$, the only thing standing between me and my goal was fifty-four miles of the trail. Unlike my previous trip in 2010, I had just one section to do. I had to hike from U.S. Route 522, just north of Shenandoah National Park in Virginia, to Harpers Ferry. The section divided up nicely into five segments—the shortest being about six miles and the longest fourteen. I had five days to hike those five segments. There would be no rest days. If it rained, I would hike. I had run out of time.

I planned to hike alone for the first three days, Sunday through Tuesday. Erin would fly in Tuesday night, and she and I would do the final two segments Wednesday and Thursday. The extended forecast for the week called for temperatures in the fifties and sixties, overcast with the chance of light rain. It would be ideal for hiking. The rest of my family would begin to arrive Friday. By then, I planned to hike only one mile from the ATC headquarters down to a park in the Old Town section of

Harpers Ferry near the confluence of the Potomac and Shenandoah Rivers. My family and friends would hike the final mile with me. Sunday's forecast called for clear skies and seventy degrees. Perfect!

I hiked the eight miles from Route 522 to Virginia Route 55 on Sunday the third. It was raining when I resumed hiking Monday, my second day out, but the rain was expected to end during the day. It didn't matter. I had to hike twelve miles to U.S. Route 50 in a place called Ashby Gap, rain or shine.

The rain ended late that morning, but the sky was overcast, threatening to open up at any moment. Few hikers were on the trail, and the air was completely still. It seemed as if I had the entire trail to myself. The hiking was easy, and I had a lot of time to think. I had completed a little over four miles by late morning when a single thought erupted in my brain. I suddenly realized there was a very important person who I had failed to invite to my celebration. My dad.

It didn't matter that he had died nearly thirty years earlier. The emotion that overcame me was as raw as it had been on the November afternoon in 1981 when he died. I stopped, and the tears began flowing. I took off my pack, sat on the ground, and cried my eyes out.

Percy Haskell was an easy man to fear and a difficult one to like. A lifetime of manual labor—farm work, woods work, construction jobs, and repairing railroad tracks—had made him incredibly strong. He was an imposing man who stood six feet one and weighed a solid two hundred pounds. He used his size and strength to intimidate those who were closest to him, especially members of his immediate family. His expectations were very high, and "compromise" was not in his vocabulary. You didn't dare to cross him, because he was always the alpha dog.

As the youngest member of my family, I had the good fortune of not being my dad's prime target early on. While my three older siblings frequently bore the brunt of his wrath, I certainly witnessed it. And I could do the math. There would be several years when I would be the only one of his children in the house.

After my siblings had moved out and I knew my turn had come, I solved the problem in the only way I could. I ran away.

Not in the traditional way; but while I was in high school I became so involved in extracurricular activities that I was out of the house from early in the morning until late in the evening. I developed a network of surrogate families who fed me dinner or let me stay with them until I could get a ride home. Having access to a family car after I got my driver's license during my junior year also helped keep me out of the house. I reasoned that the less time I was around my dad, the less chance there would be to get on his bad side. I knew that as long as I kept my grades up, he would not shorten the leash.

My plan worked perfectly. I was on the debate team and played in the band for all four years. I was editor of the student newspaper and president of the student council during my senior year. I had gone to Boys State after my junior year and was selected to the All-State Band my senior year. Meanwhile, academically, I was still at the top of my class.

The final piece of my plan was making sure that I went away to college so I would not have to live at home. I had no interest in commuting to the University of Maine at Orono as my siblings had done. I knew it took four or five hours to drive from Levant to Boston. Perfect. To Boston University I went.

After I had settled into college and had started my own journey into manhood, I finally had a chance to reflect on my relationship with my father. While his methods were harsh, his message was clear: make something of yourself. He urged the four of us to avoid any distractions that would prevent us from achieving our goals. Those distractions included the ones that most parents warn their children about—drugs and alcohol being foremost among them. But for my father, the list was a bit longer, and included things like laziness and complacency. Young love was another of his taboos because he knew that love led to sex, and sex led to children, and children changed everything.

To my dad, education was the key to success. He had gone to college on the GI Bill when Bob and Elaine were toddlers, and had earned an associate's degree in agriculture. He was the only one in his family of five to get a degree. In contrast, all four of his children have earned bachelor's degrees, and two have obtained graduate degrees. Had it not been for my dad, that probably would not have happened. Even for my generation, college was more the exception than the rule among young people in rural Maine.

By my senior year in college, I was just beginning to appreciate the influence my dad had had on my life. Then, around noon on November 8, 1981, a Sunday, my brother called to tell me our dad had suffered a massive heart attack. He died, at fifty-five, the following day. My last conversation with Percy Haskell had taken place the previous Friday. I told him I had been elected to Phi Beta Kappa. I never thanked him for helping me get there.

Even though my father was outwardly hard as nails, there was a deeply caring and emotional person bottled up inside. Tears would stream down his face while we were watching an emotional movie, such as *Born Free,* on television. But you did not point that out to him, because men of his generation weren't supposed to cry. He certainly loved his family, but the only way he could show that was by being tough.

Two of my defining moments with my dad occurred on Mount Katahdin. I hiked up that mountain with him when I was twelve and again when I was fourteen. For me, and I presume for him, those hikes marked my coming of age. I was old enough to keep up, hold my own, and endure some pain in the process. I knew he was very proud of me those days, although he never said so. That wasn't his style.

As I sat in the middle of the trail, on the verge of completing a journey that I think my father would have appreciated, my tears expressed my nearly thirty years of frustration that he was not part of my life. He never got to see me become a man and a father myself.

I wiped my cheeks dry, stood, and put my pack back on. I still had forty-one miles of the trail to hike, and nearly forty people would arrive in a few days. I had to get going. My dad would have had it no other way.

I finished that day's twelve-mile hike in Ashby Gap, then I did the thirteen miles from Snickers Gap on Virginia Route 7 to Keys Gap on West Virginia Route 9 on Tuesday. Thirty-three miles down, twenty-one to go.

I picked up Erin at Washington Dulles International Airport on Tuesday evening. I was especially happy that we would be hiking together for a couple of days. Erin had accompanied me on eleven AT hikes since 2001. She had completed over two hundred thirty miles of the trail in the process. In that time, we had become much more than uncle and niece or hiking partners. We had become very close friends.

We got a late start on Wednesday morning, so we decided to do the shortest segment I had left: six miles from Keys Gap on the Virginia–West Virginia border down to the ATC headquarters in Harpers Ferry. We left my car in Harpers Ferry and rode our bikes up to Keys Gap. A series of short hills made for some difficult biking. We were either walking our bikes uphill or careening down the other side. While the bike ride was exhausting, the hike that day was mercifully uneventful.

We got up early Thursday morning. Besides the last mile in Harpers Ferry, the final section I had to hike was the fourteen miles from Ashby Gap to Snickers Gap—a section known as "the roller coaster" because the trail constantly goes up and down eight hills in rapid succession, although the end points are at about the same elevation. I knew this would be a challenging stretch, and had intentionally saved it for this day so Erin and I could experience it together.

The idea was to park my car at Snickers Gap, bike the fourteen miles to Ashby Gap, hike back to the car at Snickers, and then drive to Ashby to retrieve our bikes. I knew that the road leading to Ashby Gap would mean more hard biking, because it was a series of ups and downs like the stretch we'd ridden the day before. It would probably take at least an hour and a half to bike it. Even as we pulled into the Snickers Gap parking lot at eight that morning, I was concerned we would not make it off the trail before dark. There had been many close calls, but I had never had to hike out in the dark in twenty-one years. But today the math wasn't with us. It would take too long to do all of that biking and hiking. We might indeed finish my last full day on the trail after dark.

I parked the car, and we began taking the bikes off the rack. Another car pulled into the lot, and a couple got out. It appeared that the woman was dropping off the man so he could hike on his own.

"Think she might give us a ride?" Erin asked me, her eyes saying, "I really don't want to ride my bike again."

"Never know if you don't ask," I replied.

Erin approached the couple and struck up a conversation. I watched her as I continued taking the bikes off the rack, not wanting to appear too anxious. Erin gave me the thumbs-up a minute later, and I gladly locked our bikes back on the rack. We were getting a ride. Trail magic on my last day. What a trail!

Erin and I survived the roller coaster. We were treated to a great view from Bears Den Rocks at the crest of the final hill of the day. I had savored hundreds of views like that between Maine and Georgia—expanses of woodland or farmland stretching to the horizon. The view may lack the majesty of the Rockies, but to me it's reassuring. It tells me that even though I've lived my life in one of the most heavily developed parts of the country, there are still lots of places where wilderness and agriculture reign supreme.

The sun was touching the horizon as Erin and I hiked down to Snickers Gap. If we hadn't gotten that trail-magic ride, we would have hiked out in the dark. I had one mile to go.

On Saturday morning, October ninth, I was sitting in the Baltimore–Washington International Airport terminal waiting for Donna and Jason to fly in from Boston.

My brother Bob, his fiancée Mary Fran, and my sister Elaine had arrived Friday. That's when the reality of the weekend began to set in. This was it—the event I'd been working toward for twenty-one years.

I was also tracking the progress of seven cars and two other flights that were carrying people toward Harpers Ferry from Maine, New Hampshire, Massachusetts, Connecticut, and Tennessee.

Finally, the video display told me that Donna's and Jason's flight had arrived. I looked for them among the crowd that I presumed was getting off the same airplane. It took me a second to recognize them. Donna's stride was unmistakable. Even though she hadn't run competitively for years, she still walked with the grace and confidence of an athlete. Still, I had to look twice because Donna was walking with a tall, dark-skinned young man. It was Jason—nearly as tall as his mother. He looked older than I expected, because he was still a kid in my eyes. As proud as I was of the young man he was becoming, I didn't want him to grow up.

Donna and I hugged, and Jason and I awkwardly grabbed each other's shoulders. There isn't a good way for a father and his thirteen-year-old son to greet one another. It's an awkward time. He's too old to be hugged and kissed; too young to merely shake hands.

For the past twelve years I had left these two people behind every time I had gone hiking. While Donna and I had hiked seventy-one miles of the trail in New England, the last time we had hiked it together was in 1998 when Jason was a year old. It was after that trip that both of us realized we could no longer do that because Donna couldn't bear to leave our son.

In my many years of hiking, I have been somewhat envious of the families who hike with their children. I've seen parents carrying toddlers in backpacks, and I've seen children as young as four or five having the time of their lives. We introduced Jason to hiking when he was five or six.

We'd find a short trail and try to make sure there was something worth seeing—a view or a waterfall—along the way. The hikes became longer as he grew older, and he has now climbed a number of peaks—including several four-thousand-footers in New Hampshire. While Jason always seemed to enjoy the hikes, he never looked forward to the next one. In fact, he eventually let us know that he wasn't the least bit interested in doing another.

As Jason approached his teen years, when he could accompany me on AT hikes, I faced a dilemma that I'm sure many fathers have encountered. Do I force him to do something with me that I love, or, in this case, do I let him stay home? I chose the latter course for a couple of reasons. I don't think children should be forced to do something just because their parents think it's fun. And the AT is no place for someone who doesn't want to be out there. I hope that Jason will someday appreciate hiking as much as I do. He has plenty of time to decide if he wants to be a hiker. But Jason's decision to sit out my hikes and stay home meant that Donna would stay with him. That's why I had hiked so much of the trail by myself.

At a little after nine o'clock on Sunday morning, the tenth day of October, my group gathered in the hotel parking lot. The morning was warmed by a bright sun that promised a fine autumn day in the central Appalachians. Despite having to deal with the heavy traffic and full flights of the Columbus Day weekend, everyone I had been tracking Saturday morning had arrived in Harpers Ferry by that evening. Three other families from Maryland and Virginia had also found their way to the hotel. Considering that these people were my family and friends, I probably didn't have to stand on ceremony. Still, there were some things I wanted to tell them.

"The first thing I want to say is that I'm just overwhelmed," I began. "Thank you all so much for being here.

"Hiking the Appalachian Trail is a thoroughly singular event. It's your feet, it's your blood, sweat, and toil that gets you over it. However, anyone who's hiked the trail will tell you that there are two things that are absolutely crucial to completing it.

"The first is trail magic. Trail magic is the good things that happen along the way that you don't expect and that somehow get you over a difficult section or get you out of jam or just lift your spirits enough so you can continue on.

"The second is the people who support you during your hike. For thru-hikers, that may be the people at home who make sure there's a package of supplies waiting at the next post office. For me, having hiked the trail for the past twenty-one years, I can say that I have pretty much taken advantage of just about everybody in this group."

Everyone laughed.

"Many of you provided me with transportation at some point, or you let me crash on your floor. For those of you who dared to hike with me, I very much enjoyed your company on the trail. But even more than these tangible items, it was people like you asking me, 'So, how was the trail this year?' or 'How much more do you have to go?' that gave me the encouragement I needed to keep hiking.

"If it hadn't been for you, I couldn't have done it. Thank you all so very much."

There is a tradition among hikers who are called the "two-thousand-milers" and who plan to complete the entire Appalachian Trail. They are photographed at the Appalachian Trail Conservancy's headquarters as they pass through Harpers Ferry. Since most two-thousand-milers are thru-hiking, Harpers Ferry and that photo symbolize the halfway point of their journey. Section hikers like me can hit Harpers Ferry at just about any time. I was there on my last day.

More than eleven thousand people had hiked the entire AT during its first seventy-three years by that Sunday in October. I was about to join that rather select group. I certainly hadn't hiked it the fastest, nor had I been the slowest. I was nowhere near the oldest, although, at fifty, I was hardly among the youngest. However, there was one record that I believed I could claim as my own—the hiker with the largest number of loved ones in that ATC photo. There were thirty-seven people and two dogs in my photo. Until someone proves otherwise, that record is mine.

The photo taken, it was time to finish the trail. My group began the mile-long hike down to the historic center of Harpers Ferry. The actual point where I would finish was near the bridge that crosses the Potomac River to Maryland. There is a little park where the Potomac and Shenandoah rivers converge. The trail changes from a gravel path to a brick walkway just before the bridge. I had stopped at the end of the bricks four years before. Today, when I stepped from the gravel to the bricks, my hike of the Appalachian Trail would be complete.

I had thought about just how arbitrary that point really was. It is a piece of ground that many people pass over every day. Most of them probably don't even know they're on the Appalachian Trail. Yet, it was the spot on the earth that largely defined what I had accomplished in twenty-one years.

It occurred to me that the entire trail is an arbitrary thing. There is no God-given reason why it runs north and south between two mountains named Springer and Katahdin. Benton MacKaye could have planned an east-west trail. And because of many relocations, what was once the trail is no longer. Yes, the trail does exist in the physical universe, but the AT is much more than that. It exists more profoundly as a concept than it does as an actual footpath. The path may change, but the idea of hiking the Appalachian Trail, thanks to MacKaye's vision, remains the same.

I marveled at the people who were strung out ahead of me as our group hiked beside the sparkling Shenandoah River while descending into Harpers Ferry. I had intentionally stayed at the back of the pack so everyone could be assembled near the bridge when I finished. This vantage point enabled me to take in everyone who was there. With the exception of my mom and dad, nearly everyone who was special to me was in front of me.

There are only a few moments in your life—generally a wedding or graduation—when everyone who is dear to you is near to you. But most everyone has other special moments they want to share with those they love, and finishing the AT was that kind of an occasion for me. I loved every one of those people for being part of this special day.

For twenty-one years I had imagined what it would feel like to take my last step on the Appalachian Trail. Now that time was near. The trail led onto Church Street, and we passed the magnificent stonework of St. Peter's Roman Catholic Church. All of Harpers Ferry was below us, almost as if we were floating above it in the stillness of this pleasant Sunday morning. The trail descended steeply on well-worn stone steps toward the center of the Old Town. We passed historic buildings and turned onto the cobblestones of Potomac Street. The trail continued past the firehouse where John Brown had been captured a hundred fifty-one Octobers before. I walked under the railroad overpass. The park where I would finish came into sight, and the moment I had been waiting for was at hand.

The group was assembled on the grass beside the gravel path. My sister, Elaine, began chanting, "Go, Jim. Go, Jim," and the rest of my group joined in. Others who were at the park stopped to see what all of the commotion was about.

What would I do when I got to the brick walkway? Would I say something profound? Would I make a joke? Would I claim I was tired and couldn't go any farther? I really didn't know.

As it turned out, I did very little. I stopped just short of the bricks and stood there in silence. I looked down at my boots that had brought me so far. Then, realizing I had nothing profound or funny to say, I simply took a long and determined step onto the brick walkway and raised my arms in victory. People cheered, and there were smiles and hugs and handshakes all around.

The Appalachian Trail was behind me. I was ready for the next chapter in my life.

# Epilogue

Goals are a funny thing. You work long and hard to reach one, savor your accomplishment for a while, and then set a new one. It's a way of getting on with your life. Most people can rest on their oars for just so long.

Although I focused on my goal of completing the Appalachian Trail for many years, it wasn't long after I took my final step in 2010 that I realized my life was not over—that I needed another goal, or two or three. In pursuing them, I continue to write the next chapters in my life.

Besides the ongoing challenges of parenting a teenager and doing my day job, I am preparing to launch a website, www.trailconnections.com, that will be devoted to helping hikers find trailheads and crossings along the Appalachian Trail and locate services in nearby towns.

I also want to climb all of the four-thousand-foot peaks in New York and New England by 2020, my sixtieth year. I had already climbed thirty-three of them by 2010 because most of those are on the AT. I have climbed twenty-six since then. That leaves fifty-seven more to do over the next six years.

Piece of cake.

# Acknowledgments

***T**wo Tents* began with a conversation I had with my brother, Bob Haskell, during the summer of 2008. While I still had well over three hundred miles of the trail to complete, the end was in sight. I regretted not keeping a journal about my section hikes during the previous nineteen years, and I wondered if I could recall enough details from my experiences to actually fill a book. Bob encouraged me to jot down a few notes from my various hikes so we could determine if there would be enough material. Two hundred single-spaced pages later, we knew the problem wouldn't be having enough material. It would be how to condense and convey the stories that I did have.

Since then, Bob has been much more than my editor. He has been my mentor, problem solver, facilitator, taskmaster, time traveler, theorist, pragmatist, and friend—all rolled into one. In that time, we have shared motel rooms from New Hampshire to Virginia as we've retraced some of the stretches I have hiked. Had I been left to my own devices, *Two Tents* would have been about a thousand pages of nearly incomprehensible prose. If you enjoyed reading this book, you have Bob to thank.

I would also like to thank the three early readers of *Two Tents*: Joyce DeHaan, Tasha Enseki, and Kim Lundgren. Thanks to their feedback, I made many changes to the content and order of the material. Their contributions to this book have been invaluable. Tragically, Kim unexpectedly passed away in early 2015. She had been my colleague at the Salem Harbor Community Development Corporation and then in my consulting business afterward. She was a great friend and role model, and I'll miss her deeply.

I received publishing guidance from Jim LeVay whose wealth of experience in that business gave me a great deal of insight into a process

I knew little about. Later on, a thorough read by Ray "Hamlet" Anderson provided me with a thru-hiker's perspective and helped me fine-tune the book.

I was fortunate enough to discover the folks at Maine Authors Publishing to help me with the final editing and production of *Two Tents.* Jane Karker has developed a model for helping authors self-publish their books that I wish was available to many more people. Her shop provides the technical resources, including copyediting and graphic design, that enable an author to publish a quality piece of work, and she provides sound marketing guidance as well. I especially want to thank Katherine Mayfield, who copyedited and Lindy Gifford who was the graphic designer for *Two Tents* on behalf of Maine Authors Publishing and whose suggestions were invaluable as I finalized the manuscript.

I can't say enough about my wife Donna and her willingness to let me spend the time that I needed to complete my journey and then write about it. I know she understands that hiking the AT is vital to my wellbeing. I also know that my spending a week away from home two or three times a year put a huge burden on her. It made her a single parent when we had agreed to raise our son as a couple. Her willingness to pick up my slack made it possible for me to hike the trail and write this book.

Although they didn't actually help me write *Two Tents*, I truly appreciate the many people who made my section hikes of the Appalachian Trail possible—those who provided me with transportation, accommodations, and sustenance. Even though I am generally a shy person, I haven't been reluctant to ask relatives and friends to go out of their way to help me get to and from the trail. That they did so with good humor and encouragement is even more appreciated. Without them, I could not have hiked the AT, and therefore, written *Two Tents.*

I was especially pleased that my wife's sister Barbara and her husband Dave were among those who walked my final mile with me in Harpers Ferry, West Virginia, on October 10, 2010. Barbara branded me with the nickname Sherpa Jim soon after we met. It was the beginning of an endearing and enduring friendship. Had I known that Barbara would be taken from us less than four months after that memorable day, I would have hiked with her a little longer. Rest in peace, Auntie Xena. We love you.

While much of *Two Tents* is based on my memories of events that occurred during twenty-one years, I have tried to corroborate those recollections as much as possible. I have frequently referred to online resources such as Wikipedia, Mapquest, and the Urban Dictionary. Google became my friend. Information about sunrises and sunsets came from sunrisesunset.com, and information about the risings and settings and other phases of the moon were obtained from the U.S. Naval Observatory's website. I scoured the websites of the Appalachian Trail Conservancy (ATC), the Appalachian Mountain Club (AMC), and the Potomac Appalachian Mountain Club (PATC) for bits of information. I frequently referenced the *DeLorme Atlas & Gazetteer* for information about several of the states along the AT corridor, and the AMC's *White Mountain Guide* for trail information in New Hampshire. I could not have done without the Appalachian Trail Guides that are published by the ATC and some of the maintaining clubs. The AT Guides were not only invaluable to me while writing *Two Tents*. They actually saved my life several times while I was hiking the trail.

In the opening chapter, I referenced material on the Shenandoah National Park and Bear Mountain Inn (New York) websites. For "Looking for Love," I obtained information about Amicalola Falls State Park from the website of the Georgia Department of Natural Resources.

Writing "Feuding Founders" gave me the opportunity to read Benton MacKaye's brilliant "An Appalachian Trail: A Project in Regional Planning" that was published by the *Journal of the American Institute of Architects* in October 1921. I also relied heavily of Brian King's "Trail Years: A History of the Appalachian Trail Conference" that the ATC published in a special commemorative issue of the *Appalachian Trailway News* in July 2000. Also helpful in writing that chapter was *Great Stories of Hiking the Appalachian Trail,* edited by Debra Smith, originally published in 1975 and again in 2010.

"Feuding Founders" tells about of the origins of the AT, but that is only a tiny piece of the story. Were it not for the dedication of the Appalachian Trail Conservancy and the thirty-one clubs that maintain the trail, the AT would have been overgrown and forgotten decades before I started my hike. Every step that I took on the trail was made possible by people willing to lug chainsaws, axes, and long-handled pruning shears many miles from the nearest road. The real heroes of the trail are the volunteers who maintain it and the clubs that ensure the entire trail is cared for.

I learned a lot about high-tech and ultralight backpacking while writing the "Trail Technology" chapter. I found information about satellite GPS messengers at the findmespot.com website. Information about ultralight hiking has already filled several volumes. I made sense of all of that information through the ultralightbackpacker.com and backpacking.net websites.

For my encounter with the presidential candidate in "Memorable Men," I referenced historyorb.com and u-s-history.com for the topics he and I would most likely have discussed. In "Carnivores and Canoes," I relied on the Great Smoky Mountains National Park's website for information about encounters with bears.

The story about Steve Longley was greatly helped by Bob Proudman's "The Kennebec River Ferry" that the ATC published in the March–April 2008 edition of *AT Journeys*. In early 2013 Steve passed away suddenly at the age of fifty-five. That's when I learned he was the son of former Maine Governor James Longley. To the thousands of hikers he paddled across the Kennebec, he was simply "The Ferryman." The line that I wrote, "If anyone deserves sainthood, it's Steve Longley," has taken on a whole new meaning. Steve, you were one of the best.

I would never have learned about the Battle of Saltville had I not stumbled upon the Museum of the Middle Appalachians on a rainy afternoon in 2005. I visited the museum again in the summer of 2011. Furthermore, David E. Brown has written two articles about the battle: "Was There a Massacre in Saltville in 1864?" which was published in 1999, and "5th Regiment Cavalry, U.S. Colored Troops" published in 2010. "Remembering Saltville," a story by Tonia Moxley published by the *Roanoke Times* in September 28, 2001, was also helpful.

The list of Native American tribes living along the AT corridor was compiled using the native-languages.org website. Bob and I ate at the Log Cabin restaurant in Elkton, Virginia, during one of our research trips. Trust me. The barbecue was wonderful.

Finally, I would be remiss not to give credit to my first wife, Aimee, for her contribution to my section hikes and, therefore, to this book. It was her chance encounter with a down-in-the-mouth thru-hiker that gave us the idea to section-hike the entire Appalachian Trail in the first place. We hiked it together for only one season before going our separate ways. But I am certainly grateful to Aimee for helping to plant the seed from which this tree has grown.

## Jim Haskell's Hikes
## Mount Katahdin, ME to Harpers Ferry, WV

| Starting Point | Ending Point | Mileage* | Year | Days on trail |
|---|---|---|---|---|
| Katahdin Stream | Baxter Peak | 5.2 | 1990 | 1 |
| Katahdin Stream | Daicey Pond Campground | 2.0 | 1990 | 1 |
| Daicey Pond Campground | Abol Bridge | 7.3 | 1990 | 1 |
| Abol Bridge | Cooper Brook Road | 39.8 | 1992 | 5 |
| Cooper Brook Road | Katahdin Iron Works Road | 28.0 | 1993 | 3 |
| Katahdin Iron Works Road | Maine Route 15 | 29.9 | 1994 | 3 |
| Maine Route 15 | Moxie Pond Rd. | 24.8 | 1995 | 3 |
| Moxie Pond Rd. | US Route 201 | 11.9 | 1992 | 2 |
| US Route 201 | Pierce Pond Dam | 3.8 | 1996 | 1 |
| Pierce Pond Dam | Pierce Pond Lean-to | 0.2 | 2010 | 1 |
| Pierce Pond Lean-to | Long Falls Dam Road | 13.5 | 1996 | 1 |
| Long Falls Dam Road | Maine Route 27 | 19.1 | 1997 | 2 |
| Maine Route 27 | Caribou Valley Road | 8.3 | 1998 | 1 |
| Caribou Valley Road | Maine Route 4 | 23.9 | 2001 | 3 |
| Maine Route 4 | Maine Route 17 | 13.1 | 1991 | 1 |
| Maine Route 17 | South Arm Road | 13.3 | 1991 | 1 |
| South Arm Road | East B Hill Road | 10.1 | 1996 | 1 |
| East B Hill Road | Maine Route 26 | 10.3 | 1990 | 1 |
| Maine Route 26 | Speck Pond Trail | 4.6 | 1990 | 1 |
| Speck Pond Trail | Mahoosuc Notch Trail | 3.6 | 1995 | 1 |
| Mahoosuc Notch Trail | Goose Eye Trail | 4.1 | 1991 | 1 |
| Goose Eye Trail | Success Trail (NH) | 3.3 | 1996 | 1 |

*current mileages may vary due to subsequent trail relocations.

| Starting Point | Ending Point | Mileage* | Year | Days on trail |
|---|---|---|---|---|
| Success Trail | Austin Brook Trail | 3.4 | 1994 | 1 |
| Austin Brook Trail | US Route 2 | 12.2 | 1990 | 2 |
| US Route 2 | New Hampshire Route 16 | 20.9 | 1991 | 3 |
| New Hampshire Route 16 | Parapet Trail | 6.8 | 1990 | 1 |
| Parapet Trail | Madison Springs Hut | 1.0 | 1995 | 1 |
| Madison Springs Hut | Mt. Washington summit | 5.6 | 1990 | 1 |
| US Route 302 | Mt. Washington summit | 12.6 | 1991 | 2 |
| US Route 302 | Garfield Trail | 17.6 | 1991 | 3 |
| Garfield Trail | US Route 3 | 10.1 | 1992 | 2 |
| US Route 3 | New Hampshire Route 25A | 35.6 | 1991 | 5 |
| New Hampshire Route 25A | Lyme-Dorchester Rd. | 14.0 | 1995 | 2 |
| Lyme-Dorchester Rd. | Three Mile Road | 10.9 | 1995 | 1 |
| Three Mile Road | Connecticut River (VT) | 9.4 | 1993 | 1 |
| Connecticut River | Vermont Route 14 | 8.7 | 1993 | 1 |
| Vermont Route 14 | Gifford Woods State Park | 32.4 | 1994 | 3 |
| Gifford Woods State Park | US Route 4 | 1.9 | 1994 | 1 |
| US Route 4 | Upper Cold River Road | 10.9 | 1995 | 1 |
| Upper Cold River Road | Vermont Route 140 | 11.3 | 1994 | 1 |
| Vermont Route 140 | Homer Stone Brook Trail | 6.7 | 1997 | 1 |
| Homer Stone Brook Trail | US Forest Service Road 10 | 2.6 | 1994 | 1 |
| US Forest Service Road 10 | Vermont Routes 11/30 | 17.1 | 1996 | 2 |
| Vermont Routes 11/30 | Old Rootville Road | 4.8 | 1997 | 1 |
| Arlington-West Wardsboro Road | Old Rootville Road | 12.7 | 1997 | 1 |
| Arlington-West Wardsboro Road | Vermont Route 9 | 22.6 | 1999 | 3 |

| Starting Point | Ending Point | Mileage* | Year | Days on trail |
|---|---|---|---|---|
| Vermont Route 9 | Massachusetts Route 2 (MA) | 18.6 | 1996 | 2 |
| Massachusetts Route 2 | Mount Greylock summit | 5.8 | 1993 | 1 |
| Mount Greylock summit | Massachusetts Route 8 | 7.7 | 1993 | 1 |
| Massachusetts Route 8 | Massachusetts Routes 8/9 | 9.3 | 1993 | 1 |
| Massachusetts Routes 8/9 | Pittsfield Road | 9.6 | 1996 | 1 |
| Pittsfield Road | County Road | 4.0 | 1998 | 1 |
| County Road | US Route 20 | 5.4 | 1999 | 1 |
| US Route 20 | Main Road, Tyringham | 8.6 | 2003 | 1 |
| Main Road, Tyringham | Beartown Mountain Road | 6.3 | 1999 | 1 |
| Massachusetts Route 23 | Beartown Mountain Road | 5.8 | 1996 | 2 |
| Massachusetts Route 23 | West Sheffield Road | 9.0 | 1998 | 1 |
| West Sheffield Road | Jug End Road | 3.9 | 1998 | 1 |
| Jug End Road | Connecticut Route 41 (CT) | 16.9 | 1998 | 2 |
| Connecticut Route 41 | Falls Village | 8.1 | 1990 | 1 |
| Falls Village | Housatonic High School | 1.8 | 1992 | 1 |
| West Cornwall Road | Housatonic High School | 7.6 | 1991 | 1 |
| West Cornwall Road | Connecticut Route 341 | 15.9 | 1998 | 1 |
| Connecticut Route 341 | County Road 20 (NY) | 21.0 | 1999 | 2 |
| County Road 20 | Stormville Mountain Road | 10.8 | 1999 | 1 |
| Stormville Mountain Road | New York Route 52 | 1.4 | 2000 | 1 |
| New York Route 52 | New York Route 301 | 12.1 | 2000 | 1 |
| New York Route 301 | Bear Mountain State Park | 18.8 | 2000 | 2 |
| Bear Mountain State Park | Arden Valley Road | 17.7 | 2000 | 2 |
| Arden Valley Road | Warwick Turnpike (NJ) | 21.8 | 2000 | 2 |

| Starting Point | Ending Point | Mileage* | Year | Days on trail |
|---|---|---|---|---|
| Warwick Turnpike | New Jersey Route 94 | 6.0 | 2003 | 1 |
| New Jersey Route 94 | New Jersey Route 23 | 21.4 | 2002 | 2 |
| New Jersey Route 23 | Culver Tower | 12.4 | 2003 | 1 |
| US Route 206 | Culver Tower | 2.0 | 2003 | 1 |
| US Route 206 | Lookout Rock, Wind Gap (PA) | 44.8 | 2001 | 3 |
| Lookout Rock, Wind Gap | Hahn's Lookout | 0.2 | 2009 | 1 |
| Hahn's Lookout | Katellen Trail | 3.6 | 2001 | 1 |
| Katellen Trail | Hawk Mountain Road | 41.8 | 2002 | 3 |
| Hawk Mountain Road | Pennsylvania Route 61 | 13.5 | 2003 | 1 |
| Pennsylvania Route 61 | Pennsylvania Route 183 | 14.4 | 2003 | 1 |
| Pennsylvania Route 183 | Pennsylvania Route 501 | 9.3 | 2003 | 1 |
| Pennsylvania Route 501 | Pennsylvania Route 443 | 12.8 | 2004 | 1 |
| Pennsylvania Route 443 | Pennsylvania Route 325 | 15.0 | 2004 | 1 |
| Pennsylvania Route 325 | Pennsylvania Route 850 | 26.9 | 2004 | 2 |
| Pennsylvania Route 850 | Boiling Springs | 16.9 | 2005 | 1 |
| Boiling Springs | Pennsylvania Route 94 | 8.5 | 2005 | 1 |
| Pennsylvania Route 94 | Shippensburg Road | 19.2 | 2005 | 2 |
| Shippensburg Road | Caledonia Park | 10.6 | 2005 | 1 |
| Caledonia Park | Old Forge Road | 10.6 | 2005 | 1 |
| Old Forge Road | Pen-Mar (MD) | 8.3 | 2006 | 1 |
| Pen-Mar | Wolfsville Road | 9.4 | 2006 | 1 |
| Wolfsville Road | US Route 40 | 8.5 | 2006 | 1 |
| US Route 40 | Gathland State Park | 12.3 | 2006 | 1 |
| Gathland State Park | Harpers Ferry (WV) | 10.0 | 2006 | 1 |
| **Northern Section Totals:** | | **1,158.2** | | **139** |

## Jim Haskell's Hikes
## Springer Mountain, GA to Harpers Ferry, WV

| Starting Point | Ending Point | Mileage* | Year | Days on trail |
|---|---|---|---|---|
| Springer Mountain | Unicoi Gap | 50.7 | 1992 | 6 |
| Unicoi Gap | Wallace Gap (NC) | 53.0 | 1993 | 5 |
| Wallace Gap | Fontana Dam | 59.8 | 1995 | 6 |
| Fontana Dam | Newfound Gap | 39.2 | 1996 | 4 |
| Newfound Gap | Hot Springs | 66.4 | 1997 | 6 |
| Devil Fork Gap | Hot Springs | 35.2 | 2000 | 3 |
| Devil Fork Gap | Nolichucky River | 32.2 | 2001 | 4 |
| Nolichucky River | US Route 19E (TN) | 45.2 | 2002 | 5 |
| US Route 19E | Waycaster Spring | 22.1 | 2003 | 2 |
| Waycaster Spring | Wautauga Dam Road | 10.1 | 2004 | 1 |
| Wautauga Dam Road | Tennessee Route 91 | 16.0 | 2004 | 1 |
| Tennessee Route 91 | US Route 421 | 7.0 | 2004 | 1 |
| US Route 421 | Damascus (VA) | 17.8 | 2004 | 1 |
| Damascus | Virginia Route 728 | 14.5 | 2005 | 1 |
| Virginia Route 728 | Virginia Route 600 | 9.8 | 2005 | 1 |
| Virginia Route 600 | Virginia Route 603 | 16.9 | 2006 | 2 |
| Virginia Route 603 | Dickey Gap | 8.5 | 2006 | 1 |
| Dickey Gap | Mount Rogers National Rec. Area HQ | 14.6 | 2006 | 1 |
| Mount Rogers National Rec. Area HQ | Virginia Route 627 | 12.6 | 2007 | 1 |

*current mileages may vary due to subsequent trail relocations.

| Starting Point | Ending Point | Mileage* | Year | Days on trail |
|---|---|---|---|---|
| Virginia Route 627 | Reed Creek | 5.2 | 2007 | 1 |
| Virginia Route 42 | Reed Creek | 5.5 | 2007 | 1 |
| Virginia Route 42 | Virginia Route 615 | 25.7 | 2007 | 2 |
| Virginia Route 615 | US Route 21 | 6.9 | 2007 | 1 |
| US Route 21 | Virginia Route 611 | 9.0 | 2007 | 1 |
| Virginia Route 611 | Virginia Route 605 | 9.6 | 2008 | 1 |
| Virginia Route 605 | Virginia Route 100 | 24.1 | 2009 | 2 |
| Virginia Route 635 | Virginia Route 100 | 21.8 | 2010 | 1 |
| Virginia Route 635 | Virginia Route 621 | 29.8 | 2008 | 3 |
| Virginia Route 621 | Virginia Route 624 | 14.6 | 2008 | 1 |
| Virginia Route 624 | Virginia Route 311 | 5.9 | 2008 | 1 |
| Virginia Route 311 | US Route 220 | 19.6 | 2009 | 2 |
| US Route 220 | Black Horse Gap | 13.6 | 2008 | 1 |
| Black Horse Gap | Bearwallow Gap | 8.1 | 2008 | 1 |
| Bearwallow Gap | Cornelius Creek Shelter | 15.1 | 2008 | 1 |
| Cornelius Creek Shelter | Petite's Gap | 10.0 | 2008 | 1 |
| US Route 501 | Petite's Gap | 9.9 | 2008 | 1 |
| US Route 501 | Punchbowl Gap | 10.9 | 2008 | 1 |
| Punchbowl Gap | US Route 60 | 10.2 | 2009 | 1 |
| US Route 60 | Salt Log Gap | 8.5 | 2009 | 1 |
| Salt Log Gap | Virginia Route 56 | 17.2 | 2009 | 1 |
| Virginia Route 56 | Dripping Rocks | 15.3 | 2010 | 1 |

| Starting Point | Ending Point | Mileage* | Year | Days on trail |
|---|---|---|---|---|
| Dripping Rocks | Rockfish Gap | 14.6 | 2010 | 1 |
| Rockfish Gap | Turk Gap | 11.4 | 2010 | 1 |
| Turk Gap | Blackrock Area Parking Lot | 9.6 | 2010 | 1 |
| Blackrock Area Parking Lot | Loft Mountain | 7.5 | 2009 | 1 |
| Loft Mountain | Powell Gap | 10.1 | 2009 | 1 |
| Powell Gap | South River Picnic Area | 9.2 | 2009 | 1 |
| South River Picnic Area | Milam Gap | 11.4 | 2009 | 1 |
| Milam Gap | Skyland Resort | 10.7 | 2009 | 1 |
| Skyland Resort | Beahm's Gap | 12.4 | 2010 | 1 |
| Beahm's Gap | Keyser Run Rd. | 9.9 | 2009 | 1 |
| Keyser Run Rd. | Compton Gap | 9.0 | 2009 | 1 |
| Compton Gap | US Route 522 | 5.6 | 2009 | 1 |
| US Route 522 | Virginia Route 755 | 8.4 | 2010 | 1 |
| Virginia Route 755 | US Route 50 | 12.1 | 2010 | 1 |
| US Route 50 | West Virginia Route 7 (WV) | 14.1 | 2010 | 1 |
| West Virginia Route 7 | West Virginia Route 9 | 13.5 | 2010 | 1 |
| West Virginia Route 9 | ATC Headquarters Side Trail | 5.6 | 2010 | 1 |
| ATC Headquarters Side Trail | Harpers Ferry | 0.7 | 2010 | 1 |
| **Southern Section Totals:** | | **1,003.9** | | **97** |
| **Grand Totals:** | | **2,162.1** | | **236** |

## Jim Haskell

Climbing Mount Katahdin when he was twelve opened up the world of hiking to Jim Haskell. Besides completing the Appalachian Trail, he has climbed sixty of the sixty-seven highest mountains in New England, and hopes to complete all of the four-thousand-footers in New England and New York by his sixtieth year.

Leaving his native Maine in 1978, Jim studied history at Boston University and earned a master's degree from Suffolk University. Jim has been a community development executive and consultant for thirty years. Jim lives with his wife Donna and their son Jason north of Boston. *Two Tents* is his first book.

## Chelsea White

(cover illustration)

Chelsea White grew up in Carmel, Maine, where her love of drawing took root from the time she could pick up a pencil. Lions, horses, wolves, and the wild aspects of the Maine landscape are among her favorite subjects, which she has cultivated for most of her life. She began learning about painting and illustrating at Hermon High School. She studied art at Gordon College in Wenham, Massachusetts, graduating in 2012. She is expanding her artistic horizons while working with a nonprofit theater arts company. Chelsea presented Jim Haskell, her uncle, with the painting that illustrates this book's front cover when he completed the Appalachian Trail in 2010.